Also available in the
Classics of Anglo-Catholic Devotion series

The Eucharistic Year: Seasonal Devotions for the Sacrament
by A. H. Baverstock

Keynotes of the Catholic Faith (forthcoming)

The King's Highway

A Simple Statement of
Catholic Belief and Duty

George D. Carleton

With an Introduction by
Julien Chilcott-Monk

TUFTON
B O O K S

First published in 1924 by the
Church Literature Association
This edition first published in
2001 by Tufton Books
(Church Union Publications)
in conjunction with
The Canterbury Press Norwich
St Mary's Works, St Mary's Plain,
Norwich, Norfolk NR3 3BH

George D. Carleton © 1924, 1928, 1937, 1940
Reprinted 8 times
Introduction © Julien Chilcott-Monk 2001

British Library Cataloguing in Publication Data

A catalogue record for this book is available
from the British Library

ISBN 0–85191–039–4

Printed in Great Britain by
Bookmarque Ltd, Croydon, Surrey

INTRODUCTION

When I entered Kelham (the Society of the Sacred Mission's Theological College and Mother House at Kelham, Newark in Nottinghamshire) in the early 1960s, one book in the library immediately stood out as a book I recognized from my father's own library. It was, of course, *The King's Highway* by then also available in both Japanese and Swahili! I remember that my father had earlier impressed upon me the soundness of the Catholic teaching and instruction to be found in the book. The style of writing is, inevitably, very much of its own day, but that, surely, is just another of its great joys.

The King's Highway was first published in 1924 by the Church Literature Association, one of the predecessors of Tufton Books and an imprint of the Church Union, and was reissued many times before and after the Second World War. Most recently a limited reissue was printed for the Anglican Catholic Church of Canada in 1993. During the 'go ahead' 1960s the book was beginning to be regarded as unacceptably dated, a time when *The English Missal* was considered dangerously old-fashioned. But *The King's Highway* is by no means a book to be read only by those who would have *The English Missal*, it is pertinent to the Catholic Anglican of any tradition and, indeed, to any Catholic or to any Anglican!

In Fr Carleton's Preface to the first and subsequent editions, he states his intentions thus:

> I have tried to set forth in this book in simple words a statement of Catholic belief and duty; not seeking to prove my statement by arguments, but only to explain the faith and to illustrate it from Holy Scripture.

INTRODUCTION

> I have endeavoured to follow the high road of revelation and redemption, which is marked out for us by the common consent of the Catholic Church and the witness of Scripture; disregarding the side-paths and wrong roads which branch off from the high road at every point.

And the theme of the roadway to the Kingdom is taken up by Bishop John in his Recommendation. More than ever the Catholic Anglican has urgent need of a good guide to this roadway in these confused and turbulent times within the Church. They are confused and turbulent times because society itself has evangelized the Church and has caused the Church to remodel itself upon the secular—from the diocesan authority upon best business practices to the statements about Christian morality upon that which society at the moment favours and embraces.

Fr Carleton aims to 'set forth ... a statement of Catholic belief and duty ... *in simple words*' [my italics]. However, modern Catholic Anglican readers will have to apply themselves in the study of *The Kings Highway* because it is a substantial guide to the Christian faith. This intellectual effort will be much rewarded and will reap dividends in the practice of contemplation, in the honing of one's rule of life, and in the understanding of the tenets of the Faith. And how refreshing this is in age of superficiality of thought, when the cartoon instructs us to kneel or to stand, to sing or be silent; and when new prayers and hymns are other either little more than advertising jingles or political slogans. Perhaps I exaggerate in making the point; but, sadly, there is a point to make.

In his Preface, Fr Carleton goes on to say:

> The book was written in part for the instruction of certain natives in South Africa, who were preparing for ordination. My hope is that it may serve as a map of the road for Anglo-Catholic wayfarers. It is not intended for the edification of skilled theologians, who do not need a book of this simple character, nor for the conversion of gainsayers, save in so far as every statement of the Catholic faith has converting power.

INTRODUCTION

Well, it is with this foundation that so many good, Catholic Anglican African priests were made and, happily, this tradition has been maintained in that continent to the present day. Do not be concerned by the seemingly condescending tone of 'certain natives'; remember that this book was first published in 1924. Indeed, Fr Carleton was renowned for his enthusiasm for and encouragement of the theological training and ordination of African priests. Fr Carleton sees the book as a simple affair and 'not intended for edification of skilled theologians' but rather a good guide for those before they begin their ordained ministry and for other 'Catholic wayfarers'. I fervently hope that all new Catholic Anglicans will read this book and read again, and that even those who believe themselves to be 'skilled theologians' will also read and read again. Those who have been Catholic Anglicans for some time will already know the book and will not resist its reissue.

It is my great privilege, as publishing co-ordinator for Tufton Books, to see *The King's Highway* once again widely available and to have the book so warmly endorsed at the outset of the venture, by Bishop John.

Julien Chilcott-Monk
St Bartholomew, 2001

A RECOMMENDATION

For some time now I have felt that there is a need for a succinct and readable summary of the Catholic Faith to recommend to Confirmation candidates and others. I am therefore very pleased to learn that *The King's Highway* is to be reissued.

I first encountered *The King's Highway* during my undergraduate days in the 1950s and found it a treasure trove of information, a source of inspiration and an aid to contemplation. There may be some emphases which today's reader may find uncomfortable—the rules of fasting and in particular fasting before receiving Holy Communion; the statement that 'divorce and remarriage are contrary to the divine will'. Perhaps that is no bad thing! We would do well to recover the disciplines it commends for the sake of our spiritual health and the well-being of our Church. We need to keep to the high road in an age noted for its 'side paths and wrong roads'—if not complete cul-de-sac!

This is a book for reference, of course, but also for regular use. To parish priests it will be useful when teaching and preaching. Lay people, in their personal reading, will find in it a clear outline of the treasures of our Faith. It can be a source for meditation and contemplation on the great events of our salvation. It is an excellent aid in the development and maintenance of a rule of life.

This is a book which embraces and explains the Faith handed down by generations of Christians through the ages. It is firmly orthodox, and its teaching can be trusted. It is thoroughly based on Scripture, backed by appropriate Biblical references throughout. I can confidently recommend *The King's Highway* to anyone seeking to learn about the Christian Faith, its teaching and

A RECOMMENDATION

disciplines and also to practising Christians seeking to deepen their devotion, maintain their discipline and increase their faith.

John Gaisford
(formerly the Bishop of Beverley)
Our Lady, Queen of Heaven, 2001

CONTENTS

I. GOD AND MAN

II. SIN.

III. THE PREPARATION FOR CHRIST.

IV. THE INCARNATON.

V. THE ATONEMENT.

CONTENTS

VI. The Church and Sacraments.

VII. Baptism and Confirmation.

VIII. Sin, Repentance, and the Sacrament of Penance.

IX. The Sacrament of the Altar.

X. Holy Order.

XI. The Unity of the Church

CONTENTS

CONTENTS

XIX. DEATH AND AFTER DEATH.

XX. THE END.

An highway shall be there, and it shall be called The Way of Holiness. The wayfaring men shall not err therein. The redeemed shall walk there: and the ransomed of the Lord shall return, and come with singing unto Zion.[1]

Jesus saith, I am the Way and the Truth and the Life: no one cometh unto the Father but through me.[2]

Having boldness to enter into the holy place by the Blood of Jesus, by the Way which he dedicated for us, a new and living Way, through the veil—that is to say, the Way of his Flesh: let us draw near.[3]

We will go along the King's Highway: we will not turn aside, to the right hand nor to the left.[4]

---

[1] Isa. xxxv. 8-10.   [2] John xiv. 6.
[3] Heb. x. 19-22.   [4] Num. xx. 17.

THE KING'S HIGHWAY

I

GOD AND MAN

1

EVERYONE starts life's journey with the knowledge that he is
distinct from all other human beings. When we first began
to think, we already had that knowledge. We did not put it
into words, but each of us could have said : I am a person;
I can think, and love, and make up my mind by deliberate
choices and decisions, and I am conscious of my own self
distinct from all others.

Considerably later came the discovery that we are animals,
more wonderful and having greater powers of mind than
other animals, but yet akin to them in our structure and in
the materials of our bodies, and like them especially in being
mortal. The thought that death is certain came to us with
an unpleasant shock. It seemed to upset the idea, which
was natural to us, of eternal and unchanging personality—
that is, I am I, and I shall never cease to exist; I cannot think
of myself either ceasing to exist or becoming another person.

We were conscious of our immortal souls before we realised
that we had mortal bodies.

Distinct from ourselves, we knew of other people and of
God. Doubtless we should not have had any clear thought
of God if we had not been told about him; but, when we were
told, the thought of God was an easy one to our minds. There
was that within us which made it easy. We were ready from
the beginning to know God, as a personal being like ourselves
only immensely greater.

And as it was with us, so it is also with all men. Before
they are taught the truth, there is present some dim con-

sciousness of a personal being higher than man, which prepares them for the knowledge of God.

But everyone needs to learn a further lesson: that God is the centre of all things, and not he himself. The old astronomers thought that this earth was the centre of the universe, and that around it moved the sun and moon and stars. Similarly, everyone is inclined to think of himself as the centre, and of all other beings, and even of God, as existing only in relation to him and for his sake. It was a great achievement when the astronomers realised that the earth moves around the sun, and not the sun around the earth. And it is a great achievement when we realise that we and all other beings move, so to speak, around God, and not God around us; that we exist for God, and not God for us; that man has no power but that which comes from God; and that the only reason or purpose of man's life is in relation to God. Practical religion begins with the recognition of this great and fundamental truth. But there are many, even many Christians, who have not learnt it; and hence they mean but little when they say, " I believe in God."

We have clear knowledge about God because we have been taught about him by others; and the truths they taught us were in the first instance taught to mankind by God himself. For mankind needed a revelation from God. Man cannot by searching find out God.[1] God is greater than the human mind can comprehend. We can know about him only those truths which he has made known. We could not know anything for certain about him if he had not shown himself.

God has taught about himself. The universe, and especially mankind itself, is a revelation of God[2] to those who have eyes to see. Human reason has argued that there must be a cause for the existence of all things; and that there are signs of plan and design everywhere which seem to show that all things were caused to be by a personal Being. He that made the eye, shall he not see?[3] He that gave life, is he not living? He that made thinking men, is he not a

[1] Job xi. 7. [2] Rom. i. 20. [3] Ps. xciv. 9.

thinking person? The Creator surely has not made beings greater than himself. The very fact that men have minds which can think of God is an argument that there is a God to be thought of, and that he is the cause of the thought and of the mind that thinks it. Whence could men get such a thought, unless from God?

But such reasonings would be of little avail, if we had not more definite knowledge about God than that which we can gain from the study of the universe and of ourselves. Human reason by itself cannot get further than to say: "It is probable there is a God." The universe does not tell much about God, except to those who already have learnt to know him.

But God has enabled men to know him; not only through creation, but also by his revelation of himself to the prophets of Israel, which is written for us in the Old Testament,[1] and again by his full revelation of himself in Jesus Christ his Son, which is preserved for us in the Catholic Church.[2]

And God, who has given the revelation, gives men the power to accept it, and take it to themselves. This power we call Faith. Faith is a gift of God, as also is reason. Faith is not opposed to reason, but it is independent of it. Reason leads the mind towards God; faith enables the soul to know God.[3]

II

I believe in one God. So we say in the Creed, and without further explanation of what God is in himself, we pass on to the thought of God as he has shown himself to mankind. And rightly so. For we know about God chiefly through what he has done and is doing for us, as Creator, Redeemer, and Sanctifier. First, I learn to believe in God the Father, who hath made me and all the world; secondly, in God the Son, who hath redeemed me and all mankind; thirdly, in God the Holy Ghost, who sanctifies me and all the members of the Christian Church.[4]

Our subject in this book is what God has done and is doing for us, and what we therefore ought to do for God.

[1] Chaps. iii. 3; xiii. 2.   [2] Chaps. xii. 1, 2; xiii. 1, 3.
[3] Chaps. vi. 4; xii. 3; xvi. 2.   [4] Church Catechism.

3

Let us put together very simply, as an introduction, some of the main truths which we know about God through his revelation of himself received by faith.

We believe that God exists, and that he is the rewarder of them that seek after him.[1]

He is the one and only God, the one supreme ruler over all people and all things, from the beginning of creation and for ever. God is eternal; he never had a beginning, and he will never have an end. He always was God, and he always will be God. He is the king eternal, incorruptible, invisible, the only God; he is the blessed and only potentate, the king of kings and Lord of lords, who only hath immortality, dwelling in light unapproachable; whom no man on earth hath seen, nor can see; to whom be honour and power eternal.[2]

God is spirit, and they that worship him must worship him in spirit and in truth.[3] We cannot see what is spiritual with our eyes, as we see material things. We can worship God, but, because he is spirit, we cannot see him in this world. We can see only the signs and effects of his power and his goodness.[4] It is promised that we shall see God in heaven.[5] By heaven we mean the presence of God; we shall be in heaven when we have attained to the blessed vision of God and to perfect union with him. But, though we cannot now see him, he is everywhere. God is not only above all things as the supreme ruler, but also he is in all things, and all things are in God. The spirit of the Lord filleth the world.[6] In him we live and move and have our being.[7] He is nearer to us than the air we breathe. All things exist because God is in them as the continual cause of their existence.

In God is all knowledge and wisdom and truth. Nothing is hidden from him. He sees all that has happened, and all that will happen. All the past and future is present to his mind. He knows all about us, even our secret thoughts. He knew each one of us before he made us, and he knows

[1] Heb. xi. 6. [2] 1 Tim. i. 17; vi. 16. [3] John iv. 24.
[4] John iii. 8. [5] 1 John iii. 2; Rev. xxii. 4.
[6] Wisd. i. 7. [7] Acts xvii. 28.

4

what will be the end of each one. He sees what we are, and what we are becoming.[1]

God is perfectly holy and good, and his will is to make every one holy and good like himself. Holy, holy, holy is the Lord of hosts.[2] He is the standard of holiness : we know what holiness is only because we know God. And he is the source of holiness : whatever good there is in us comes from him.

God loves all things that he has made, for God is love.[3] He loves us, even when we do not love him. He loves us, not because we are worthy to be loved by him, but because his very nature is love. God has revealed himself as our Father. He is not only the cause of our existence, but also he acts towards us as a loving father, guiding, correcting, and helping his children.

And God is almighty. His power is always able to fulfil his will; but he does not will what is evil, because he is holy as well as almighty : he cannot act contrary to the holiness of his nature.

Sometimes, when we look at all the misery that is in the world, we are inclined to imagine that God, who lets the misery go on, is not almighty and cannot prevent it; or that he is not loving and good, and does not care. But when we come to understand the Christian religion, we learn that the root-cause of the misery of the world is sin, and that sin is not God's will, but rebellion against his holiness and love.[4] We learn that God has limited the exercise of his almighty power, through the greatness of the powers he has given to men. And we learn that, in spite of the present misery, God must be loving, because he himself came into this world to share life's burden with us, and to suffer death because of sin. The cross of Christ is the revelation of the love of God.[5]

God has taught us that he is one God in three Persons, and three Persons in one God. That is to say : there is the Father, and the Son, and the Holy Spirit;[6] and the

---

[1] Ps. xciv. 11; cxxxix. 1-6; Heb. iv. 13.
[2] Isa. vi. 3; Rev. iv. 8.   [3] 1 John iv. 7 *ff*.   [4] Chap. ii. 1, 5.
[5] Chap. v. 2.   [6] Matt. xxviii. 19; 2 Cor. xiii. 14.

Father is God, the Son is God, and the Holy Spirit is God. And yet the Father and the Son and the Holy Spirit are not three Gods. God is one God only.

The Father in himself is God. The Son is God, because he receives his Godhead eternally from the Father. The Holy Spirit is God, because he receives his Godhead eternally from the Father through the Son.

God the Father, God the Son, and God the Holy Spirit, are equal in power and love and holiness. The Father never was without the Son and the Holy Spirit. The three Persons are eternal together.[1] They are distinct from each other in person, but one in nature, and always united in thought and will and action, and in their mutual love.

This is the doctrine of the Holy Trinity, which all Christians believe, because God has taught it in his Church. We cannot understand it completely at present. We cannot make any clear picture in our minds to represent the Holy Trinity, and it is hard to think without making pictures. But we can see how men came to believe the doctrine. First they learnt to know and believe in the one God. Then they came to know Jesus Christ, and to believe that he was God; and they learnt from his teaching that he was not the Father.[2] Finally they learnt to believe in God the Holy Spirit, whom Jesus Christ sent from the Father to abide in the Church.[3] And thus, step by step, they came to believe in the three Persons; and, knowing that there can be only one God, they expressed the truth about him in the word Trinity, Three-in-One.

Such are some of the main truths which we know about God. We should think about them often, so that our minds may be filled with reverence and holy fear.

But someone may ask: It is really necessary to know such deep doctrines as these? Is it not sufficient to live a good life? The answer is: Yes, it is necessary to know all about God that our minds are able to grasp. First, if we really believe in God, we must surely desire to know all we can know about him in whom we believe. We must love the

---

[1] Athanasian Creed.   [2] John v. 19.   [3] John xv. 26.

Lord our God with all our mind, as well as with all our heart and all our strength;[1] we owe to God right belief, as well as true devotion and faithful service. Secondly, we cannot know what is a good life in the sight of God unless we have a definite knowledge about his power and love and holiness. To know the love of God, without due understanding of his holiness, makes our idea of his love soft and sentimental, so that we lose the awe we should feel towards our heavenly Father. To know his holiness without his love turns our awe into slavish fear, and makes us think of him as hard and austere,[2] demanding too much from us. To know his power only gives us no power to love him. Such as we think God to be, such we tend to become. He has shown himself to us, that we may become like him. Therefore, whatever he has shown, it is necessary for us to know. Thirdly, when we ponder the Christian revelation, we find that it is one whole, and each part is related to all other parts. At whatever point we begin to consider it, we are led on to the consideration of the whole. The doctrines that seem easier to us are found to depend on those which are more difficult. And every truth we learn about Jesus Christ leads us in the end to the thought of the Blessed Trinity whom he revealed to mankind.[3]

But, better than knowing *about* God, we are able to know him, our heavenly Father, as really as we know an earthly father. And this is life eternal, that we should know the only true God.[4] The greatest mind cannot probe the full meaning of what has been revealed about God; but the heart of a child can find its way straight to the heart of God. This is the knowledge which may be hidden from the wise and prudent, and yet be revealed unto babes.[5] If anyone seeks with his whole heart to know God, he will not be disappointed;[6] for it is God's will to reveal himself to all who truly seek him. God wills that all men should be saved, and come to the knowledge of the truth.[7] And the more we know him, the more we shall love him; and the more we love him, the more we shall want to serve him.

---

[1] Mark xii. 30. [2] Matt. xxv. 24 [3] Chap. xii. 3. [4] John xvii. 3.
[5] Matt. xi. 25. [6] Matt. vii. 7-8 [7] 1 Tim. ii. 4; Chap. xii. 1.

III

God created all things. Because of his will to create, all things were in his mind, and by his will they were made.[1]

God the Father made all things, visible and invisible.[2] Nothing existed except God until he began the work of creation.[3]

God the Father made all things through God the Son, who is called the Word of God. In the beginning was the Word, and the Word was with God, and the Word was God; all things were made through him.[4] As a word comes from a thought, so God the Son comes from God the Father; and as a thought is shown by a word, so all things were first in the mind of God the Father, and then were shown in creation by being made through the Son.

God the Holy Spirit is the Giver of life.[5] It is he who gives life to all living things.

God's work of creation is a work of love. There was no necessity obliging God to create; he had no need of creatures. Within the Blessed Trinity the three Persons had sufficient and perfect scope for their mutual knowledge and love. God began the work of creation, not to supply any deficiency within himself, but because he willed to bring creatures into existence to share in the benefit of his love.

The work of creation goes on continually. God is always using one thing to make another. He uses seeds to make plants, and the male and female to produce offspring. Also he makes use of one form of living creature from which to produce a higher form; and in this way all the different forms of living things in the world have come into existence naturally, by the gradual process which we call Evolution. But always it is God himself who does the work. He did not make the world like a watchmaker, who makes a watch, and winds it up, and leaves it to run by itself. Nothing can be made, and nothing can remain, without the will of God making it and maintaining it. What we call the Laws of

---

[1] Rev. iv. 11.   [2] Nicene Creed.
[3] Told in parables in Gen. i.-ii.
[4] John i. 1-3; *cf.* Col. i. 16-17.   [5] Nicene Creed.

Nature are God's laws; that is, they are our descriptions of ways in which we see God acting as the creator and upholder of all things.

God has created angels and men. He made them good like himself, and he intended them for that perfect happiness which he has, and which can come only through likeness to him. Evil came in, as we shall see,[1] among both angels and men; and along with evil there came also unhappiness and pain, and death as we know it now. But these came, not according to the purpose of the holy God, but through opposition to his will, and through the self-will of angels and men thwarting his good purpose.

The angels are spirits. The holy angels worship and serve God in heaven. They fulfil his commandments, and are the agents of his will towards this world and mankind. They are the ministers of God that do his pleasure;[2] in the forces of nature we discern angelic power. They are worshipping spirits, who are sent forth to do service to men.[3] We know not how many angels there are, but Holy Scripture speaks of great multitudes,[4] and in almost every book records their ministrations in heaven and on earth. Among them are the guardian angels, whose office is to watch over human beings and protect them from harm. The angels of God's little ones always behold the face of the Father in heaven.[5]

Human beings are of a twofold nature, both spiritual and bodily. In their bodily nature they are akin to the animals; in their spiritual nature they are like the angels.

God has given to angels and men, alone of his creatures, the power of choosing to obey his will or of choosing to disobey. All things else, the world in its course, the stars in the sky, the trees and plants and stones, are as God wills them to be, and therefore fulfil the purpose he had in making them. They continue according to his ordinances; for all things are his servants.[6] They have no choice to do otherwise. But angels and men have the power of conscious

---

[1] Chaps. iii. and xix. 1. [2] Ps. ciii. 21.
[3] Heb. i. 14. [4] Heb. xii. 22; Rev. v. 11.
[5] Matt. xviii. 10; Acts xii. 7; xxvii. 23. [6] Ps. cxix. 91.

choice.   God has given them the power to say, "I will obey thee," or to say, "I will not obey thee." This power is called Free Will.   The reason why God has given it to them is that he wants from them the free loving obedience of children, and not the forced submission of helpless slaves. He wants them to have the happiness of serving him by their own consent, and of knowing that they are so doing.

It has not been made plain to us how our wills can be entirely free.   On the one hand, we seem to ourselves to be able to think and act as we choose.   In spite of the influences of heredity and environment, our power of self-direction is sufficiently free for us to be held responsible for our deeds by our fellow-men.   Social life is built on the supposition of our freedom and responsibility.   If we were in reality tied by our circumstances, or by irresistible fate, there would be no point in education, or in the many exhortations in Holy Scripture that spur us on to high endeavour.

On the other hand, we know that God is ruling over all. He foreknows and ordains the course of the world and of human life.   Nothing can happen, whether good or evil, outside of his will and all-embracing providence.

Either of these truths is plain to us, when considered by itself, as we look only at ourselves or only at God; and, to our imperfect powers of thinking, each truth seems to exclude the other.   But as each is taught by God, we must be content to accept them together, both God's determining and man's free choice; while as yet we are not able to see clearly how they are to be reconciled with each other.   In Holy Scripture the two are stated together without explanation, as, for example, in the words : The Son of man goeth as it hath been determined; but woe unto that man by whom he is betrayed.[1]

What God has made plain to us is the point of practical importance, that we are sufficiently free to be held accountable by him for the conduct of our lives in this world.   We must each of us appear before his judgment-seat, to give account for the deeds done in the body.[2]   Therefore our deeds must in real truth be our own, for God's justice cannot hold us responsible for that which is not ours.

[1] Luke xxii. 22.   [2] 2 Cor. v. 10.

I come from God. I belong to God. I go to God.

I come from God. My bodily life and my spiritual life come from God who made me. I am God's child; he is my Father, the author of my being. From all eternity God intended that I should be created. He thought about me, he foresaw my life, before I was conceived. When the right time came he brought me into existence, by means of my parents and the mysterious laws of human birth. He created me, to be another child for him to love. But I am not lost in the crowd. His love is upon me, just as if there were no other beings in the whole world.

I come from God. I am made in the image of God my Father.[1] As a mirror reflects my likeness, so I have been created to reflect the likeness and character of God. Be ye perfect, said Christ, even as your heavenly Father is perfect.[2] And if I know that I have no ability in myself to fulfil this high ideal, or if I am conscious that as a matter of fact the image of God in me is obscured, and that I am very far from being like him, I know also that God is willing and able to make me that which by my own power I cannot be. The gospel of God, the good news to mankind, is this : that through the life and death and resurrection of God's Son, Jesus Christ our Lord, we can be enabled to reflect as in a mirror the glory of the Lord, who is the true image of God, and be transformed into the same image, from glory to glory.[3]

I come from God. I have the power of knowing my Father, and of entering into communion with him. Prayer[4] is talking with God, the intercourse of the Father with his child. The sacraments[5] are the means of union with God, by sharing in the eternal life of God which is in Jesus Christ. And when by prayer and sacraments I know God, I have the power also of loving and of serving him. And my love and service are valuable in his sight, because he loves me.

[1] Gen. i. 27; v. 3; ix. 6.   [2] Matt. v. 48.
[3] 2 Cor. iii. 18; Col. i. 15.
[4] Chap. xiv. 1; xv. 1, 3.   [5] Chap. vi. 1-3.

I belong to God. If I make anything, a table or a chair, it is mine, because I made it for myself, and have not given it away. Even if it be stolen from me, it is really my property still. Similarly, I belong to God, because he made me for himself. I do not belong to the devil,[1] even if he has stolen me from God, and holds me at present in his power. I belong to good, not to evil; to God, not to Satan. The Son of God died on the cross to deliver me from the power which Satan had usurped over mankind, and to win me back to my true owner and master.[2]

I belong to God; not to my employer or any other person. I have no right, and I have no need, to be the slave of another. That is not God's will. No one may make himself a god over me; nor may I take anyone to stand to me in the place of God.

I belong to God; not to myself, to do what I like, without regard to his will. God created me to carry out his purpose; as for my own purpose I made the table or the chair. It must serve me, wherever I place it; for it is without a life or will of its own. But God has given me the power of loving and serving consciously. He respects the power he himself has given me. He does not force my will, but he enables me to choose what is right, as a loving child. And I want to choose what is right, because I know I come from God and belong to God.

I belong to God. That fact must govern my whole outlook on life. My one great purpose must be to do the will of God, to have regard to him in all that I think and say and do, and to know and love and serve him now and for all eternity. I must fear God and keep his commandments, for this is the whole duty of man.[3] The only way in which I can make the best and most of my life, and be happy now and for ever, is by fulfilling the purpose for which I was made. All my desires and actions will be right or wrong according as they make for or against this one ruling principle of human life.

I belong to God. If I am a willing servant of God, then

[1] Chap. ii. 2.   [2] 1 John iii. 8; Heb. ii. 14-15.
[3] Eccles. x. 13.

12

I am free. The only way to true liberty is to accept the service of God. His service is perfect freedom, because in his service I can find deliverance from the bondage of sin and selfishness, and from all that hinders me from being my true self. This is the glorious liberty of the children of God.[1]

I go to God. Death is not the end. I am an immortal soul. God created man to be immortal, and made him an image of his own eternity.[2]

I go to God. Death is sure, and after death cometh judgment.[3] I am responsible to God for the conduct of my life here, because I am free, and he has given me power to choose rightly. I am responsible to God, because I know him and his holy will. He will look into my life, to see what has been its purpose, its ruling principle—for him, or for self without regard to him. He will look into my soul, seeking there the likeness of himself.

I go to God, the judge of all;[4] to enter upon my eternal destiny, the destiny I have made for myself—with God, or apart from God; heaven or hell[5]—for all eternity.

I go to God; to find (may he grant it of his mercy) that he is my exceeding great reward.[6]

---

[1] Rom. viii. 21.
[3] Heb. ix. 27; Chap. xix. 1, 3.
[5] Chap. xx. 5-6.

[2] Wisd. ii. 23.
[4] Heb. xii. 23.
[6] Gen. xv. 1.

II

SIN

I

WE have seen what is the true purpose of human life: to live not for oneself, but for God. If men and women in every age had fulfilled this purpose, this world would indeed be a heaven upon earth. The will of the Creator was this: happy people in a happy world.

The will of the good God has not been fulfilled. God saw everything that he had made, and behold, it was very good.[1] But plainly, evil is now present everywhere in God's good world. We see evil of every kind; physical evil, in pain and sickness and death; moral evil, in sin and selfishness and self-will, in unhappiness and remorse, and the sense of our failure to rise to what we know we ought to be; evil in social and commercial life; evil in the relations of class with class, of nation with nation; gross evil amongst the heathen, and evil more subtle but not less deadly in civilisation. The world is not what the dwelling-place of creatures made in God's image ought to be.

And so the question is forced upon us: Why is there all this evil in the world of a good God? Whence has it come: from within us, or from without us? In particular, why is there that evil and that inclination towards evil in the heart of man which we call Sin? We cannot think that it was implanted in us by God, who is holy. We mean by sin whatever is contrary to God's holy will, and we cannot think that God is the source of what is contrary to his own will. We find the root of sin in the misuse by man of the free will that is his noblest power, and we cannot think that it is

[1] Gen. i. 31.

14

SIN

God who has disposed us to turn his own best gift against him. Why is it, then, that we choose evil, though we know what is good? In a word, whence comes sin?

The problem of the origin of evil is one which has always perplexed the minds of men. In every age they have tried, and have failed, to find a full explanation of it by the light of natural reason.

The Old Testament taught men the holiness of God and his hatred of sin, but it did not solve the problem of sin's origin.

The Christian revelation gave God's remedy for sin, but we must frankly confess that not even Christianity tells us how sin first began. This need not surprise us. Christ came to give us sufficient light to enable us to walk securely on the high road that leads man back to God, but not to solve every puzzle that the restless mind of man can raise.[1]

Christ did not tell us the origin of evil, perhaps because our minds are not yet capable of comprehending it; perhaps because the presence of evil within us, our bosom enemy, deprives us of the power of seeing it as it really is; or perhaps because evil cannot be reasonably explained, being itself unreasonable, the one unreasonable thing in the world. Anyway, since Christ has not told us the origin of evil, we may be sure that it is not necessary for us to know it. We must be content to wait until we come to the unveiled knowledge of God, and in the light of that knowledge see much that is now hidden from us.

II

The first chapter, then, of the history of evil is sealed from us. That history opens for us at the second chapter, and there we read that, before mankind was created, evil was already present in the spiritual world. Some of the angels, though created good, and capable of attaining to perfect and permanent holiness, had changed—we know not how or why—and became evil, rebelling against God.

[1] Chap. xii. 1.

These angels, fallen from their glory, are called devils; their leader is Satan.

There was war in heaven, Michael and his angels going forth to war with the dragon; and the dragon warred and his angels; and they prevailed not, neither was their place found any more in heaven. And the great dragon was cast down, the old serpent, he that is called the Devil, and Satan, the deceiver of the whole world; he was cast down to the earth, and his angels were cast down with him.[1] So Holy Scripture says, speaking to us of the spirit-world in picture language.

The evil angels, cast forth from the presence of God, turned their malignant energies against the newly created race of men. Here in this world the war continues, and we are told it will continue until the end of the world[2]—the war of evil against good, of the evil spirits against God. In this war mankind is the battle-ground, rather than the protagonist. Evil strives against good within and around man, seeking to gain possession of him and make him its prey.

Let us make no mistake about it. The devils do exist, intelligent beings, bearing ill-will towards God and men. Some people are doubtful about the existence of the devils; but Holy Scripture is as clear in teaching about evil spirits as it is in teaching about the holy angels. It is one of the cunning devices of Satan to persuade men that he does not exist; and he does not cease to have power for ill when his existence is disbelieved. Woe to the inhabitants of the earth : because the devil is gone down unto you, having great wrath, because he knoweth that he hath but a short time.[3] Behind the rage of sinful men, and the hostility of the forces of this world against Christ and his Church, the Christian discerns the might of Satanic enmity.[4] Our adversary, the devil, as a roaring lion, walketh about, seeking whom he may devour.[5]

We know not why God has allowed this thwarting of his will. We know not why evil is allowed by the Almighty God

[1] Rev. xii. 7-9.   [2] Rev. xix. 11-21.   [3] Rev. xii. 12.
[4] Acts iv. 25-29; Rev. ii. 10.   [5] 1 Pet. v. 8.

16

still to continue, nor why it seems so often to prevail. But we do know, from the Christian revelation, that it will not triumph in the end.[1]

III

The third chapter in the history of evil is the Fall of Man.

Evil did not have its first beginning in man; it came to him from outside, through the ill-will of evil spirits. It was Satan who brought evil into the world, and won the consent of mankind to sin, by which the world and mankind were spoilt, and guilt and misery found entrance among the children of men.

The first people whom God made in the world were good and innocent and happy. They were not perfect, but they were capable of attaining perfection. They were not highly developed—it was but the childhood of the race—but they were capable of developing in knowledge without sinning. They needed to come into contact with evil, and to know its strength : until they did so, they were but babes. But contact with evil assailing from outside is a very different thing from inward consent to it. It is not necessary for a man to sow his wild oats in order to grow up. Since there is evil in the world, knowledge of it and of its power is necessary to make a man a complete man; but this knowledge can be as real if a man refuses the evil by the right use of his will, as if by the wrong use of it he surrenders to evil and embraces it. Nay, more : it is the man who rejects the assaults of evil who knows its full strength, and attains to the spiritual development that results from the full exercise of his powers of resistance. He who falls yields before he had learnt all that his striving against evil might have taught him.

Similarly, the development of the race of man, in knowledge and in the exercise of his powers, might have come to pass without sin. But, in fact, this was not so. The intellectual rising of the race was accomplished by a moral fall. Knowledge of evil was gained by consent to it and rebellion against God, not by resisting it in obedience to

[1] Rev. xii. 10-12; xix. 2.

God. Like the devils, men changed and became bad,
deliberately using their will in opposition to God's will,
under the first stress of temptation. It was not altogether
their fault: they were tempted by Satan. But for all that
they were guilty, because they were responsible for their
own acts, being free agents. They had the power, if they
would, of refusing Satan's temptation; but they chose to
consent to him. The citadel was captured through consent
of the garrison. Nor might they cast the blame of their
sin upon God, as if he were responsible for all that happened
because all was present to his mind from the beginning.
God's foreknowledge does not take away man's responsibility.

The Fall of Man means that the first step in the development of the race was marked, without any need, by a mis-
directing of human will, and a turning away from the true
purpose of life. The development of mankind was begun;
but already man, intended for God, had turned against God.

This is set forth for us, in a parable, in the third chapter of
Genesis. There we see man's happiness in innocence,
the image of God in him unstained, his enjoyment of God's
presence—man living for God.

The temptation came through Satan, who is portrayed
as a serpent. It was allowed by God, since temptation (but
not sin) was necessary for man's education and probation.
He could not reach his perfection unless he felt the power of
sin in temptation and conquered.

The temptation came, as all temptation comes, through
natural desires not wrong in themselves: the tree was good
for food, and pleasant to the eyes, a tree to be desired to
make one wise. There is no sin in such desires. Sin can come
only by the act of our will consenting to our desires contrary
to the known will of God.[1]

Then we see the gradual yielding to temptation. It is
caressed in the mind: I wish it were not wrong. The mind
is obscured through the desire: Yea, hath God said . . . ?
Perhaps it is not really wrong. Perhaps sin is not so very

[1] Chap. viii. 1.

dreadful after all : Ye shall not surely die. Pride and self-will are aroused : Ye shall be as gods. I will do what I like, I will be a god unto myself. I will not submit to constraint or limitation, I will turn to my own way.

The effects of sin follow immediately upon the sinful act. The development of the mind is accompanied by the loss of innocence : they knew that they were naked. The sense of guilt : they heard the voice of God saying, Where art thou? The slavish fear : they hid themselves from the presence of the Lord God. The cowardice, blaming others : the woman gave me of the tree . . . ; blaming the devil : the serpent beguiled me; blaming God : the woman whom thou gavest to be with me . . .

And the final scene is of mankind being driven from the presence of God, by God's command, which yet was no arbitrary command, but the necessary consequence of their own act. They cannot remain in the presence of God, because they are no longer fit for it. They cannot remain with God, because they have turned against him. They are separated from him, because by their own choice and act they have separated themselves.

That is how Holy Scripture tells the story; and we can each of us test the truth of the parable by our own personal experience, when first we passed from the happy innocence of undeveloped childhood to the consciousness of our awakening powers, but in doing so took the road of sin.

And so ends the third chapter of the history of evil. Man is spoilt and lowered through turning away from the true purpose of life. God is outraged, and his will set at naught; and the devil, though convicted by God, has for the time got his own way and worked his will on mankind. Man cannot undo his act himself and return to God. What remedy, then, can there be, unless God, who is almighty, provide a means whereby Satan can be overcome, and the outrage against God compensated by an obedience on the part of man greater than his disobedience, and man endued with a strength and righteousness which he has not in himself?

IV

The fourth chapter carries on the history of sin in its effects upon the whole race down to the present time.

Sin is a universal and perpetual disease, and it shows itself in thoughts and words and deeds which are the symptoms of the deep-seated evil within.

And sin is an inherited disease. As the seeds of bodily disease are sometimes tranmitted from the parent to the unborn child, so the evil inheritance of sin was handed on trom generation to generation. In every generation the offspring of men have been born, having already from their parents the infection of sin in their souls. From birth, and even before birth, men have a disposition to sin within them, and are by nature inclined towards self rather than towards God. Selfishness is natural in a fallen race. How little it surprises us, when we note the first signs of naughtiness or selfishness in the unfolding life of a little child. We see our own history, and indeed the history of the whole race, being repeated in him. Our first parents misused their free will, choosing what they knew was wrong; and their children continue in the same path, seeing the higher road, but following the lower. All we like sheep have gone astray; we have turned every one to his own way.[1]

And we may not put the blame of our sins upon those who have gone before us. It is true that we are part and parcel of the race, and inherit its evil tendencies. But mankind, even apart from Christ, is not totally depraved through the fall; and mankind in Christ has been enabled to attain to much that is very good. The good as well as the evil has been transmitted to us. We inherit myriad influences both good and bad; and our will is enabled by God to turn from the evil, and to allow the good to be developed in us. No man is fated to reproduce in himself a degenerate father. And again, if it be true that the natural will is always prone to choose the evil, it is still more true that the grace of Christ, which is given to us Christians, is stronger than nature: it is supernatural; and through it our own weak and faulty

---

[1] Isa. liii. 6.

will can be strengthened and corrected. I can do all things in him that strengtheneth me.[1]

And similarly, no Christian can ever rightly ascribe the blame of his sins to his companions, his education, or his surroundings. Though often there are adverse influences in a man's circumstances, yet still he can make choice to yield or to resist. Nobody's circumstances are entirely favourable, and God, who knows the difficulties and hindrances of each one, provides the necessary aid for those who seek it.[2]

We have said that the taint of evil which came in at the beginning has remained in mankind. This is true, in spite of the fact of man's progress. His mental powers, which we saw awakening at the fall, have shown a continual development. Through them has come civilisation, and all the triumphs of science, literature, and art. The child-race has been growing towards manhood's powers. Also in every age the history of mankind shows that even fallen man is capable of heroic virtues. Loyalty and patriotism, courage and fortitude, endurance of pain, natural affections, the sense of justice, the sincere pursuit of truth—these and many more give proof that, although fallen, man still retains the image of God. And all this is the fulfilment of part of God's will for mankind. Man's powers and virtues were God's gifts and the development of them has come to pass through his working. But, mixed with this real advance, there has always been that which is not according to God's will, and has not come from him, that is, Sin. God intended that there should have been a rise all along the line, but it has not been so. Side by side with the development of what is good in man, we are faced with his growth in evil. And all that is best in man is spoilt by the fact that man, having lost the true knowledge of God, has always tended to find the central object of his life in himself, and not in God.

Every man enters the world, not as God meant him to be, but with his soul darkened, and his will weak to choose the right. And the inherited weakness within man opens the door for the entrance of evil influences, so that in every

[1] Phil. iv. 13.   [2] 1 Cor. x. 13.

generation men have renewed the fall individually, by sinful self-pleasing and continual self-assertion against God. And, but for the grace of God finding a remedy for sin, men must have so continued always, missing the true purpose of life, and acting against their own truest interests.

Men have in every age been tempted by Satan and the devils. The enmity of the evil spirits did not cease with their first victory. They have always the will to do harm to men in body and soul. and they have not only the will, but often also the power. Sometimes they are able even to take complete possession of their victim, as we read in the gospels.[1] This fact is hard for those to credit whose experience is limited to lands where Christian influences abound, but not for those who have intimate knowledge of the heathen world. Much evil of all kinds is due to the activities of evil spirits. We are too much inclined to look only for what we call natural causes of the ills which we see, while as a matter of fact those natural causes may be themselves the symptoms of underlying spiritual evil. For example, our Lord teaches plainly that in some cases bodily sickness is caused directly by evil spirits, and therefore can be cured only by supernatural means.[2]

But though the devils have such evil will and power, men are not simply helpless or without defence against them. It is only by our inward consent to evil that the enemy can find entrance. If there are hosts of evil spirits assailing us and seeking to find means to do us harm, they are not almighty, they are not equal with God. And they are opposed, army against army, by the hosts of the holy angels, who are able to drive Satanic power from us, and to keep safe from harm all those who have taken their stand on the side of God and righteousness, and who refuse to consent to the wickedness of Satan and his servants.

We are not to hold Satan responsible, any more than God or our forbears, for the sins we do. If our first parents sinned at Satan's instigation, yet they sinned without any compelling cause, of their own fault. And though it may be that we should not sin if we were not tempted, still Satan

[1] Mark v. 2, 9, etc.   [2] Mark ix. 29, and Chap. xix. 2.

22

S I N

could have no power over us if we did not consent to him, of our own fault. Christians are not the slaves of the devil, unless by their own choice and act they have bound themselves anew with his chains.

Because of sin, the friendship of men with God, and of men with other men, has been broken.

Men have fallen away from the happy fellowship with God for which they were made. Like a dark cloud that hides the sun, sin has come between man and God, preventing man from seeing God and knowing his will clearly, and shutting him off from the ever-radiating love of God. The world lies under the wrath of God.[1] Man cannot remove that cloud of sin; and God, because he is holy and true, cannot pretend that it does not exist. God who is holy cannot be pleased with sin which is contrary to his nature; God who is loving cannot but hate sin which is harmful to his creatures; God who is true cannot ignore sin. Sinful man takes from God the honour which is due from the creature to the Creator, outraging his love, ungratefully using against him the powers he has given. Sinful man has separated himself from God, and is fit only for continued separation, fit only for hell—that is, eternal separation from God.[2]

We can see the effects of the fall most clearly in the state of the heathen, who have not been brought within reach of God's remedy for sin. Although made in the image of God, they know not God who made them, nor the meaning of life, having no hope, and without God in the world.[3] But indeed we can see the evidences of man's spiritual separation from God in everything around us, and even in our own hearts, Christians though we be. Unless God had implanted in us a higher nature than that which we received from our parents, we should be unable to know God or to please him.[4] and, even with that higher nature, there still remains in us Christians the faulty disposition which we have inherited, so that we are not able to turn away from sin and Satan except by the continual help of God.

[1] John iii. 36; 1 John v. 19.   [2] Chaps. v. 2; xx. 5.
[3] Eph. ii. 12.   [4] Rom. viii. 7-8.

And as men were separated from God by sin, so also they
became separated from one another. The natural brotherhood of man with man is broken, for the children of God
have no real bond of union with each other, if they are
alienated from the one Father of all. From the first root
of sin sprang all malice and dissension, all strifes and wars,
and all that is evil and cruel in modern civilisation. Men
are at enmity with one another because they are at enmity
with God.[1] Men sin, not only against God, but also against
their fellow-men. They harm and spoil one another, by
deliberate malice, or by the evil effects of their sins, or by the
unintended influence of their sinful characters and example.
The disease of sin is contagious; the infection passes from
one to another like a plague. No man can sin unto himself
alone. Sin ever tends to spread, and to spoil, and to separate.

v

The parable of the Prodigal Son is our Lord's fullest
teaching about sin.[2] One may interpret it as applying either
to oneself or to the whole race of men.

There was a young man who said to his father, "Father,
give me the portion of goods that falleth to me." The sin lay
not in desiring the good things, all our powers of mind and
soul and body, which it is God's will to give us; the sin lay
in the perverted will of the lad, to have those gifts for his
own, to use as he liked, apart from the will of the Father.
The begining of sin is self-will, the desire to be independent
of God.

So he got what he asked for. His powers came to him, as
they have come to us all. And after not many days—those
days in which he, or we, kept in touch with religion, while
in fact the heart was already turned away from God—he
went his own way openly into the far country. And the
father let him go : the Almighty God cannot keep us against
our will, without taking from us that highest of all the gifts
he has given us, our free will.

[1] Rom. i. 28 ff.   [2] Luke xv. 11-32.

24

S I N

He went into the far country, which is reached by no longer journey than a change of mind; that far country in which we are as soon as we have turned away from God. And there he had the pleasures of sin for a season,[1] for the devil does not always cheat us of what he promises us, the poor price for which we barter our eternal happiness. The lad had the good time he expected to have. The pleasures of fleshly indulgence, the ambitions of this world, the exaltation of self, whatever wrong purpose in life lies nearest to our heart, perhaps we shall have it if we seek it. Perhaps also, unlike the lad, we shall preserve our social respectability, and even practise the outward observances of religion to the end. But all the time he was, and we shall be, in the far country, against God and apart from God, by our own choice. And there that punishment of sin will come upon us which is the necessary consequence of what we are.

He wasted his substance. There are more ways of wasting our substance than by riotous living; for if a man uses his powers in any other way than in obedience to God and in fulfilment of God's purpose in giving them, he wastes them. He wastes them, even if he effects his own purpose, even if he achieves his ambition, even if he gains the whole world.[2]

He began to be in want. The soul apart from God begins to starve, for the wholehearted service of God alone can satisfy: the pleasures of sin are only for a season.

And finally he joined himself to a citizen of that country. The desire to please oneself and go one's own way ends in the slavery of sin and degradation. He wanted to be free and independent; he despised the glorious liberty of the children of God; and so he lost freedom and became a slave, even as it is written: Every one that committeth sin is the bond-servant of sin.[3]

[1] Heb. xi. 25.   [2] Matt. xvi. 26.   [3] John viii. 34.

III

THE PREPARATION FOR CHRIST

I

MAN had chosen the downward road from Jerusalem, the city of God; and he had fallen among thieves, who stripped him of his raiment—his God-given raiment of righteousness —and inflicted grievous injuries upon him, leaving him half-dead, too weak to help himself or to return to his home, unable to cure his wounds, in desperate need of the Good Samaritan.[1]

Or, in another picture, man was in the power of Satan, the strong man armed, who like a robber-chief was holding mankind prisoner in his stronghold. Men were captives, tied and bound by the chains of their sins. There was needed one stronger than Satan to conquer him, if men were to be set free. And God alone is stronger than Satan. It was necessary that God should come to the rescue; else there could be no deliverance.[2]

Mankind needed rescue, remission, restoration: rescue from the power of Satan, remission of the guilt of sin, restoration from the effects of sin. Of himself man was unable to find this deliverance, however great his desire, however earnest his efforts. If God would come, there could be rescue, remission, and restoration; but no one else could break the power of Satan.

And the gospel, the good news of the love of God towards sinful man, is this: God was willing to come. He did not abandon mankind because of sin. He hated the sin, but loved the sinner; and so great was his love that he was willing to come to do the threefold work that needed to be done, and to start mankind afresh.

[1] Luke x. 30 *ff*.   [2] Mark iii. 27.

26

God wills all men to be saved. He 'has done the needed work *for* us, conquering Satan at the cost of the death of Jesus; and he will also to do the needed work *in* us, binding up our wounds, and pouring in the oil and wine of divine grace, that we may pass out of the death of sin into the new life of righteousness.

The wages of sin is death;[1] but thanks be to God who gives us the victory through our Lord Jesus Christ.[2] The free gift of God is eternal life in Christ Jesus our Lord.[3] Where sin abounded, grace did abound more exceedingly: that, as sin reigned in death, even so might grace reign through righteousness unto eternal life through Jesus Christ our Lord.[4]

II

From all eternity[5] God, foreseeing the sin of man, had provided the remedy of sin; and when sin was first committed, we hear God promising that a Saviour will come to bruise the serpent's head.[6] We see the salvation of the world already beginning.

The preparation of the world for the coming of the Saviour took many more thousands of years than have elapsed since his coming. In covering that long period briefly we can think only of a very few points.

Although the world went astray from the truth, yet it did not lose the knowledge of God altogether. God left not himself without witness, in that he did good, and gave rain from heaven and fruitful seasons.[7] All creation bore witness to the Creator. As St. Paul says: The invisible things of God, even his everlasting power and divinity are clearly seen, being perceived through created things.[8] Not by any means that all men had eyes to see. Indeed, most men became vain in their reasonings, and their senseless heart was darkened, and they changed the glory of the incorruptible God for the likeness of an image of corruptible man.[9] But even idolatry in its blindness was a dark expression of the

[1] Rom. vi. 23. [2] 1 Cor. xv. 57. [3] Rom. vi. 23.
[4] Rom. v. 20-21. [5] Eph. iii. 11. [6] Gen. iii. 15.
[7] Acts xiv. 17. [8] Rom. i. 20. [9] Rom. i. 21, 23.

27

universal belief of mankind, and kept alive the belief in the existence of some divine power greater than man.

Similarly the instinct of mankind to offer sacrifice, though misdirected through the belief in many gods, was a true instinct. It came from a deep-rooted feeling of man's dependence upon some higher power. There seem to have been three main ideas underlying all sacrifices. First, that man needs to enter into communion with his god. Men sought to do this by means of the sacrificed victim, of which both men and the deity were understood to partake together in the sacrificial feast. Secondly, that man approaching his god must come with an offering in his hand. They felt that the god made great demands upon his worshippers, and that they belonged to him, and must pay homage and tribute. Thirdly, that man has reason to fear his god, and must avert his anger by sacrifice. Thus, though darkened by superstition and ignorance, the sacrifices even of the heathen pointed to and kept alive the true ideas of communion, worship, and propitiation for sin.[1]

As the ages passed, the minds of the wisest men were led gradually to disbelieve in the many gods of popular religion. Great teachers arose, especially among the ancient Greeks, who, through their search for one source of all things in the world, came near to the truth that there is one God; the highest and best that the mind of man can conceive, from whom all things come, and in whom all things exist. To such thoughts as these St. Paul appealed at Athens, when he said : God is not far from every one of you; for in him we live and move and have our being; as certain even of your own poets have said. For we are also his offspring.[2] Although this was the teaching only of the learned and spiritually minded, and although even they did not know that the one God whom they were feeling after was a Person and a loving Father; yet we see here unmistakable signs of the preparation of the world by God, through human reason, for the revelation of himself in Christ.

And again, the heart of man in the pagan world was seeking for God, seeking for one outside itself in whom to rest.

[1] Chap. ix. 4.   [2] Acts xvii. 27, 28.

28

There were some who realised that man continually failed
to attain to his own ideals. They saw man going from this life
into the dark unknown, without having fulfilled any purpose
worthy of his powers. They were asking : How may a
man make the best of his life? They felt the beauty of
goodness, and were seeking to know what goodness is. Amid
many mistakes and doubts and denials, the feeling was
growing that the distinction between right and wrong could
have no other basis than in the mind of God himself, that
God is good, that he demands righteousness and virtue from
man, and that human goodness is nothing else than being like
God. They felt that man needed God, if he was to live
true to his own best self.

But who or what was God? Where was God to be found?
Man's reason and man's sense of need were not in themselves capable of truly finding God. Mankind never could
have found God, had not God come to man and revealed
himself in Christ. But the awakening of the need of a sure
knowledge of God was part of God's preparation of the
world for Christ. He who was about to satisfy the need
first led men to the sense of need. The Word of God, before
he became flesh and dwelt among us, was already the light
of men, the source of all true thoughts and feelings and
desires that they had. He was the light that lighteneth every
man that cometh into the world,[1] the light that already was
shining amid the darkness of a fallen race.

III

The direct line of God's preparation of the world for
Christ lay in his choice of one nation, the Israelites or Jews,
out of all the nations of the world, to be his own people,
whom he educated gradually in the true knowledge of himself
and of his will.

Every nation has some God-given quality in which it excels
others. While the Greeks excelled in powers of reason and
imagination, and the Romans in powers of government, God
gave the Jews above all nations the instinct to seek him
and the power to know him.

[1] John i. 4, 5, 9.

God established his covenant with Israel. The covenant was a solemn agreement between the nation and God, which assured the people of the favour of God their Father, on condition that they were obedient to him, forsaking their false gods, and serving the one true God only.

We read that, in the far-distant times of the patriarchs, Abraham had the knowledge of the true God; and the promise was made to him first, that in him and in his seed all the nations of the earth should be blessed.[1] And God said to him: I am God Almighty; walk before me, and be thou perfect; and I will make my covenant between me and thee.[2]

The history of Israel as a nation begins in the time of Moses, when God stretched forth his hand and brought the people out of Egypt, and established his covenant with the nation at Mount Sinai.[3] The Israelites were then like children learning their first lesson about their Father. In Canaan they were always being tempted to fall back to the idolatrous ways of the heathen around them, and to go after other gods. The first lesson they had to learn was this: I am the Lord thy God; thou shalt have not other gods besides me.[4] We see how hard they found the lesson by their continual backslidings, recorded in the Old Testament.[5]

As the national life developed, many further lessons had to be learnt; the character of God, his righteousness, his holiness; and that he alone is God, the ruler of the destinies of all nations, and the judge of all; and not, as they had thought at first, the God of the Israelites only. They were taught that God required of them morality of life, and that social unrighteousness, commercial dishonesty, and the oppression of the poor were not only offences against one another, but also sins against God.[6]

The hardest lesson was taught them by the cruel discipline of the exile in Babylon. Uprooted from their home, far away from the holy associations and traditions of the land of their birth, deprived of their temple sacrifices and all the

---

[1] Gen. xxii. 18.   [2] Gen. xvii. 3.
[3] Exod. xxiv. 7, 8.   [4] Exod. xx. 2, 3.
[5] Judges, Samuel, Kings.   [6] Amos, Hosea, Isaiah.

outward helps to worship, they had to learn that they could still call upon their God, and find him in a strange land.[1]

On the return from exile, the whole Jewish nation became definitely a church, the church of the true God in a pagan world. Being weak and oppressed politically, they devoted themselves to the observances of the law of God, and waited with growing expectation for the coming of the promised Deliverer,[2] and for the establishment of a new covenant between them and God, as had been promised them; Behold, the days come, saith the Lord, that I will make a new covenant with the house of Israel, and with the house of Judah: I will put my law in their inward parts, and in their heart will I write it; and will be their God, and they shall be my people; and they shall all know me, from the least of them unto the greatest of them, saith the Lord; for I will forgive their iniquity, and their sins will I remember no more.[3]

The history of this preparation of the chosen race is written in the Old Testament, which was divided by the Jews into three parts: the Law, the Prophets, and the Psalms.[4]

The Law was gradually put together from the time of Moses, and included enactments of various kinds. God taught the people through the Law great moral precepts such as the Ten Commandments;[5] and also laws for the regulation of social and political life, laws regulating the sacrifices and religious festivals of the nation, and laws about customs which separated the people from other nations, such as the observance of the sabbath, and the strict regulations about certain foods which no Jew might eat.[6] The peculiar point about the Jewish Law, as compared with the laws of other nations, is that it was accepted as the direct declaration of the will of God for his people. Each smallest regulation was regarded as a law of God.

[1] Isa. xl. *ff*.
[2] Ezekiel, Ezra, Nehemiah, Daniel, Maccabees.
[3] Jer. xxxi. 31-34; Heb. viii. 8-12.   [4] Luke xxiv. 44.
[5] Exod. xx.
[6] Genesis, Exodus, Leviticus, Numbers, Deuteronomy.

The Prophets comprise two sections. First, the historical books of the Old Testament.[1] They differ from the histories of other races in being written from God's point of view, not man's. They trace the gradual education of the people by God. They explain the events of the national life as acts of obedience or of disobedience to God. They narrate the varying fortunes of the people as the direct outcome of God's dealing with it in accordance with its attitude toward him.[2] Secondly, this part of the Old Testament contains the writings of the prophets and the records of their teaching.[3] The prophets were teachers sent by God, and inspired by him to teach the people about him, his righteousness and his love, his holiness and his hatred of sin.

The Psalms or Sacred Writings is the name applied to the rest of the Old Testament.[4] It was the latest part to be compiled. It included history and moral teaching and wise sayings. The best-known part of it is the Book of Psalms, which are the expression of the aspirations of the most spiritually minded of the people towards union with God, and their praises and prayers and meditations. This book provided the hymns which were used in the nation's worship of God in the temple and the synagogues.

Running through the Law, the Prophets, and the Psalms, there was the continual expectation and promise of a Saviour who was to come. The Jews were led always to look forward to a golden age, the days of the Messiah—that is, the days of the anointed one whom God would send to his people. Sometimes the Messiah is pictured as a great king, a mighty conqueror like the hero-king David,[5] who should be God's agent in delivering the nation from its oppressors, and setting up the kingdom of God over all nations; sometimes as a prophet like Moses,[6] who should fully teach the ways of

[1] Joshua, Judges, Samuel, Kings.   [2] Judg. ii. 11-23, etc.
[3] Isaiah, Jeremiah, Ezekiel, and the Minor Prophets.
[4] Ruth, Chronicles, Ezra, Nehemiah, Esther, Job, Psalms, Proverbs, Canticles, Ecclesiastes, Daniel; and (but not in the Hebrew Old Testament) the Apocrypha.
[5] Ps. lxxxix. 3, 4; Isa. ix. 7; Jer. xxiii. 5; Heb. i. 8.
[6] Deut. xviii. 15; Heb. i. 1, 2.

32

God to men; sometimes as a priest greater than Aaron,[1] who should really bring the people, and with them all the nations, into the presence of God, by taking away the sins which the continual sacrifices pointed to but could not remove. Sometimes they thought of the Messiah as one who should come in clouds of divine glory attended by the holy angels,[2] sometimes again he is depicted (but this the Jews did not recognise as a picture of the Messiah) as the suffering servant of Jehovah, despised and rejected and slain by his fellow-men.[3]

This expectation of a Saviour became part of the mind of the whole nation. Thus God prepared for the Saviour's coming. The Saviour, we know, was Jesus Christ, the Son of God, Prophet, Priest, and King; but above all the Saviour and Redeemer, not of the Jews only, but also of the whole world, through whom all nations may become part of the chosen people of God.[4]

We can now understand what St. Paul meant when he wrote of the Jews as Israelites, whose is the adoption, and the glory, and the covenants, and the giving of the law, and the service of God, and the promises; whose are the fathers, and of whom is Christ as concerning the flesh, who is over all, God blessed for ever.[5]

The nation which had such great privileges and such a high destiny was, therefore, the more blameable when in the end it proved unworthy of its high calling. Christ came as one of the chosen people, but when he came unto his own, they that were his own received him not.[6] All along, God's purpose of rescue, remission, and restoration was hindered and delayed by new sins and self-will even in his highly favoured people. While always there were some who were obedient to the Law and the Prophets, there was also always a greater number who were perverted by Satan and were disobedient, turning to their own ways. And at last, when their Messiah came, only a very few accepted him. The Jewish nation as a whole failed to recognise their Saviour.

[1] Ps. cx. 4; Heb. v. 6.
[2] Dan. vii. 13; Matt. xxvi. 64.   [3] Isa. liii.
[4] 1 Pet. ii. 10. On the use of the Old Testament in the Christian Church, see Chaps. xiii. 2; xiv. 2.   [5] Rom. ix. 4, 5.
[6] John i. 11.

33

IV

The final preparation of the chosen people was the preaching of John the Baptist, which is narrated at the beginning of each of the four gospels.

John the Baptist was the last of the long line of Jewish prophets; and he was more than a prophet.[1] He was the immediate forerunner of the Saviour, preparing his way. He was sent, in the days of the Messiah, to prepare the people for the salvation and the judgment that were at hand.

He came with a message that men should repent. The heart of the people still needed to be prepared for Christ. Repent ye, he cried, for the kingdom of heaven is at hand.[2]

He taught[3] that the coming of the Saviour would mean the coming of divine judgment upon the nation. As wheat is separated from chaff in the threshing-floor, so those who repented, and therefore were able to welcome Christ, would be separated from those who rejected him. Repentance was necessary, else the coming of the Saviour would not be for joy and blessing, but would bring upon them the infliction of the wrath of God. Every tree that bringeth not forth good fruit shall be hewn down and cast into the fire.

He taught them that they could not rely for their salvation on their privileged position as children of the covenant in which they fondly trusted. Think not to say, We have Abraham as our father. Nothing but personal repentance could prepare each one for the kingdom of God.

And by repentance St. John the Baptist meant three things. First, conversion, a change of mind, turning from their own ways to the ways of God. Secondly, the humbling of their pride by open confession of their sins, and submission to the baptism of repentance. This baptism was only an outward sign of conversion: the Christian sacrament of baptism was not yet. He taught : There cometh one that is mightier than I; he shall baptise you with the Holy Ghost and with fire. Thirdly, repentance meant a new life of righteousness and unselfishness in their daily dealings with one

---

[1] Matt. xi. 10.   [2] Matt. iii. 2.   [3] Matt. iii. 7-12.

another.[1] Christian repentance, as we shall see,[2] includes all these, but more than these.

The result of St. John's mission was that many of the people, and even the outcast sinners, heeded God's warning spoken by him; but the Pharisees, the leaders of the Jewish religion, and the Sadducees, the leaders in political and social life, remained still in their proud impenitence.[3] Already God's judgment was begun.

Then it was shown to St. John that the promised Saviour whom he had been proclaiming was none other than the holy Jesus whom he had known from childhood. St. John pointed out Jesus to his own followers, saying : Behold the Lamb of God, which taketh away the sin of the world.[4]

And then the work of the forerunner was finished. God's work of preparation was done. God was with man. Those who rejected him would do so through their own fault.

---

[1] Luke iii. 10-14.
[2] Chaps. vii. 3; viii. 2.
[3] Matt. xxi. 31, 32.
[4] John i. 29.

IV

THE INCARNATION

I

WHEN the fulness of the time came, God sent forth his Son, born of a woman.[1] For us men and for our salvation God the Son came down from heaven, and was made man.[2] In the beginning was the Word, and the Word was God; and the Word became flesh, and dwelt among us.[3] From all eternity he was God, receiving his divine life and nature from God the Father. When the time of preparation of the world was fulfilled, he became man. He did not cease to be God, but he joined together human nature with divine nature in his Person, that all mankind might be brought into union with God through him. This is called the Incarnation, a word which means Being made flesh.

Born of a woman. The final act of God's age-long preparation for the Incarnation was that he made choice of a woman, from whom his Son should take human nature and be born. That woman was a Jewish maiden named Mary. Of all women who had lived in the world, she alone was made worthy in her spotless purity and holiness of so great an honour. No one else has been so highly favoured by God.[4] No one else has received so great grace. Through the grace of God given to her she was enabled to live all her life without any stain of sin coming upon her.[5] And thus she was wonderfully prepared by God for her wonderful motherhood.

As Mary has been so highly exalted by God, she is worthy to receive from us greater honour than any other human

[1] Gal. iv. 4.   [2] Nicene Creed.
[4] Luke i. 28.   [5] Chap. xix. 6.   [3] John i. 1, 14.

being or any of the holy angels. Always we speak of her as blessed Mary; as she herself said : All generations shall called me blessed.[1] She is blessed in her purity and humility; blessed in being the Mother from whom God the Son took a human body and mind and soul, and all that makes up our human nature; above all, blessed in her perfect obedience always to the will of the heavenly Father.[2]

Blessed Mary was a virgin when she became the Mother of Jesus.[3] She was betrothed to a man whose name was Joseph. The archangel Gabriel was sent by God to her with this message : Hail, thou that art highly favoured; blessed art thou among women. And behold, thou shalt conceive in thy womb, and shalt bring forth a son, and shalt call his name Jesus. He shall be great and shall be called the Son of the Most High; and of his kingdom there shall be no end. And Mary said : How shall this be, seeing I know not a man? And the archangel answered : The Holy Ghost shall come upon thee, and the power of the Most High shall overshadow thee; wherefore also that which is to be born shall be called holy, the Son of God. And Mary said : Behold the hand-maid of the Lord; be it unto me according to thy word.[4] At that moment,[5] by the consent of Mary to the will of God, the Incarnation of his Son began within her womb; and God was with man.

During nine months her unborn Child was being formed of her substance. Then the divine Saviour was born, at Bethlehem in the land of Judea; and the wondrous birth was celebrated by choirs of angels singing : Glory to God in the highest, and on earth peace among men in whom he is well-pleased.[6] The Word was made flesh, and dwelt among us; and we beheld his glory, glory as of the Only-Begotten from the Father, full of grace and truth.[7]

When God the Son became man, it was not a new person who was born into the world. The Child of Mary still was

<hr/>

[1] Luke i. 48.   [2] Mark iii. 35.
[3] Luke i. 26; Matt. i. 18-25.   [4] Luke i. 26-38.
[5] Celebrated by the Church on the Feast of the Annunciation, March 25.
[6] Luke ii. 1-14.   [7] John i. 14.

God, as he had been from all eternity; but now he was God made man. He was the same Person as before, but now he was as truly human as divine. Jesus Christ was one Person, having two natures. Therefore it was natural that the manner of his birth should have been different from that of all men. If blessed Mary had conceived by a husband, her child would have been human only. From ordinary human generation human persons are produced. But he who was born of Mary was not a new human person appearing in the world : he was the Son of God, uniting himself with human nature.

And, having become man, he has never laid aside the human nature which he took into union with his Godhead. Jesus Christ our Saviour is truly God and truly man, altogether God and altogether man, now and for ever. He is the link between God and man, joined with God the Father by his divine nature, and joined with all men by his human nature.

II

St. Joseph, to whom the miracle of the virgin-birth had been told by an angel, took St. Mary as his legal wife before the Child was born, and he became their protector.[1] St. Joseph is held in reverence by Christians because of his devotion to Jesus and Mary. But, although St. Mary lived in his house, she remained a virgin always. So the Church has believed and taught from the earliest times.

When Jesus was eight days old, he was circumcised according to the law of the Old Testament, and was given his name.[2] The holy name of Jesus means God or Saviour.

For thirty years[3] he lived a hidden life, having his home at Nazareth with St. Mary and St. Joseph.[4] The ordinary duties and occupations of home-life are made holy for us, because God has shared in them. Our Lord passed from infancy to boyhood, and from boyhood to manhood; and at each stage of his growing powers he fulfilled perfectly the

[1] Matt. i. 18-25.
[2] Luke ii. 21.
[3] Luke iii. 23.
[4] Matt. ii. 23; Luke iv. 16.

will of the heavenly Father, showing forth at each stage the perfection of human nature.[1] We see in his perfect life on earth the fulfilment of the true purpose of human life, obedience to the will of God. As a child, a youth, a man, he is our pattern.

Though he was the Son of God, he was subject to his Mother and St. Joseph.[2] He was educated as a Jewish boy in the religion of the Old Testament, and shared in the worship of the temple and the synagogue.[3] He was not counted great among men. He did not choose worldly honour as his lot. He was willing to be known as the son of Joseph.[4] His lineage was kingly: it is believed that both St. Joseph and St. Mary were descendants of David,[5] but his home was poor and humble. He associated himself, not with the ruling class, or the very wealthy, but with the great majority of men, those who have to earn their living by their own labour. He learnt and practised the trade of a carpenter,[6] and thereby taught us the dignity of labour. Nothing which God has shared can be without dignity.

When Jesus was thirty years old, St. John the Baptist had already begun his preaching of repentance in preparation for the Messiah's coming. Jesus submitted to baptism at the hands of John. That baptism was a sign of repentance, and Jesus accepted it, although there was no sin in him that needed repentance. He accepted it because, being in all things obedient to God's will, he was obedient in this also to God's prophet. He said to St. John : Thus it becometh us to fulfil all righteousness.[7] Here we see him as already the Sin-bearer, allying himself with that sinful humanity which he had taken to himself. Already he is the Lamb of God, taking away the sin of the world.[8]

When he was baptised the Holy Spirit came down upon him; and both he and St. John heard a voice from heaven saying : Thou art my beloved Son, in whom I am well-pleased.[9] The Holy Spirit had indeed been dwelling in

[1] Luke ii. 49, 52.
[2] Luke ii. 51.
[3] Luke ii. 42; iv. 16.
[4] Luke iv. 22.
[5] Matt. i. 1; Rom. i. 3.
[6] Mark vi. 3.
[7] Matt. iii. 13-15.   [8] John i. 29.
[9] Mark i. 11; Matt. i. 17.

our Lord's human nature from its beginning, but at this time he received from the Holy Spirit powers which he had not exercised before. It was his ordination for his office and work as the Messiah: as Prophet, Priest, and King. Somewhat in the same way now Christian men, who have already received the Holy Spirit, are given special powers by him when they are ordained to be priests.[1]

Our Lord was then led by the Spirit into the desert; and there he was tempted by Satan to use his powers, and to plan his career as Messiah, for his own selfish advantage and to gain wordly honour.[2] But our Lord, in whom was no sin,[3] resisted the temptation, and chose the way marked out for him by the Father's will—the way that led him to the Cross. He was in all points tempted like as we are, yet without sin.[4]

From that time he began his three-years' ministry to the Jews. He came into Galilee, and began to preach the gospel of the Kingdom of God, and to work miracles.[5]

III

Our Lord began his teaching with the words: Repent ye, for the kingdom of heaven is at hand.[6]

He had come to establish on earth a kingdom which should never pass away, as had been foretold by the prophets.[7] This kingdom of God was to be a kingdom on earth, but not a kingdom of this world.[8] It was to be a kingdom consisting not of one nation only, but made up of members out of every nation; a kingdom maintained not by force and power, but by the obedience of those who would accept him as their king, and obey his laws, and learn his spirit. It was to be the means by which truth and righteousness and peace should be established, and God's will be done on earth as it is in heaven. The kingdom has its imperfect beginning amongst sin-stained men here, and will be perfected for ever in the

---

[1] Chap. x. 3.   [2] Matt. iv. 1-11.
[3] John viii. 46; 1 Pet. ii. 22; 1 John iii. 5.
[4] Heb. iv. 15.   [5] Mark i. 14, 15.   [6] Matt. iii. 17.
[7] Isa. ix. 7, etc.   [8] John xviii. 36.

40

complete company of the redeemed in heavenly glory and triumph.[1]

Our Lord began, like St. John the Baptist, by preaching repentance, and the necessity for a change of heart; for, after all their preparation, the people's ideas about the kingdom were still worldly and unspiritual. They needed still to learn that unless a man be converted and become as a little child, he cannot enter the kingdom of God.[2] Therefore, in a great many parables,[3] our Lord set forth the spiritual nature of the kingdom, and of what character its members must be; and that though in the end it would become great and world-wide, yet its growth would be slow, gradual, and secret.

Our Lord proclaimed the laws of the kingdom, asserting again with new authority[4] the moral laws of the Old Testament, and teaching men to apply them not only to outward actions, but also to inward desires and thoughts. Thus he taught them that Thou shalt do no murder, meant also that men must not give way to hatred and revengeful thoughts; and that Thou shalt not commit adultery, forbade all indulgence of evil desires of the flesh.[5] He summed up the old Law in these two sayings : Thou shalt love the Lord thy God with all thy heart and with all thy soul and with all thy mind; and, Thou shalt love thy neighbour as thyself, or in other words, Whatsoever ye would that men should do unto you, do also unto them.[6]

He taught also that sacrifice and ceremonial observances are not acceptable in God's sight without the love of God and the inward sincerity of a converted heart.[7]

And he spoke of the end of this world, when he would come again to judgment, to establish for ever the kingdom of God made perfect; saying that his servants must ever be watching for his coming, and not live thinking only of the things of this world; lest when he came he should find them unfit to enter into his glory.[8]

[1] Chap. xx. 1, 6. [2] Matt. xviii. 3. [3] Matt. xiii., etc.
[4] Matt. vii. 29. [5] Matt. v. 17-48; and Chap. xvii.
[6] Matt. xxii. 34-40; vii. 12. [7] Mark vii. 1-13; xii. 28-34.
[8] Mark xiii.; Matt. xxv.; and Chap. xx. 1, 2.

41

The most important point about the kingdom is the character of the king, for the character of Jesus is the revelation to us of the character of God our Father. Our Lord came to show us the Father. No man hath seen God at any time : the only-begotten Son hath declared him.[1] We never could have been sure and certain about God's nature and character and will unless God himself had come and taught us in human words which we could understand. God in heaven was too high and holy for sinful man to understand. Therefore he, as it were, translated himself into an easy language, the mother-tongue of human nature; so that, both by knowing Jesus and by hearing his words, men might truly know God. He that hath seen me, he said, hath seen the Father; for he was himself the image of the invisible God.[2]

And, being both God and man, he brought men back to God by bringing them to himself. He claimed that all men should become his disciples and submit their minds to him, turning from their own darkness to him who is the Light of the world.[3] He called them to accept him as their Master, surrendering their wills to his will, and following him even to suffering and to death.[4] He taught that they could not save themselves by righteous deeds or respectability of life, but must give their hearts to him, and come to him with faith and love, trusting to him for their salvation. Come unto me, he cried, all ye that labour and are heavy laden, and I will give you rest. Take my yoke upon you, and learn of me; for I am meek and lowly in heart : and ye shall find rest unto your souls. For my yoke is easy, and my burden is light.[5]

To all who would come to him, however degraded and outcast, he promised salvation in this life, and glory hereafter, in the company of his redeemed ones. He would give them life : life not of this world, but the divine life that was in himself.[6] He would unite them inwardly with himself,

[1] John i. 18.
[2] John xiv. 9; Col. i. 15; Heb. i. 3; and Chap. xii. 1.
[3] John viii. 12.   [4] Mark viii. 34.
[5] Matt. xi. 28-30.   [6] John v. 26; x. 10.

and so they would be united with their heavenly Father. He would give to them the grace and truth which were in him,[1] that so they would be enabled to escape from sin, and share his holiness, and fulfil the purpose of their creation according to the will of God.

This is a very brief summary of the teaching of Jesus Christ. We need to study his teaching in detail, as it is written in the gospels. It comes to us with divine authority. When Jesus Christ spoke, it was God himself who was speaking through human words; Jesus Christ made no mistakes. Unlike other teachers, he said nothing that was untrue, or that was only half-true. We can trust his teaching entirely, for it is the voice of God.[2]

But the words of Christ cannot come home to our hearts as divine unless our hearts are in tune with God, and our wills ready to submit to him. Jesus said to the Jews: He that is of God heareth the words of God; for this cause ye hear them not, because ye are not of God.[3] And, If any man willeth to do God's will, he shall know of the teaching, whether it be of God.[4] The message of Christ can commend itself only to those who are spiritually prepared to receive it.[5]

IV

Jesus Christ did many wonderful works of mercy during the years of the ministry. He healed the sick, he gave sight to the blind, he raised the dead to life, he delivered those who were possessed by the devil. Wherever he went, the sick and suffering thronged him; and, where there was no hindrance through unbelief,[6] they drew new life and health from him.

These miracles of healing may be regarded in several ways. They were proofs of his love for suffering humanity. He healed those who sought his help, because he was moved with compassion for them.[7]

[1] Chap. vi. 1. [2] John iii. 34. [3] John viii. 47.
[4] John vii. 17. [5] Matt. xiii. 11-17.
[6] Mark vi. 5, 6. [7] Mark i. 41.

And they were evidence that Jesus was the true Messiah sent from God. Thus, when the Baptist sent to ask him, Art thou the Messiah? he answered the messengers: Go, and show John the things which ye do hear and see; the blind receive their sight, and the lame walk, the lepers are cleansed, and the deaf hear, and the dead are raised up, and the poor have good tidings preached unto them. And blessed is he, whosoever shall find none occasion of stumbling in me.[1]

Again, these works were the first-fruits of the victory of Christ in the war which he was waging against the powers of evil. The strength of Christ was greater than that of Satan; the powers of the kingdom of God were mightier than the powers of the realm of darkness. If I, said Jesus, cast out devils by the Spirit of God, then is the kingdom of God come upon you.[2]

And they were also parables in act, signs which showed Jesus as the light[3] and the life[4] of mankind. The miracles of bodily healing were proofs of the presence in Jesus of power to work healings more wonderful, to restore souls dead in the darkness of sin to spiritual life and light, by bringing them the forgiveness of God. Thus, he said to a palsied man, Thy sins are forgiven; and when the bystanders doubted the reality of his power, he healed the man's bodily ailment also, as a sign that the Son of Man has power to forgive sins.[5]

Jesus Christ did all these works, both of healing and of pardon, by the power of God which was in his human nature. Power went forth from his body to make sick people well;[6] and there was authority in his word to bring them forgiveness.[7] Therefore, those who were sick in body, and those who were sick in soul, did not only pray to God for relief, as the Jews had done before ever Jesus Christ came; they came to Jesus, who was himself truly man, and they found that there was virtue in his manhood to heal them. The power of God was stored up in Jesus, like water in a never-failing

---

[1] Matt. xi. 4-6. [2] Matt. xi. 28. [3] John ix. 5.
[4] John xi. 25. [5] Mark ii. 10.
[6] Mark v. 30. [7] Luke vii. 48.

reservoir, for the refreshment and help of men in body and soul. The humanity of Jesus was full of grace and truth.[1] From him flowed to men that grace and truth which are the life and light of God. And the force that made the healing waters flow was the force of faithful prayer, the human prayer of the Son of man.[2]

We read also in the gospels that Jesus had power to rule over the powers of nature, calming the winds and walking on the storm-tossed sea.[3] There are some people who find this hard to believe; who, indeed, doubt all works of his for which they cannot find natural explanations. But to us Christians, who believe the one greatest of all miracles, the Incarnation of the Son of God, it would seem a strange thing that Perfect Man should have been in this world and not have done greater works than imperfect men can do.

v

Our Lord did not work only by himself. From among his followers he chose twelve men, that they should be with him as an inner circle of disciples, and that he might send them forth to preach as his apostles, with his authority to heal diseases and to cast out devils.[4]

Not only were they to be his helpers during these three years, but also he intended them to be the first to continue and to extend his work after his own ministry was ended. Christ in his own person began the work,[5] he willed to extend it continually for all time by working through human agents, to whom he would give a share in the powers which were in his human nature. He said: He that believeth on me, the works that I do shall he do also; and greater works than these shall he do; because I go unto the Father.[6] And again: As the Father hath sent me, even so send I you.[7]

In other words, Christ came into the world to establish the Church, to be the kingdom of God on earth.[8] He came to form an ever-extending society of believers, in which

---

[1] John i. 14. [2] Mark ix. 29; xi. 23, 24.
[3] Mark iv. 39; vi. 48. [4] Mark iii. 14-15. [5] Acts i. 1.
[6] John xiv. 12. [7] John xx. 21. [8] Matt. xvi. 18-19.

should be stored up for all men the treasures of grace and truth which first were in himself alone.[1] And the apostles were to be the first members and the first rulers, the foundation and also the builders, of the Church.

But before the Church could be formed, the apostles themselves needed to come to a true belief in Christ. They had to be weaned from their wordly ideas about the kingdom of God, and to be brought to faith in Jesus as the true Messiah and Saviour. Their education by Christ took time : their advance towards faith was slow. The great moment was reached when St. Peter, the chief of the apostles, was the first to confess his faith in Jesus, saying to him : Thou art the Messiah, the Son of the living God. Then our Lord had a firm foundation on which to build. He answered Peter : Thou art Peter, that art the rock; and upon this rock I will build my Church.[2]

From that time our Lord was occupied in preparing the apostles for the work that lay before them. Again and again we see him pressing home to their minds one great lesson—self-sacrifice towards God and humble service towards men;[3]—If any man would come after me, let him deny himself, and take up his cross and follow me.[4] Whosoever would become great among you shall be your minister, and whosoever would be first among you shall be servant of all. For verily the Son of man came not to be ministered unto, but to minister, and to give his life a ransom for many.[5] If I, the Lord and the Master, have washed your feet, ye also ought to wash one another's feet. For I have given you an example, that ye also should do as I have done to you.[6] If they were to be the princes of the kingdom of God, the leaders in Christ's Church, it was not enough that they should believe in him : they must learn his spirit, and become like him.

[1] Chap. vi.   [2] Matt. xvi. 13-20.   [3] Matt. xvi. 21.
[4] Mark viii. 34.   [5] Mark x. 43-45.   [6] John xiii. 14-15.

THE INCARNATION

VI

What think ye of the Christ, whose Son is he? said our Lord to the Jews.[1] And Judaism made answer: He is the Son of David, man and super-man, divine in being more Godlike and more fully inspired by God than any other child of man; but still only divine in the sense in which all men may be so called, in so far as the image of God is reproduced in them. But the Christian Church confesses that Christ, who was manifested in this world, belonged from all eternity not to this creation, but to the other side of the infinite gulf that lies between all created beings and the uncreated self-existent God. We believe in one Lord Jesus Christ, the only-begotten Son of God, begotten of his Father before all worlds, God from God, Light from Light, true God from true God, begotten not made, being of one essence with the Father.[2]

And why do we so believe in Christ as God? Not simply because of the perfection of his teaching and example. To those who have ears to hear, indeed, that teaching contains in itself the evidence that it is divine as no other teaching ever was;[3] and to those who have eyes to see, that example is nothing less than the perfect pattern of human life lived by God himself. But still, we believe the teaching and accept the example because we believe in Christ. Men cannot really adopt and submit of standards of conduct so high above the reach of the natural man, unless they have accepted Jesus Christ as God.

Nor do we believe in Christ simply because of his miracles. It is not only Christ who has displayed powers that we call miraculous. And Christ himself, although he said, The works that I do bear witness that the Father hath sent me,[4] does not seem to have desired men to believe on him merely on account of his works.[5]

Nor even because of the fact of his resurrection from the dead; although if it were not for that fact we could not believe on him.[6] If Christ hath not been raised, our faith

---

[1] Matt. xxii. 42.
[2] Nicene Creed.
[3] John vii. 46.
[4] John v. 36.
[5] John x. 37, 38.
[6] Chap. v. 3.

47

is vain;[1] for the whole fabric of our belief is built up on that, the most certain fact in history. But no man could be persuaded of the resurrection of Christ if he thought of Christ as being merely a man like himself. He would explain away the historical evidence, however certain it might appear, unless he had also within himself that which prepared him for conviction of its truth.

Nor again because of the age-long preparation of the world for Christ's coming; or the long history of the Christian Church, and the witness of the Christian life, showing what men can become, and do, and suffer, who confess Christ crucified as God.

All these and other considerations have, indeed, contributed largely to the forming of our belief in Christ. But all would not avail to convince us, and to bring us to his feet in unquestioning submission and worship, apart from our personal knowledge and experience of him. That I may know him, and the power of his resurrection, and the fellowship of his sufferings—that is St. Paul's aspiration,[2] who had never seen Christ in his earthly life. It is just in so far as anyone has thus known Christ by mystic communion, and has had personal experience of his love and power, that he has real and unshakable conviction of Christ's Godhead.

The disciples came to believe in Christ because they knew him personally, because they were in his company. From that companionship they learnt to know that he was the true Messiah, although he did not fulfil what had been their expectations about the Messiah. They did not believe in his Godhead until after the resurrection : and then it was not rational proofs that convinced them; but one after another believed because the risen Lord met with them. Personal communion with him brought conviction of his resurrection and of his Godhead. Thomas saith unto him : My Lord and my God : making the leap of faith that was called forth, not by the proofs of the passion-marks in Christ's body, but by the power of the presence with him of the risen Lord.[3]

[1] 1 Cor. xv. 17.   [2] Phil. iii. 10.   [3] John xx. 28.

And those whose is the blessedness of believing without having seen,[1] like St. Paul, and countless multitudes in every generation of the Church, owe their belief to their communion with Christ, the same yesterday, to-day, and for ever,[2] which is given through prayer and the sacraments of the Church, in the power of the Holy Spirit. The Christian cries : I know him whom I have believed.[3] And he believes in him with conviction because he knows him.

Mary Magdalene, seeking to cling to Jesus at the tomb,[4] the merely human Jesus, as she thought, whom she had loved so devotedly, is the representative of those who have not attained to spiritual communion with the risen Lord. No, Mary, thou loving penitent, cling not thus to him, but ask : How could this loved one free your soul, as he has freed it from your sins, if he is only man? Is it merely his human example that has cleansed your guilt away? How is he what he is to thee, more than husband, lover, friend, or master? How is he the same also to every true disciple that he is to thee, if he is not more than man? How can he claim, and prove his claim, to satisfy every soul and every need, if he is only a very good man, only in degree more Godlike than we are? How is this man the satisfaction of every aspiration and every faculty we have or can have? Because he is our God and our Lord.

To the doubter and the imperfect believer, then, the Church says : Come and see;[5] even as Jesus said : Come unto me.[6] Come, not merely to study his character in the pages of Holy Writ, nor merely to examine arguments and proofs about him, though such study also is good and necessary; but come unto him, seek to find him where he is, seek to know him and this power within yourself. Our Lord himself calls us to this experimental finding of him, which indeed is not our act, but the work of God within us :—
I am the bread of life; he that cometh to me shall not hunger, and he that believeth on me shall never thirst. All that which the Father giveth me shall come unto me : and

---

[1] John xx. 29.
[2] Heb. xiii. 8.
[3] 2 Tim. i. 12.
[4] John xx. 17.
[5] John i. 39, 46; iv. 28.
[6] Matt. xi. 28.

him that cometh unto me I will in no wise cast out. No man can come to me, except the Father who sent me draw him. It is written in the prophets, They shall all be taught of God. Everyone that hath heard from the Father, and hath learned, cometh unto me.[1] And so it comes to pass that he that believeth on the Son of God hath the witness within himself.[2]

---

[1] John vi. 35, 37, 44, 45.   [2] 1 John v. 10.

V

THE ATONEMENT

1

WHILE our Lord was ministering to the Jews by his words
and works, the powers of evil were not idle. The light was
shining, but the surrounding darkness was striving to over-
whelm it.[1]

The Pharisees and Sadducees, who generally were at
variance with each other in religious and political views,
were leagued together in a common opposition to Jesus.[2]
They called him a law-breaker,[3] and an agent of the devil.[4]
They hated and feared him. They saw in him not the
expected Deliverer, but a revolutionary who would upset
religious, political, and social life throughout the whole
nation, in which they had pride of place and power, and to
which they were bound by their upbringing and national
feeling and self-interest.[5] Being too unspiritual to see the
holy beauty of his character and teaching, and being blinded
by envy[6] of his popularity with the common people, and
enraged by his condemnation of themselves, they easily
persuaded themselves that he had not been sent by God;
and they determined to compass his death.

And of the multitude that crowded around Jesus, only a
few were willing to accept him as their Lord and Master.
They were eager to receive benefits from him, to be healed
of their infirmities, to listen to his words, and to follow him
if he would lead them to the possession of a worldly kingdom.
But they refused him and turned away from him when they

[1] John i. 5.   [2] Mark iii. 6; Matt. xvi. 1; xxii. 34.
[3] John v. 18.   [4] Mark iii. 22.
[5] Mark xii. 1-12.   [6] Mark xv. 10.

51

perceived that his kingdom was not of this world,[1] and that he made great spiritual demands upon those who would be his disciples, claiming from them personal repentance and obedience and self-surrender.[2]

He came unto his own, and they that were his own received him not.[3] In the tragedy of the rejection of Christ we see the supreme example of the constant ingratitude of the world towards its truest benefactors.

Therefore our Lord's life on earth was full of sorrow. He was grieved continually at the hard-heartedness of men, who loved themselves more than God.[4] He was grieved that they refused the salvation he offered them, that they would not come unto him that they might have life.[5] The Sacred Heart of Jesus was burdened by the sinfulness of mankind, and the greatness of his love for man was the measure of his pain. Christ walked among men as a Man of sorrows, acquainted with grief.[6]

Christ was betrayed to the Jewish leaders by Judas Iscariot, one of the twelve apostles.[7] He was condemned by them on a charge of blasphemy, because he made what they regarded as a false claim to be the Messiah.[8] Not having the power of life and death, they brought Jesus before Pontius Pilate, the representative of the Roman Empire, to which the Jewish nation was subject. Here they accused Jesus of political sedition against the Roman Empire.[9] Pilate did not believe the charge,[10] but he sentenced Jesus to death because he was afraid of being reported to the Emperor if he acquitted Jesus.[11] And then in great haste for fear of a rescue by the populace,[12] our Lord was done to death, on Mount Calvary near Jerusalem, by crucifixion, the shameful death of a criminal.[13]

By the hands of lawless men, says Holy Scripture,[14] he was crucified and slain. And behind the acts of men we discern

---

[1] John vi. 15, 66.
[2] John vi. 66; Mark x. 22; Luke ix. 57-62.
[3] John i. 11.
[4] John v. 44.
[5] John v. 40.
[6] Isa. liii. 3.
[7] Mark xiv. 10.
[8] Mark xiv. 61-64.
[9] Luke xxiii. 1-3.
[10] Luke xxiii. 4, 14, 22.
[11] John xix. 12, 13.
[12] Mark xiv. 2.
[13] Luke xxiii. 33.
[14] Acts ii. 23.

the power of Satan. Christ's death was the utmost that Satan's malice could achieve against the Son of God. He could organise against Jesus the passions of sinful men. He could do to death his body. But he could not injure the sinless soul of Jesus. Not even the terrors of such a death could bring to Jesus any temptation that could make him fall. Before he entered upon his last and fiercest temptation, in the Garden of Gethsemane, he had said : The prince of this world cometh, and he hath nothing in me.[1] And though it cost him a sweat as of great drops of blood, he conquered, as we Christians also can conquer in our temptations, by the power of prayer : being in an agony, he prayed more earnestly, saying, Father, not my will, but thine be done.[2]

II

It was the will of the heavenly Father that his Son should die. Though it was through the lawlessness of men and the malice of the devil that he was crucified, yet he was delivered up by the determinate counsel and foreknowledge of God.[3] The Son of man, said our Lord, goeth as it hath been determined.[4] Not that God the Father simply willed the sufferings of Jesus. How could the sufferings of his Son be in themselves pleasing to him who is infinite love? But his love for sinful men was so great that he willed their salvation even at the price of the death of Jesus. Herein is love, not that we loved God, but that he loved us, and sent his Son to be the propritiation for our sins.[5]

It is a deep mystery, how the death of Jesus can take away the sins of the world, and how the sins of the world can be taken away only by the sacrifice of the Son of God made man. There is a simple hymn which says :

> He died that we might be forgiven,
>   He died to make us good;
> That we might go at last to heaven,
>   Saved by his precious blood.

[1] John xiv. 30.   [2] Luke xxii. 39-44.   [3] Acts ii. 23.
[4] Luke xxii. 22.   [5] 1 John iv. 10.

There was no other good enough
To pay the price of sin;
He only could unlock the gate
Of heaven, and let us in.

These words tell us nearly all that has been taught by God about that death in which we trust for our salvation. And it is enough for the heart of the sinner, who accepts in faith that the Son of God loved him, and gave himself up for him.[1] The truth of it, and the life-giving power of it, he will learn by his own experience of deliverance.

But the mind of man seeks, and rightly seeks, to probe into the deep things of God.[2] One out of the many ways in which men have reasoned about the death of Christ is this:

God is perfectly righteous and true, as well as perfectly loving and merciful. Man had sinned, and by sin had done injury and outrage to God's glory. Justice required that the sinner should himself atone for his sin. Forgiveness by God, in the sense of letting man off his punishment, might have been merciful, but would not have satisfied truth and justice. If a debtor is forgiven his debt, and if he is thenceforth able to avoid incurring new debt, still the debt already incurred remains unpaid. The obedience to God of a forgiven sinner, even the perfect obedience of all the rest of his life, would not avail to pay off the debt he owes—that is, the honour that was due from him to God, and which he withheld during the time of his sinfulness. All his future obedience day by day can do no more than pay what is daily due from him to God; he can acquire no surplus with which to pay his back debt.

How, then, was God to have the honour that belonged to him, which eternal righteousness demanded that man should pay, but which he had not wherewith to pay? How, indeed, unless God should become man, to do for man and in man what man must do, but cannot do of himself? If God joined himself with all humanity, then justice could be satisfied. Humanity having divine strength could do what man in his own weakness could not do.

The perfect obedience even unto death of Jesus Christ,

[1] Gal. ii. 20.   [2] 1 Cor. ii. 10-12.

54

the Son of God made man, was of so great merit that it outweighed all the debt that mankind owes to God. That was the way in which, through divine love, divine justice was satisfied.

God, holy and true, could not simply ignore sin; for that would have been to act contrary to his holiness and truth. But God, who is love, could pay the price of sin, conquering Satan and redeeming mankind from his power; and God could become man, in order that the payer and the conqueror should be man. And when mankind joined with God in Christ had paid the price, by perfect obedience to the uttermost, then God's love, which sent the Son, was free, without violation of right, to remit the guilt and the eternal punishment due to sin. God laid upon him the iniquity of us all.[1]

But it is not the whole truth to say that Christ has died as the sacrifice for sin, as it were, apart from us. We must not separate the thought of Calvary from that of Pentecost and the Church which is the body of the risen and ascended Lord, in which we are united with Christ as his members.[2] There is no condemnation to them that are in Christ Jesus,[3] any more than to Christ himself; for they are in him, and are one with him. God sees them only as made one with him who in our common humanity has paid the debt. And men, receiving a higher life than that of nature, through union individually with Christ risen from the dead, can be restored from the effects of the fall; and not only restored but raised to a state higher than that from which they fell. The Christian may say, in words of St. Paul: I have been crucified with Christ; yet I live; and yet no longer I, but Christ liveth in me; and that life which I now live in the flesh I live in faith, the faith which is in the Son of God, who loved me, and gave himself for me.[4]

There have been other ways, besides this, in which men have tried to explain how Christ's death brought the forgiveness of sin and their at-one-ment with God. But no explanation can express to the mind of man the fulness of the

[1] Isa. liii. 4-6.   [2] Chap. vi. 2.
[3] Rom. viii. 1.   [4] Gal. ii. 20.

mystery accomplished: for it is a mystery. All explanations, however true they may be, are only partial: the mystery is inexhaustible in its truth and power. We can rest content with the fact that through the sacrifice of the death of Jesus there is deliverance from the bondage of sin and the penalty of eternal death; and to the reality of this fact each can find witness within his own soul.

And as it was the love of God the Father that sent the Son, so also it was the love of the Son that brought him into the world to be a willing sacrifice. Our Saviour went the way determined for him by the Father; but he trod that way of sorrows willingly. He gave himself to death of his own free will. He said: The Son of man came into the world to give his life a ransom for many;[1] and again, The good shepherd layeth down his life for the sheep; no one taketh it away from me, but I lay it down of myself.[2]

When the time was come, he steadfastly set his face to go to Jerusalem, where his enemies were;[3] and he went of his own accord, knowing what would befall him there. He said to his disciples: Behold, we go up to Jerusalem; and the Son of man shall be delivered unto the chief priests and scribes; and they shall condemn him to death, and shall deliver him unto the Gentiles to mock, and to scourge, and to crucify him; and the third day he shall be raised up.[4]

If he had so willed, he could have escaped: he could have avoided the Cross.[5] But he had not come to please himself.[6] He was obedient unto death, even the death of the Cross.[7] The supreme end to which obedience can go is not only the readiness to die, but the fulfilment of that readiness by the actual surrender of life. And the supreme end to which love can go, to which love must go in a sinful world, is suffering and self-sacrifice; greater love hath no man than this, that a man lay down his life.[8]

[1] Mark x. 45; cf. Matt. xxvi. 28. [2] John x. 11, 18.
[3] Luke ix. 51. [4] Matt. xx. 17-19. [5] Matt. xxvi. 53-54.
[6] Rom. xv. 3. [7] Phil. ii. 8. [8] John xv. 13.

III

When Jesus Christ died upon the Cross on the first Good
Friday, his body was buried in a tomb;[1] and his soul passed
to the abode of the dead : which is what we mean when we
say in the Creed : He descended into hell. Christ has
experienced every stage of human existence, both on this side
of the grave and beyond. Where we shall go, there Christ
has been before us. In this, as in all else, he has been made
like to his brethren whose nature he shares.[2]

We read in Holy Scripture that he preached to the spirits
of the dead.[3] He proclaimed the good tidings of the
redemption which he had wrought by his death, and he
offered them salvation in himself. When he had overcome
the sharpness of death, he opened the kingdom of heaven to
all believers.[4]

The Godhead was joined with both the body and the soul
of Christ, and it was separated from neither when they were
parted asunder in death. His body, even in death was the
body of the Son of God, and therefore suffered no taint of
corruption. It awaited in the tomb reunion with his soul,
and its resurrection-change. And on the third day, the first
Easter Day, Christ rose again from the dead. God raised
him up, having loosed the pangs of death; because it was not
possible that he should be holden of it.[5]

No human being was present when the soul of Jesus came
again, and his body was restored from death. That was a
sight which human eyes might not behold. We are told
only of what happened afterwards,[6] that the tomb was
found empty, and that the risen Lord showed himself to
those who loved him in a spiritual body, which was the
same body that he had before his death, but which now
had new and supernatural powers.[7]

The apostles were not expecting the resurrection, nor were

[1] John xix. 41-42.   [2] Heb. ii. 17.   [3] 1 Pet. iii. 19.
[4] Te Deum.   [5] Acts ii. 24.
[6] Mark xvi. 2-6; John xx. 1-10.
[7] John xx. 11-29; Luke xxiv. 13-43.

they disposed readily to believe it.[1] Our Lord had indeed foretold that after his death he would rise again; but they had not understood his words, so that his death left them without any hope or expectation.[2] But the Lord showed himself to them many times during forty days, both to individuals and to numerous groups.[3] It was no spiritualistic manifestation, but a real appearing oft repeated of the risen Lord in his glorified body. He conversed with them, speaking to them about the Church, the kingdom of God.[4] He submitted himself to be touched and handled by them;[5] he took food and ate it before them;[6] giving every proof of the reality of his risen body, and of his identity with the Jesus whom they had known and loved. They saw, and they believed;[7] and they became the witnesses to the fact of the resurrection.[8] They gave their whole lives to bearing witness to it before men. They suffered persecution for their belief, and finally sealed their testimony by martyrdom.

The fact that Christ rose from the dead, as he had foretold is the great proof to men that he was what he said he was. Indeed, if Christ had not risen we should be without guarantee of the truth of any of his words. If Christ hath not been raised, said St. Paul, then is our preaching vain; your faith also in vain.[9] The fact of the resurrection sets the seal to the truth of all the revelation of God in Christ.

Because Christ has risen, we know that it is possible for men to rise, and that death must not be the end. Because Christ has risen according to his word, we believe that he is able also to fulfil his promise[10] to raise us to share, body and soul, in the life of glory with him: even as he said, I am the resurrection and the life; he that believeth on me, though he die, yet shall he live : and whosoever liveth and believeth on me shall never die.[11] Christ hath been raised from the dead,

---

[1] Luke xxiv. 11; John xx. 25.
[2] Mark viii. 31; ix. 31-32; x. 34; xiv. 28.
[3] Acts i. 3; 1 Cor. xv. 5-8.   [4] Acts i. 3; Luke xxiv. 44-49.
[5] Luke xxiv. 39; John xx. 27. [6] Luke xxiv. 43.
[7] John xx. 20.   [8] Acts i. 8, 22; iii. 15; xvii. 18.
[9] 1 Cor. xv. 14.   [10] John v. 28; vi. 54.   [11] John xi. 25, 26.

the first-fruits of them that are asleep.   For since by man
came death, by man came also the resurrection from the dead.
For as in Adam all die, so also in Christ shall all be made
alive.[1] As he was stronger than death's power against himself, so he is stronger than death's power within us.   He
became man that through death he might bring to naught him
that had the power of death—that is, the devil; and might
deliver all them who through fear of death were all their
lifetime subject to bondage.[2]

Christ rose from the dead, to die no more.   Death hath no
more dominion over him.   For the death that he died, he
died unto sin once for all; but the life that he liveth he liveth
unto God.[3] Christ rose, not to take up again the earthly
life, but to enter in his human nature upon the heavenly
life.   His sacred humanity in its glory was no longer limited
by time and place, as he had willed it to be during his earthly
life.[4]

IV

On the fortieth day after the resurrection, Christ showed
himself for the last time to the apostles.   He led them out of
Jerusalem to the Mount of Olives, and while he blessed them,
they saw him lifted up from the earth, until he was lost to
their sight.[5] By this they understood that Christ was entering into his glory, and that they would see him no more with
their eyes.   Unless they had seen him acending, they could
not have realised that his earthly sojourn was ended, and
that the time was at hand when they should receive the
Holy Spirit whom he had promised to send upon them.[6]

He ascended into heaven.   Not as he came, so did he
return.   He ascended to take our humanity : he ascended
in our humanity.   God came : God-in-man returned.   The
Incarnation has not ceased.   Jesus has not put away from
him the human nature which he took once for all in the
womb of blessed Mary.   Jesus in divine glory has still his
human body and mind and soul.

[1] 1 Cor. xv. 20-22.   [2] Heb. ii. 14, 15.
[3] Rom. vi. 9, 10.   [4] John xx. 19; Luke xxiv. 31.
[5] Luke xxiv. 50, 51; Acts i. 9-11.
[6] Luke xxiv. 49; John xvi. 7; Acts i. 4, 5.

He ascended into heaven, and sat down on the right hand of God.[1] That is to say, human nature is exalted in Christ to the highest place in heaven, adored and worshipped by the holy angels, for ever united with the Deity. And there, in highest heaven, he appears before the face of God on our behalf.[2] He is our great Priest, seated on the throne of God, who is the perpetual sacrifice for the sins of the world, the one sacrifice with which God is well-pleased—humanity sinless and perfect, that has made full satisfaction for sins.[3] Our salvation depends not only on the act done once for all on Calvary, considered as an event that is past and over, but also on that same act ever-present at the throne of God, and on our union with Christ, who in the timelessness of heaven continually offers himself sacrificed for sin and consecrated to God, and presents us in union with himself. We have an advocate with the Father, Jesus Christ the righteous; and he is the propitiation for our sins; and not for ours only, but also for the whole world.[4]

And we, while we are still here on earth, may truly be united with our risen and ascended Lord. The glorified life which is in Christ is not for himself alone : it is capable of being bestowed also upon Christ's members in every place and every age, who are thereby brought into spiritual fellowship and living union with him.[5] He rose from the dead, that his life might be the source of spiritual life in us. He was raised a life-giving Spirit,[6] giving from himself even now heavenly life unto his own, to be the life of their souls. God hath given to us eternal life, and this life is in his Son. He that hath the Son of God hath the life, the life of God that is in Jesus.[7] The glory which Christ won he has won for us also, and if we will receive it he gives it to us, by uniting us severally with himself, and by imparting to us his eternal life. God, being rich in mercy, for his great love wherewith he loved us, even when we were dead through our trespasses, gave us life together with Christ (by grace have we been

---

[1] Apostles' Creed.
[2] Heb. ix. 24.
[3] Chap. ix. 4.
[4] 1 John ii. 1, 2; cf. Heb. vii.-x.
[5] Chaps. vi. 3; vii. 1; ix. 5; xx. 3.
[6] 1 Cor. xv. 45.
[7] 1 John v. 12.

saved), and raised us up with him, and made us to sit with
him in the heavenly places in Christ Jesus.[1]

Heaven is not far away. Christ ascended to heaven, that
even now we might be with him where he is.[2] Our life, the
life which we live as members of Christ, is hid with Christ
in God. For Christ is our life, the life by which we live.[3]
Christ lives in us, and we in him.[4] When his visible presence
was about to be taken away, he said : Lo, I am with you
always.[5] He is present still, because his Spirit is present :
If I go not away, the Comforter will not come unto you;
but if I go, I will send him unto you.[6] It is the work of the
Holy Spirit to make Christ really present to the faithful in
every place and age. I will pray the Father, said Christ, and
he shall give you another Comforter—another like myself—
that he may be with you for ever, even the Spirit of truth.[7]
And so was fulfilled that other saying of Christ's : I will not
leave you desolate; I come unto you.[8]

This mystical union between us and the ascended Lord,
this sharing in his risen life by the power of the Holy Spirit,
is effected in us through our being brought into membership
of the Church, and through our participation in the sacraments with repentance, faith, and love.[9]

V

It was on the Jewish feast of Pentecost, fifty days after
the resurrection, that the Holy Spirit came upon St. Mary
and the apostles and the other faithful disciples of Jesus in
Jerusalem. On that day the Catholic Church began.[10]

As the Holy Spirit had come upon Jesus himself at his
baptism, so now he came upon those who believed in Jesus;
and they received the baptism of the Holy Ghost and of fire,
of which St. John the Baptist had spoken.[11] Christ had
promised them : Ye shall receive power, when the Holy
Ghost is come upon you; and ye shall be my witnesses both

---

[1] Eph. ii. 5, 6.   [2] John xiv. 3.   [3] Col. iii. 3, 4.
[4] Gal. ii. 20; John vi. 56, 57.   [5] Matt. xxviii. 20.
[6] John xvi. 7.   [7] John xiv. 16, 17.   [8] John xiv. 18.
[9] Chap. vi.   [10] Acts ii. 1-4.   [11] Matt. iii. 11; Acts i. 5.

61

in Jerusalem, and in all Judea, and in Samaria, and unto the uttermost part of the earth.[1] And so it came to pass. The body of believers was empowered by the Holy Spirit to continue Christ's work on earth, to preach in his name, to make disciples from all the nations of the world, and to baptise them in the name of the Father, and of the Son, and of the Holy Ghost.[2] The grace and truth, which were first brought to men in the human nature of Jesus himself, were now also in the Church, Christ's mystical body, in which the Holy Spirit dwells, and in which he works for the salvation and the sanctification of mankind.[3]

In the power of the Spirit, the apostles, and those whom they in their turn sent forth,[4] went everywhere preaching the word,[5] and bringing men into the fellowship cf the Church. We read, in the Acts of the Apostles, how the Church extended from the Holy Land to Antioch and Ephesus and the towns of Asia Minor; and thence to Macedonia and Greece, and to Rome, the capital of the world.[6] It was a progress continual and triumphant in the face of opposition and persecutions; a progress which, in spite of human frailty and many backslidings, has continued to the present day, and will continue until the whole world is evangelised.[7]

We read how St. Peter was the first to open the door of the Church to others than Jews, thereby setting the Church free from the bonds of Jewish nationalism, and showing it to be Catholic, universal, God's means of salvation for all the nations.[8] We read how St. John laboured for Christ,[9] and how his brother St. James was the first of the apostles to be slain for Christ's sake;[10] and how St. Paul, the last called to be an apostle, was converted from being a persecutor by the risen Lord himself, and become the great apostle of the Gentiles.[11]

We have also the writings of the apostles, in the epistles of the New Testament; and we can see in them how the

---

[1] Acts i. 8.   [2] Matt. xxviii. 19, 20.
[3] Chap. vi. 2.   [4] Chap. x. 1.   [5] Acts viii. 4.
[6] Acts xi. 19; xvi. 12; xvii. 16; xviii. 19; xxviii. 14.
[7] Matt. xxiv. 14.   [8] Acts x. 47.   [9] Acts iii. 1; viii. 14.
[10] Acts xii. 2.   [11] Acts ix., etc.

Christian faith and life were taught to many groups of Church-members in different places, each with its own peculiar circumstances, difficulties, and temptations; but all one body in faith and organisation and life.[1]

And we may sum up the message of the apostles to the Church in the words of St. John, the last survivor of their company : That which we have seen and heard declare we unto you also, that ye may have fellowship with us : yea, and our fellowship is with the Father, and with his Son Jesus Christ.[2]

[1] Chap. xiii. 3.   [2] 1 John i. 3.

VI

THE CHURCH AND SACRAMENTS

I

WE are brought into union with the risen Lord, and share in his heavenly life, through the power of the Holy Spirit, by our participation in the sacraments of the Church with repentance and faith.

By the word Sacrament, we mean an outward means by which God gives us inward and spiritual grace. And by grace we mean the heavenly life of Christ, given to us who are made one with him. God hath given to us eternal life, and this life is in his Son : He that hath the Son hath the life.[1] The Word was God . . . in him was life . . . and the Word was made flesh . . . full of grace.[2] The life, when it is given to us, we call grace.

Why has God given us sacraments? Why did our Lord Jesus Christ ordain outward means by which to give us grace? Because this is the method which the nature of man demands. We ourselves are sacraments—outward body and inward soul joined in one, in a union which we cannot explain. From one point of view, we appear to be altogether material; from another altogether spiritual. We are not spirits, like the angels; but we are beings in whom the spiritual is so entirely united with the material that the actions of our souls necessarily find expression through our bodies, as a thought is expressed by a word.

Because we are sacraments, God deals with us sacramentally. God is spirit;[3] but when he took upon him to deliver man, he did not abhor the Virgin's womb.[4] Jesus

---

[1] 1 John v. 11, 12.　　[2] John i. 1, 4, 14.
[3] John iv. 24.　　[4] Te Deum.

64

Christ is himself the greatest of all sacraments. This shall be the sign unto you, said the herald-angel at Bethlehem, ye shall find a babe.[1] The babe was the outward and visible sign of the reality given to man, God with us. His human nature was the means by which God gave himself to us.

In him was life, and the life was the light of men.[2] And, through the Incarnation, that light illuminated men's inward souls by means of the truth spoken outwardly by the human lips of God in human words to human ears;[3] and that life was communicated to men's souls by means of the grace brought to them in the Son of God made flesh. God came into touch with men so visibly and outwardly, as well as inwardly and spiritually, that St. John could say: That which we have heard, that which we have seen with our eyes, that which we beheld, and our hands handled, declare we unto you.[4]

II

Like Jesus Christ himself, the Church of Christ is of twofold nature, a sacrament. There is the visible organisation, the kingdom with its laws and officers; there are the outward forms and creeds and services. These are the means by which the inward realities of grace and truth, of life and light, reach each member.

God's direct way of giving grace and truth to men, during our Lord's visible sojourn on earth, was by bringing them into touch with his human nature; and now God's direct way of giving them grace and truth is by bringing them into union with the Church in its visible organisation. The latter way is the continuation of the former. God's way of dealing with sacramental man has been uniform throughout. The Church is the extension of the Incarnation. Like as Christ himself is, so is the Church—the treasury of grace, and the home of truth, and therefore the ark of safety for all alike who would escape from the sinfulness of the world.

Our Lord was the way and the truth and the life.[5] He said: No one cometh unto the Father but through me.[6]

[1] Luke ii. 12. [2] John i. 4. [3] Chap. xii. 1.
[4] 1 John i. 1. [5] John xiv. 6. [6] *Ibid.*

And now the Church is the way in which God wills all men
to be saved, and through which they shall receive the truth
and the life, the light and the grace, of God.

For the Church is the Body of Christ. That is St. Paul's
title for it.[1] What does he mean? He means that the
Church is as truly and as closely united with Christ as the
limbs of a body are with the head; that Christ and the Church
are inseparably one, because of the one life in Christ and in
the members of his body. For as the body is one, he says,
and hath many members, and all the members of the body,
being many, are one body; so also is Christ . . . Ye are the
body of Christ, and severally members thereof.[2]

At first Christ himself alone was the whole of the Church.
In the womb of blessed Mary, Christ took human nature into
union with God; and that is what the Church is—human
nature restored to union with God through Christ. But
as yet the Church was one member only. From Pentecost
onwards the Church began to grow and develop into many
members, by the continual admission of those who were
brought one by one into union with the Church, and into
union with Christ, and therefore into union with God, by the
sacrament of baptism, which makes them members of the
Church and gives them the life of Christ.[3]

To take another illustration: As a family consists at first
of husband and wife only, and those to whom they will give
life are as yet unborn, so the whole family of the Church was
at first Christ himself only, and then gradually included all
his spiritual offspring, all who were born again in baptism,
receiving the new birth by union with Christ, and living by
the life that is in him.[4]

Or again, in our Lord's words: I am the vine, ye are the
branches: he that abideth in me and I in him, the same
bringeth forth much fruit; for apart from me ye can do
nothing.[5] The vine is the whole vine, before it has the many
branches; and the branches are branches of the vine, because
they have the one life of the vine.

[1] Rom. xii. 5; 1 Cor. x. 17; Eph. iv. 16; v. 23.
[2] 1 Cor. xii. 12-27.   [3] Chap. vii. 1.
[4] John iii. 3, 5.   [5] John xv. 5.

So long as a body, or a family, or a vine exists, it is one whole, having one common life as the cause of its oneness. Similarly, the Church also is one Church, and one for ever, for the promise stands that the Church will never cease to exist.[1]

The limbs of a body, the members of a family, the branches of a vine, are parts of the one whole so long as they remain unseparated from it and sharing its life. Similarly, those who have been made members of the Church belong to it permanently, and are parts of it, unless they have separated themselves or been separated from it, thereby losing their share in its life. Even then, in one sense, they are still members of the Church; just as we may correctly say that a torn-off branch is still a branch of the vine, or an amputated limb is still a limb of the body, or an alienated member still belongs to the family. But, so far as any benefit to them is concerned, they have ceased to be parts of the whole from which they are separated, because they are cut off from the unity of the whole and from the source of its life.

But the one whole still remains. The body or the family or the vine still remains, smaller indeed, but still a living whole, after the loss even of several of its parts. So, although many have fallen away from the Church, its unity still abides, and would abide, even if every member of it on earth broke away from it by a universal apostasy. For the Church in this world is not the whole of the Church. All the generations of faithful members that have been in the Church on earth remain its members still, united with Christ the Head of the body, and living by his life. Men may break away from the unity; but that does not destroy the one Church.[2]

God's way of salvation through Christ is not simply to save individuals separately, but to save them by bringing them into membership of Christ's body, the Church. God gives life to the body; he gives life to each member by making him a partaker of the life that is in the body. The Church is God's new chosen people,[3] his new family, for which Christ died, which he has saved, to which he gives life; he saves us individually by making us members of that people

[1] Matt. xvi. 18.   [2] Chap. xi. 5.   [3] 1 Pet. ii. 10.

67

and that family. Christ is the Head of the Church, says
St. Paul, being himself the Saviour of the body. Christ
loved the Church, and gave himself up for it; that he might
sanctify it by the washing of water with the word, that he
might present the Church to himself a glorious Church.[1]
Of that glorious Church we are members, and by our
membership of it we have been brought into the state of
salvation and sanctification.

This does not mean that those who are outside the Church
are of necessity without any share in the grace and truth that
are in Jesus Christ. Doubtless, when our Lord was on
earth, many Jews received blessing from God, both in body
and soul, who sought him with sincerity in the best way
they knew, although they lacked knowledge or opportunity
to come to him through Jesus. God is not less gracious now.
He himself is not tied and bound to the sacramental method
which he has given us, so that he cannot bestow his gifts on
whom he wills and as he wills. But those who, knowing
what they are doing, wilfully turn away from the Church
and sacraments, cannot expect to share in God's mercies of
grace and truth, any more than those who wilfully refused
to come to Jesus when he was on earth.[2]

III

As the Church is sacramental in its nature, so also it is
sacramental in its manner of working. In the Church the
material and the spiritual, the human and the divine, are
joined together by God. The means of union with, and of
abiding and growing in, Christ and the Church are sacramental. Therefore we must cleave to the sacraments in order
that we may maintain living membership in the Church;
and we must maintain our membership in the Church, in
order that we may live in Christ and Christ in us. Our
salvation and our sanctification depend upon our sharing
in the sacraments of the Church.

The word Sacrament was applied in olden days to all
things that fulfilled our definition—that is, to everything that

[1] Eph. v. 23-27. [2] Chap. xi. 3.

was an outward means by which God gave grace. But in later times it has become more usual to speak of seven sacraments, to which only the word is now applied.

The seven sacraments are : Baptism,[1] which joins us to the Church, and gives us the life or grace of Christ; Confirmation,[2] which strengthens the life by the power of the Holy Spirit; Holy Communion,[3] which nourishes and supports the life with heavenly food; Absolution,[4] which restores the life, when by sin we have broken or marred our union with Christ, the source of our life; Unction,[5] by which grace is given to the sick and dying; Ordination,[6] by which grace is given to chosen men to share in the exercise of Christ's priestly and ministerial office; and Marriage,[7] by which grace is given for the sanctification of married and family life. Two of these seven stand out as pre-eminent, baptism which gives the new life, and holy communion which sustains it : the sacrament of entry into the Church, and the sacrament of membership.

Sacraments are necessary. To seek for our salvation and sanctification apart from sacramental grace would mean that we had closed our eyes to the fact that we are both body and soul, and that the Son of God for our salvation was made flesh. The material and the spiritual were joined together by the Incarnation once for all. We enter the holy place by a new and living way which Jesus has consecrated for us[8]—the way of his flesh, that is, his human nature and the Church his body. That is the direct way for man to the presence of God. We will go along the King's highway; we will not turn aside to the right hand nor to the left.[9]

God, who thus sanctified material things to be the means of grace for us, also makes use of human beings as his agents. When the Son of God took flesh, it was not without the consent of blessed Mary, who was God's agent in the Incarnation.[10] When our Lord fed five thousand people

---

[1] Chap. vii. 1-3.   [2] Chap. vii. 4.   [3] Chap. ix.
[4] Chap. viii. 3.   [5] Chap. xix. 2.   [6] Chap. x.
[7] Chap. xviii. 1-6.   [8] Heb. x. 20.   [9] Num. xx. 17.
[10] Luke i. 38.

miraculously, he deigned to use not only the materials that were at hand, the loaves and fishes, but also the ministry of the twelve apostles to distribute them.[1] When the body of Christ was to extend into the many members of the Catholic Church, the means of its expansion and growth was the sending forth of the apostles and their successors throughout the world; they were God's agents by whom, and by whom alone, it was his will that truth and grace should be brought within the reach of men.[2]

In the natural order, our creation, our preservation, our education, are brought about by God through human agents, and at every turn we are dependent upon our fellow-men. And so it is also in the spiritual order. God teaches this truth not by secret inspiration merely, but by the message entrusted to the Church and conveyed to us by the words of men.[3] God gives us his grace also through outward means and human agents. He brought us into union with himself by means of water and the word spoken by men at our baptism. He keeps us in union with himself by the consecration of bread and wine—in themselves the most ordinary things—to be the body and the blood of our Lord; and he effects the consecration by the agency of men, men like ourselves, to whom he gives a share in the priesthood of Christ.[4] In supernatural things as in natural we are dependent upon our fellow-men. By them, and together with them, we are saved and educated and sanctified, in the Catholic Church.

IV

But again, because we are sacramental, body and soul, a mere outward sharing in the sacraments with our bodies only is useless. There is needed also the consent and right disposition of our souls. Sacraments in themselves cannot save. They are not magical charms. There must be a true response within the soul, according to the capacity of the recipient, to the grace given by the sacraments. We can choose, not only to take part in them or to refuse them outwardly, but also inwardly to use them or to misuse them.

[1] Mark vi. 41.
[2] Chaps. xii. 2; xiii. 1.
[3] 1 Cor. iv. 1; 2 Cor. iv. 1, 7; v. 18, 20. Chap. x. 2.

The sacrament of God-with-us was to be found at Bethlehem.[1] Mary and Joseph and the shepherds and the wise men gave the true response of faith and love, and to them, therefore, he brought joy and blessing. There were also those who had no room for him at the inn;[2] there was Herod and the Jewish priests;[3] and the presence of the Saviour only increased their condemnation.

Thou seest the multitudes thronging thee, said the apostles to our Lord on one occasion, and sayest thou, Who touched me? Of all that throng only one woman was blessed, for she alone had the sense of need and the touch of faith.[4]

Two robbers once were near Jesus, crucified on either side of him. One was hardened in his sin. The other entered into Paradise, for he turned to the Saviour with repentance.[5]

And so it is still. We must come to our Lord in the sacraments with faith and with repentance.

Faith is necessary. What is faith?[6] Faith in relation to the sacraments is the power of the soul which corresponds to the sense of the body. For example : the world is full of beauty, but its beauty is hidden from a man born blind. He has not the sense of sight, whereby to take the beauty to himself. Similarly, faith is the power, the sense, of the soul, by which a man takes to himself spiritual realities.

It is not his faith that makes the realities. They are real in themselves, even if the man have no faith. It is not the sense of sight that has made the world beautiful; it is God. But the man's sense of sight makes the world's beauty of benefit to him. The Babe of Bethlehem was the Incarnate Son of God, whether men had faith or not : human faith did not affect the Incarnation, nor could lack of faith affect its reality. Similarly, it is not faith that makes the sacraments real; it is the power of the Holy Spirit. But it is a man's faith that makes the sacraments of real benefit to him, that enables him to enter into them and to take them to him-

[1] Matt. i. 23.   [2] Luke ii. 7.
[3] Matt. ii. 3, 4.   [4] Mark v. 31.
[5] John xix. 18.   [6] See also Chap. xvi. 2.

71

self. The reality of the sacraments is not created by faith, but it is discerned and enjoyed by faith.

Therefore it is true to say that we are saved by sacraments, and also that we are saved by faith. Both sayings are parts of one truth.

A boy is drowning in the water; his father throws him a rope; he grips it, and is saved. We are as the boy, the man is God, the rope is the sacraments, and the boy's grip on the rope is faith. And how much is concluded in that act of gripping! There is belief that the rope is strong enough, understanding of the purpose with which it is thrown, trust that the father is able and willing to pull him out, realisation of his own dire need and helplessness, and the action of his will responding to the means of escape offered him. Faith is all this: the sense of need, right belief in God and in the means of grace, personal trust in the Saviour, and, as the result of these, the exercise of the will. And we may ask, Which is it that saves the boy? Is it the father, or the rope, or the boy's grip? Surely all three, and no one of them alone. So we are saved by God, by sacraments, by faith. Not unless we have faith, not apart from the means of grace, and always by God, who has given us the sacraments, and by whose gift only we can have faith. Neither any good works nor any power nor faith of our own can procure us salvation; but God-given faith will enable us to receive, to grasp, to cling to the salvation which God offers. By grace have we been saved through faith; and that not of ourselves: it is the gift of God[1]

And repentance is necessary. For repentance[2] is the act of love towards God by which we turn from the self-love and the sins which have grieved him. How can we have the union with God in Christ which is offered to us by the sacraments, while we cling to the sins that separate the soul from God? How can we desire God, if we are desiring sin? How can we be turned to God and at the same time be turned to our own ways? How can we seek salvation from sin, if we think that we have no sin to be saved from? How shall God forgive us, unless we want to be forgiven? If

[1] Eph. ii. 8. [2] See also Chap. viii. 2.

72

the drowning boy says, I am not drowning, or, I am content
to drown, he may indeed be saved, but it will be against his
will.   And God does not save us by sacraments, if our wills
are in opposition to his work of salvation.

v

The Holy Spirit came upon the Church at Pentecost, to
remain and abide in it.   It was by the power of the Holy
Spirit that blessed Mary conceived and gave of her substance to form the body of her Child.   It was by the coming
of the same Holy Spirit that the Church, the mystical body
of Christ, was born into the world.

The Holy Spirit descended upon Christ himself at his
baptism to empower him as Prophet, Priest, and King.   The
Holy Spirit descended upon Christ's Church at Pentecost,
to empower it to be what Christ is! and as Prophet, to teach
God's truth; as Priest, to bring men back to God; as King,
to rule over the members of Christ's kingdom with his
authority.   And the same Holy Spirit is given to the members
of the Church individually, that they may bear their part
in the Church's work and ministry.

We may consider the work of the Holy Spirit under three
heads :

He is the Spirit of truth.   Christ said : I will pray the
Father, and he shall give you another Comforter, that he
may be with you for ever, even the spirit of truth.   He
abideth with you, and shall be in you.   He shall teach you
all things, and bring to your remembrance all that I have
said unto you.   He shall guide you into all the truth.   He
shall glorify me, for he shall take of mine, and shall declare
it unto you.[1]

He is the Giver of life.   It is by his power that material
things are made the vehicles of divine grace.   It is the spirit
that quickeneth; the flesh (that is, material nature by itself)
profiteth nothing.[2]   It is the Holy Spirit who sanctifies water
to the mystical washing away of sins, that a man may be
born of water and the spirit.   It is the Holy Spirit who

[1] John xiv. 16, 17, 26; xvi. 13, 14.   [2] John vi. 63.

gives power to the baptised in confirmation to act as
members of the priestly body of Christ; and to priests in
ordination to act as the representatives of the whole body
and of Christ himself. It is the Holy Spirit who makes
present with us in holy communion the true body and blood
of Jesus, that body and blood which by his overshadowing
were conceived by Mary. It is the Holy Spirit who moves
sinners to repentance; and the power of absolution is his,
which resides in the Church, ever since our Lord said:
Receive ye the Holy Ghost; whose soever sins ye forgive,
they are forgiven.[1]

Again, he is the Sanctifier. As many as are led by the
spirit of God, these are the sons of God.[2] Know ye not
that ye are a temple of God, and that the spirit of God
dwelleth in you?[3] The fruit of the spirit is love, joy, peace,
long-suffering, kindness, goodness, faithfulness, meekness,
temperance.[4] The love of God hath been shed abroad in our
hearts through the Holy Ghost which was given unto us.[5]
God chose you from the beginning unto salvation in
sanctification of the Spirit.[6]

If God uses human agents for the proclamation of his
truth and for the conveyance of grace to men, he does not
leave them alone. He gives them that present and continual
help without which their work could not but be fruitless.
It is the Holy Spirit who is now working by means of man
for man. All gifts and graces and powers are his and from
him, the one and the same spirit, dividing to each one
severally as he will.[7]

And the Holy Spirit works also outside the Church. For
only by God's working can unbelievers be brought into the
Church. No man can say that Jesus is Lord, but in the
Holy Spirit.[8]

And to him also is to be ascribed the grace given to those
who, loving our Lord and trying to be his disciples, yet know
not the whole faith and live apart from the Catholic Church,
through ignorance or the circumstances of their birth or

[1] John xx. 22.   [2] Rom. viii. 14.   [3] 1 Cor. iii. 16.
[4] Gal. v. 22.   [5] Rom. v. 5.   [6] 2 Thess. ii. 13.
[7] 1 Cor. xii. 11.   [8] 1 Cor. xii. 3.

up-bringing. We see the fruits of the Spirit in many who, through no fault of their own, are without sacramental grace, and we give thanks and praise to the Holy Spirit of God, whose love and power overflow the sacramental channels of his grace.

VII

BAPTISM AND CONFIRMATION

I

WE have seen that the Church is the organised society by means of which men may abide in spiritual union with Christ.[1] But before they can abide in union with Christ, they must be brought into union with him. They must be admitted into the Church. No one can make himself a member of Christ or of the Church; our salvation is not our work, but God's. The means by which God makes us members is the sacrament of holy baptism.

By baptism we are not only made part of the Church in its outward organisation, as a man is admitted to a human society by some ceremony of admission; but also an inward change is wrought in us. In all God's sacramental dealings with us a real spiritual grace accompanies the outward act.

The gift of grace which God gives by baptism is called Regeneration, which means new birth. Except a man be born anew, said our Lord, except a man be born of water and the Spirit, he cannot enter into the kingdom of God.[2] Not by works done in righteousness which we did ourselves, but according to his mercy he saved us, through the washing of regeneration, and renewing of the Holy Ghost.[3]

From our first parent Adam we have received natural life : from Jesus Christ we receive supernatural life by the new birth of baptism. Hence Christ is called the Second Adam.[4] We are made members of Christ, being by God's grace grafted into the body of Christ's Church, to which we did not belong by nature.[5] We become what we were not before,

[1] Chap. vi. 2.   [2] John iii. 3, 5.   [3] Titus iii. 5.
[4] 1 Cor. xv. 45.   [5] Rom. xi. 13-24.

76

Christians and children of God, through being united with
Christ, the Son of God. We are adopted[1] into the family
of God, being taken out of the separateness in which we were
born, and made parts of a greater whole; no longer merely
individuals to live a self-centred life, but to live in the spirit
of unselfishness as members of the new brotherhood of man
in Christ. We are lifted out of the state of separation from
God, and made at one with him, to live as obedient subjects
of God's kingdom, first in the Church here below, and
hereafter in the kingdom made perfect in heaven. By
natural birth we belong to this world : by our new birth we
belong to heaven. Heaven is our true home. We are
citizens of the heavenly kingdom,[2] even while we still
sojourn in this world.

Baptism was for each of us a new beginning, a death to our
old life and a birth into heavenly life. If any man is in
Christ, he is a new creature : the old things are passed away;
behold, they are become new.[3] We were buried with Christ
through baptism into death, that like as Christ was raised
from the dead, so we also might walk in newness of life.[4]

And when we were made one with Christ in baptism, we
entered into the benefits of his sacrifice for sin. We were
brought out of the state of sin into the state of salvation.[5]
We were brought out of our isolation from Christ into
membership of the body which is saved by Christ.[6] Therefore we received forgiveness of all our previous sinfulness,
both of any actual sins each one of us had committed,
and of the guilt of sinfulness that rested upon us all
through being born of the stock of fallen human nature.[7] We
believe in one baptism for the remission of sins.[8] And with
the remission of sins there came to us also the remission of
the eternal consequences of sin.

And, having once been admitted into this state of salvation, we remain saved souls, and the work of grace goes

[1] Rom. viii. 15, 16; Gal. iv. 4-7; Eph. i. 5.
[2] Phil. iii. 20; Heb. xii. 22.
[3] 1 Pet. iii. 21.
[4] Rom. vi. 4; Col. ii. 12.
[5] Nicene Creed.
[6] Eph. v. 23, 30.   [7] Chap. ii. 4.
[8] 2 Cor. v. 17.

forward in us, so long as we do not separate ourselves anew from Christ by wilful sin.

Hence a child who has been baptised, and died before he has committed any sin, is certainly saved. By baptism he has been brought out of the state of sin in which he was born into the state of salvation; and no new sin has come to sully the child's baptismal innocence. As regards children who die unbaptised, the Church has no revelation from God about their state after death. They have not entered upon the high road of salvation, and God has shown us no other road. We do not know. But God is love, and we may trust him that what he will do is good.

Similarly, in regard to the heathen, who have not known the gospel of Christ, the Church has no revelation from the Lord. It is written, indeed, that he who believes and is baptised shall be saved, and that he who disbelieves shall be condemned.[1] But that condemnation seems plainly to be reserved for those who reject baptism through wilful unbelief and disobedience. Our belief in the necessity of receiving baptism, since it is the means of salvation revealed by God, does not oblige us to deny the possibility of the salvation of those who through no fault of their own have died without having received it. Baptism is necessary, because it is the means to an end. Baptism is not itself the end; the end is salvation. Salvation is union with Christ and the sharing in his life. If God wills, he can make another road to this for those who have not been baptised. To us he has shown only the high road.[2]

Every person, therefore, should make sure, as regards himself, that he has been rightly baptised. If there is any doubt, he should apply to his parish priest. And Christian people should be very careful to see that no infant dies unbaptised, nor any adult who has shown a desire for baptism and even the beginnings of faith and repentance.

[1] Mark xvi. 16.   [2] See also Chap. xix. 3.

II

The sacrament of baptism was instituted by the risen Lord before his ascension. He said to the apostles: *All authority has been given unto me in heaven and on earth. Go ye therefore and make disciples of all the nations, baptising them in the name of the Father and of the Son and of the Holy Ghost.*[1]

The first administration of holy baptism was on the day of Pentecost. *What shall we do?* said the people who were converted by the miraculous signs, and by the preaching of St. Peter. And Peter said unto them: *Repent ye, and be baptised every one of you in the name of Jesus Christ unto the remission of your sins; and ye shall receive the gifts of the Holy Ghost. For to you is the promise, and to your children, and to all that are afar off, even as many as the Lord our God shall call unto him.*[2] From that time baptism has been the way of entrance into the Catholic Church, into the state of salvation.

The outward and visible means in baptism is water, which is poured upon the person, or in which he is immersed, with the words: *I baptise thee in the name of the Father and of the Son and of the Holy Ghost.* This is all that is necessary; but anointing with holy oil and other ceremonies are often added.

God requires of those who come to be baptised the same disposition that he requires for the reception of every sacrament—namely, faith and repentance. These are necessary, not only for the profitable receiving of a sacrament, but also at all times. They are the permanent disposition of the soul in which we need always to live, in response to the grace of God that is continually given to us. Whenever we lose faith, our hold on the spiritual realities is broken or weakened. Whenever we refuse to repent, we block the channel of grace.

If a person is baptised lacking faith and repentance, the grace of baptism will lie idle in his soul. He is made a member of the Church indeed; but his membership is of no

---

[1] Matt. xxviii. 18, 19.   [2] Acts i. 37-39.

spiritual value to him. The new life given to him can bear no fruit while he remains impenitent and unbelieving. God's sacraments do not benefit us without our consent and co-operation.

Yet it has always been the custom of the Catholic Church to baptise infants. The reasons for this are such as these. Under the old covenant infants were admitted to the family of God at eight days old,[1] and we cannot think that the blessings of the new covenant are more restricted than those of the old. Our Lord said : Suffer the little children to come unto me, and forbid them not; for of such is the kingdom of God.[2] And, by bestowing his blessing upon them, he showed that even unconscious babes are capable of receiving spiritual benefit. They can receive grace because, though they have not yet any active faith or repentance, yet there is not in them any self-willed impenitence or unbelief to hinder the goodwill of God towards them. The practice of infant baptism is one clear illustration of the Church's belief that in all God's dealings with us the beginning is with him, and our part is to respond to the grace given; that the sacraments are means of grace, and not mere tokens of a state of grace attained apart from them.

It is necessary that baptised infants be brought up in the knowledge of what God has done for them, and be taught their need of repentance and faith. Otherwise the fruits of the Spirit will not live and grow in them. That is the reason why some hold that an infant should not be baptised, unless in danger of death, if there is no prospect of its being brought up as a Christian. Others, however, hold that in Christian lands all infants should be baptised, as there is always some prospect of a Christian upbringing.

The Church bears witness to the need of faith and repentance by requiring that there shall be godparents at infant baptisms, to promise these necessary things on behalf of the child. Godparents must be communicants in a state of grace, and parents should not be godparents to their own children. The duty of godparents does not end with the baptism. They should pray continually for their godchildren,

[1] Gen. xvii. 12.   [2] Mark x. 14.

and they are bound to see that they have Christian education, so that the promises made at baptism shall become more than an empty form. And it is their duty to see that the children be brought to confirmation and holy communion.

Baptism is usually administered by a priest. But, in cases of emergency, any man or woman may baptise. A baptism performed by one who holds wrong belief, or who is separate from the Catholic Church, is a true baptism, if his intention is to give baptism, and if he uses water and the proper words. And the person baptised is thereby made a member of the Catholic Church, and not of the sect of the baptiser.

III

There are three promises made at baptism, by the person who is baptised, or by the godparents: Renunciation, faith, and obedience.

First, to renounce Satan, and to give up all that is sinful, fighting against evil wherever he may find it, whether in himself or around him. This promise includes a promise of repentance, for every act of repentance is a renunciation of evil.

Secondly, to believe all the truths that God has taught through the Catholic Church; and in particular the Apostles' Creed, which is a summary of many important points of Christian belief.[1]

Thirdly, to rule his life, not by his own faulty and wayward desires, but by God's holy will, thus fulfilling the purpose for which God made him.

It was on this clear understanding that we were admitted to membership of the Church. God brought us within the covenant; and every covenant has two contracting parties, with conditions and promises on either side. God enables us to promise to live the Christian life; and, because we promise, he gives us sacramental grace to fulfil our promise. We are bound to live as Christians, because by God's grace we can. And the continuance of God's favour to us is

---

[1] Chaps. xii. 3; xiii. 1.

conditional upon our using the grace given to us, and being faithful to our part in the contract.

The determination to renounce the devil, to believe God's truth and to serve him, is often called by the name of Conversion, which means Turning. Conversion is the change of will by which a man or a woman turns from sin to God, desiring and claiming to be saved through Christ, and accepting God's will as the one ruling principle of life.

Conversion may take place before baptism, as commonly in the case of the heathen, who must turn from their old ways of sin and unbelief to the living and holy God, before they are fit to receive the new life. Conversion in itself cannot save them. Although one cannot be converted unless the power of the Holy Ghost move him, still conversion is a human act; and our salvation is not wrought out by any act of ours: it is God's work received by us. Men must be saved by God: they cannot save themselves. The conversion of Saul of Tarsus is an example of a good conversion. But his conversion did not make him a member of the Church, nor give him the life of Christ and forgiveness of his sins. He needed to receive sacramental grace. The word of God came to him: And now, why tarriest thou? Arise, and be baptised, and wash away thy sins.[1]

Conversion may also take place after baptism, as is often the case with Christians who have gone astray in sin or unbelief, or who have never awakened to God's claim upon them and their need of a Saviour. They have been set upon the path of safety, yet they may have turned back, and be facing in the wrong direction, wandering through carelessness or wilfulness farther and farther from God. If so, they need to turn again, to be converted. Most of us need to make such a definite act of conversion at some time in our lives. Indeed, we may need to be converted again and again. But not all need it, for there are those who have never gone astray, and who have never defiled the innocence of their souls by wilful sin.

Conversion may be a sudden act, a complete re-direction

[1] Acts xxii. 16.

of one's whole purpose and energies. It may also be a gradual process without any marked crisis, a continual direction of the will more and more into conformity with the will of God, continually mortifying our corrupt affections, and daily proceeding in all virtue and godliness of living.[1] In the latter sense conversion is necessary for all. Indeed, every good act of repentance is really a new turning more directly towards God.

Conversion is not the same as sanctification: God alone can make us holy. Nor does conversion render us safe never to fall again; it is not possible for anyone to attain to such a happy state of security while in this life. Conversion is always a beginning only, a coming to God for him to perfect his work in us.[2] But, for many who have been baptised, it is the necessary beginning of their response to grace, a first step which they have never taken, and for lack of which many, even communicants, have never known the power and the joy of salvation in Christ.

IV

Confirmation is the sacrament by which the new life received in baptism is confirmed, or strengthened, by the power of the Holy Spirit. He is called the Comforter, a word which really means the Strengthener. We receive power when the Holy Spirit comes upon us at confirmation.[3]

The Holy Spirit came upon our Lord after his baptism, and, full of the Holy Spirit,[4] he began his work. He said to the Jews: The Spirit of the Lord is upon me.[5]

The Holy Spirit came upon the Church on the day of Pentecost, and the apostles became strong to preach the word with boldness. He came to abide in the Church, to teach it, to strengthen it, and to make it holy.

And the same Holy Spirit is given to each baptised person in the sacrament of confirmation, to teach him, to sanctify him, and to strengthen him to be Christ's faithful soldier and servant unto his life's end.

[1] Baptismal Service.   [2] Phil. i, 6.   [3] Acts i. 8.
[4] Luke iv. 1, 14.   [5] Luke iv. 18.

The institution of this sacrament by our Lord is not narrated in the gospels. There is no doubt, however, that it was instituted by him; for in the Acts we see the apostles administering the sacrament, which they would not have done if they had not his authority. Thus we read that when the apostles in Jerusalem heard that the people of Samaria had been converted through the preaching of Philip, and had been baptised, they sent unto them Peter and John, who, when they were come down, prayed for them that they might receive the Holy Ghost, for as yet he was fallen upon none of them. Then laid they their hands upon them, and they received the Holy Ghost.[1]

The outward means in the sacrament of confirmation is the laying of the hand of the bishop upon the candidates, with prayer. The example set by the apostles is followed by the bishop, who is their successor. In many parts of the Church the candidates are also anointed with holy oil that has been blessed by the bishop for this purpose; and the words used are such as these : I sign thee with the sign of the Cross, and I confirm thee with the anointing of salvation, in the name of the Father and of the Son and of the Holy Ghost. In some places, also, confirmation is administered by a priest authorised by the bishop, but the oil used is hallowed by the bishop himself.

The bishop prays that the candidates may have the seven gifts of the Spirit : Wisdom, to know and love God; Understanding of what he has done and is doing in them; Counsel, to know his will; Strength, to carry it out; Knowledge of the true faith of the Church; Godliness in life and character; and holy Fear of grieving God by disobedience or irreverence.[2]

The Holy Spirit comes to each person to abide with him. Confirmation, like baptism, may be received only once. Once we have been made the children of God, we remain his children always; and when we receive the Holy Spirit, we receive him once and for all. It is true that we may become unloving and disobedient children, and we may grieve the Holy Spirit by neglecting to use the power and grace given to us. And, if so, God's work of sanctification

[1] Acts viii. 14-17; *cf.* xix. 1-7.   [2] Isa. xi. 2.

will not go forward in us. But there is needed only our conversion, our repentance, to remove the hindrance to God's grace which our sinfulness has caused.

While we continue in faith and repentance, co-operating with the grace of God, we are being made holy by his Holy Spirit, and are being conformed more and more to the likeness of Christ. The Holy Ghost sanctifieth us and all the chosen people of God.[1]

The baptised and confirmed Christian who has received his first communion is a perfect Christian. Not that he has reached perfect holiness, but that he now has at his disposal all that he needs both for his salvation and his sanctification. He is a soldier fully armed, to fight in the army of the Lord. He is a traveller, set upon the right road, and made strong to persevere to the end, which is the perfect fulfilment in him of the divine will. He is a servant, trained and ready for the Master's work. He is a subject of the kingdom of heaven, in possession of all the rights of his citizenship. He is a full member of the Christian Church, the priestly body of Christ, to offer in union with Christ the acceptable sacrifice of worship and propitiation.

We know from history that in the earliest days baptism and confirmation were administered together, and the two sacraments were regarded as parts of one whole. In some parts of the Church this is still the case, and infants are given baptism, and confirmation, and also first communion. But in other parts confirmation and first communion are not given until the child is old enough to have been instructed in the elements of Christian belief and duty. To delay confirmation and communion until the years of maturity have been reached is a bad custom, contrary to the mind of the Church. It is right that the Christian should have received the full grace of God before he meets the temptations that come to him through the awakening powers of his body and through contact with the world.

In some parts of the Church the candidates renew at their confirmation the promises that were made at their baptism.

[1] Church Catechism.

They do not thereby undertake any new responsibility; they only acknowledge publicly, on this solemn occasion, the obligations by which they have always been bound as Christians. This renewal of the baptismal vows is a good and helpful custom. Indeed, all Christians would do well to renew them frequently before God, so that they may not slip into forgetfulness of what Christians are bound to forsake and to believe and to do. But the renewal of the vows is not a part of the sacrament of confirmation.

VIII

SIN, REPENTANCE, AND THE SACRAMENT
OF PENANCE

1

ALTHOUGH we are endowed with many gifts of divine grace in the Catholic Church, we are still liable to fall into sin. God washed us in holy baptism, and made us clean;[1] yet we can stain our souls again. He has shown us the way in which we should walk;[2] but still we can go our own way, and follow our own will, not caring about his. The grace we have received does not force us to choose the right and refuse the wrong. The powers of evil are still active against us. We are living in the midst of the influences of a sinful world. And within ourselves there remains the faulty disposition of our fallen nature, inclining us towards wilfulness and self-pleasing. There are foes around us always and we ourselves may prove traitors and welcome the enemy.[3]

And so it comes to pass that we fall into sin. In many things we all stumble.[4] Sin is any thought or word or deed against God's will. Sometimes, we sin by doing what we know we ought not to do, sometimes by omitting to do what we know we ought to do.

Temptation is not sin. Even the sinless Jesus was tempted. Temptations are the suggestions of evil that come to our minds, it may be, without our will. They become sins only when, by our frailty or deliberate choice we seek them, or desire them, or yield to them.

Temptations come to us from three sources: from Satan and the evil spirits; from the world—that is, from the influence of the low standard of conduct of those who are not

[1] Titus iii. 5.   [2] Isa. xxx. 21.
[3] Chap. ii. 4.   [4] Jas. iii. 2.

ruled by God's will; and from the flesh—that is, from our own bodily desires and the bad inclinations of our fallen nature. Temptations to sin do not come from God, but they are allowed by him for our training and education.[1] Whenever we have to make choice between two lines of conduct, the one good and the other bad or less good, God is giving us an opportunity of showing our faith in him[2] and our love, and of gaining strength by the practice of virtue. The fiercer the temptation, the greater the opportunity. Blessed is the man that endureth temptation; for when he hath been approved, he shall receive the crown of life, which the Lord promised to them that love him. Let no man say when he is tempted, I am tempted of God; for God cannot be tempted with evil, and he himself tempteth no man; but each man is tempted when he is drawn away by his own lust, and enticed.[3]

We are never obliged to sin. It is never true, for one who was in a state of grace and has fallen into sin, to say, I could not help it. The power of God is stronger than the powers of evil, and he gives us always sufficient strength to be victors in the fight, if only we will use it. There hath no temptation taken you but such as man can bear; but God is faithful, who will not suffer you to be tempted above that ye are able; but will with the temptation make also the way to escape, that ye may be able to endure it.[4]

All sins are not equally sinful in God's sight. We do some sins in ignorance or in partial ignorance, not knowing clearly that they are sins, because we have not fully learnt God's will. And sometimes we sin without really having intended to sin : we are overtaken[5] by the temptation before we know that we are being tempted. And again, we sometimes commit sins or fail in our duty because old sinful habits are strong in us, and our will is weak through having yielded to the temptation many times before. Such sins are called venial, from a Latin word meaning pardon, because they are more easily pardoned than greater and more sinful sins.

[1] Chap. ii. 3. [2] Jas. i. 3. [3] Jas. i. 12, 13.
[4] 1 Cor. x. 13. [5] Gal. vi. 1.

But also sometimes Christians give in to temptations on purpose, and with full knowledge that they are doing wrong, choosing to please themselves and to rebel against God : and this, alas ! not only in small matters, but even in the greatest. Such wilful sins, if the matter be great, are called mortal sins,[1] for they bring spiritual death, as a mortal disease brings bodily death. Whenever a person commits mortal sin, he is cutting himself off from God by his own choice, and killing the eternal life, which he has in his soul so long as he is spiritually in union with God. If anyone has done such great sin, and dies without repentance, he will be for ever separated from God in hell. Sin, when it is full-grown, bringeth forth death.[2]

The sins of Christians are more grievous in the sight of God than those of the heathen; for the heathen do not know what is right as Christians do, nor have they that grace of God to help them which Christians have through the sacraments. A heathen sins lacking the grace and truth that are in Jesus : a Christian, if he sins wilfully, sins against that grace and truth.[3]

No sins of a Christian can be regarded as being really trivial; for each smallest sin is contrary to the grace of God and the higher nature that has been given to us. If one great sin can block the channel of grace, so also can a number of lesser sins. And small sins ever tend to grow more frequent, and to lead to greater sins :

> Sow a sinful thought, reap a sinful deed ;
> Sow a sinful deed, reap a sinful habit ;
> Sow a sinful habit, reap a sinful character ;
> Sow a sinful character, reap a sinful end.

And all the acts of a Christian, even those which are not wrong in themselves, may be of the nature of sin. If they are done for his own sake, because to act otherwise would offend his culture or self-respect—and not for God's sake, simply because they are right—their motive is self apart from God, and self apart from God is the root of sin.

[1] 1 John v. 16, 17. [2] Jas. i. 15.
[3] Heb. x. 26-31 ; 2 Pet. ii. 20, 21.

II

Christians cannot obtain forgiveness a second time by being baptised again. But God has given us another sacrament by which we can receive pardon even for the worst sins, and be restored to the state of grace, as often as we truly repent : the sacrament of penance—that is, of repentance.

Let us consider now, more particularly than before,[1] what true repentance is.

Repentance cannot begin until we know that we have sinned. There must be conviction of sin. If we say that we have no sins, we deceive ourselves and the truth is not in us.[2] Next to the knowledge of God, we are most concerned to know ourselves. We can awaken our dull consciences, and know what our sins are, if we examine ourselves by the commandments of God and his Church.[3]

There are three parts in a good repentance : contrition, confession, and satisfaction.

First, contrition is repentance in the heart and will, because we know that we have offended against the holy and loving God and Jesus Christ our Saviour who died for us. If we are sorry only because we have been found out, or have got into trouble, or are lowered in our self-respect or in the eyes of our acquaintances, or because we are afraid of going to hell, we have not true Christian repentance. Perfect contrition is sorrow for sin joined with love towards God.[4]

And it obliges us to turn away from our sins, and to make up for the past by a new and better life, and to avoid whatever is likely to lead us again into the old temptations. It is plain that if anyone knows he has done wrong, and yet intends to do it again, or is careless whether he does it again or not, he is not really penitent.[5]

Contrition is not a mere feeling. Indeed, some find it very hard to feel contrite. Great depth of contrite feeling is, perhaps, only found in great saints. God does not ask of us more than we are able to give. He will accept us if we

[1] Chaps. iii. 4; vi. 4.   [2] 1 John i. 8.   [3] Chaps. xvi., xvii.
[4] Luke vii. 47.   [5] John viii. 11.

90

have an honest desire to make a good repentance and a sincere determination to amend our lives. The desire to be contrite is contrition.

Secondly, confession is repentance on the lips. If we confess our sins, God is faithful and righteous to forgive us our sins, and to cleanse us from all unrighteousness.[1]

Confess your sins one to another, is the rule in the New Testament.[2] Every confession of sin mentioned in it was open, heard by others as well as by God. Such open confession is a great act of humility. It is a hard test by which we can judge of the sincerity of our contrition, and it has the effect of deepening contrition in us.

Confession is due from us, because we are all members of one body in the Church. No man sinneth unto himself alone. The evil that we do, the evil that is in us, spreads its infection to others. If one member suffer, all the members suffer with it.[3] Our sins are not only against God, but also against the brotherhood of the Church. And by our sins we break the terms of our membership. We are not straight if we evade the frank acknowledgement of our unfaithfulness.

In the earliest days, the custom was that great sins were confessed in the public church in the hearing of all. But before long this was found to be undesirable, from fear of suggesting evil to innocent minds, except in some cases where the circumstances of the sin were already known and had caused grievous scandal. The custom grew up in the Church that confessions were usually made, not before the whole congregation, but to the priest alone as the representative of the whole body. And the priest was bound never to reveal anything that was told him in confession.

The sinner must tell out all the sins he knows he has been guilty of, since the time of his last confession, or since his baptism if he is making a first confession. He must lay bare his whole soul truly and humbly, without making excuses. He cannot, indeed, confess every sin he has done and every failure in his duty; for no amount of care in self-examination can make one conscious of the whole of one's sinfulness. But if he deliberately keeps any sin back from

[1] 1 John i. 9.   [2] Jas. v. 16.   [3] 1 Cor. xii. 26.

confession, of which he knows he has been guilty, he is failing in sincerity through fear or shame, and he will not be forgiven, but will only add another sin to his burden.

Except ye be converted, said our Lord, and become as little children, ye shall not enter into the kingdom of heaven.[1] Confession should be both easy and hard. It is easy, in that it is the God-given relief of the overburdened heart of the sinner, who tells out his sad story like a little child to his mother. It is hard, just in so far as that little child realises the mother's love and goodness. It is harder still for us, when we are grown up, and our imperfect penitence shrinks from the mortification of our pride. But, although confession of sin is hard, it is natural for us as human beings to find relief in words, if we are penitent : it is still more natural for us to do so as members of one organised brotherhood of mutual help.

And it is natural to seek the divine forgiveness in the sacrament of penance, for that is the direct means of pardon. A man may say, I prefer to receive forgiveness direct from God, meaning, apart from the sacrament. But if he had been in the Holy Land when Jesus was there, God made man, God made sacramental, he would not, supposing he were penitent, have stood apart from Jesus, trusting in the loving kindness of Jehovah. He would have been forced, by the very power of his loving penitence, to go where Jesus was, and kneel at the feet of the Son of man, and hear the absolving word spoken by human lips, and receive forgiveness sacramentally, through the human nature of Jesus— that is, by the direct means ordained by God. And similarly, it is natural now to seek for pardon, as we seek grace for every other spiritual need, through Jesus, through his body the Church, through a sacrament. The direct approach of God to us, and of us to God, is the sacramental way, which is the extension of the Incarnation.[2]

Thirdly, satisfaction is repentance in the life. This will be explained in the next section.

Repentance is not genuine if it be without its continual companions, faith and charity. How can we come to God

[1] Matt. xviii. 3.   [2] Chap. vi. 1-3.

for pardon unless we believe in God's willingness to receive us? How can we approach the sacraments, unless we believe in the power that is in them through the death of Jesus? And how dare we seek for pardon from the love of God, if we ourselves are holding back our love from God or our neighbour? We must forgive others as we hope ourselves to be forgiven.[1]

III

In preparing for sacramental confession, the Christian should first pray earnestly for grace to make a good repentance. Then he should carefully examine his conscience; seeking also to make his contrition as deep as he can, by reflecting on the love of God and the grievousness of sin in his holy sight; and lastly he should make a firm resolution to amend his life.

A form of words such as the following is commonly used in making confession : I confess to God Almighty, to blessed Mary and all the saints, and to thee, my spiritual father, that I have sinned exceedingly, in thought, word, and deed, and by omission; by my fault, by my own fault, by my own most grievous fault. Especially I confess that, since I received absolution, I have done these sins . . . For these, and for all my other sins which I cannot now remember, I am heartily sorry, and I purpose amendment. Wherefore I pray Almighty God to have mercy upon me, and forgive me my sins; and of thee, father, I ask penance, advice, and absolution. And I beg blessed Mary, and all the saints, and thee, father, to pray for me to the Lord our God. Amen.

When the sinner has confessed his sins, the priest gives his absolution, if he judges him to be penitent; and also he gives him such advice and comfort as his state requires. Absolution is the forgiveness of God bestowed upon a repentant sinner by a priest in the sacrament of penance. The word Absolution means loosing. The penitent is not only forgiven the guilt of his sins, but also he is loosed from the bonds of Satan. He is set free from the eternal consequences of sin, and restored to his rightful position as a

---

[1] Matt. vi. 14, 15; *cf.* Chap. xvi. 2.

child of God and a member of the Church. His union with God, the source of grace and life, which was broken or impaired by sin, is renewed.

The words by which the priest gives absolution are: I absolve thee from all thy sins, in the name of the Father and of the Son and of the Holy Ghost. This act of absolution brings divine forgiveness as surely and as definitely as does baptism. And it is God's act, not merely the priest's. No one but a properly ordained priest[1] has authority to give absolution: and he gives it, not in his own power, but by the authority committed to him at his ordination. The priest is not only the representative of the congregation. If so, the pardon would be but human, not divine. He is the representative of Christ.[2]

Our Lord instituted the sacrament of penance on the day of his resurrection, when he gave the powers of his priesthood to the Church, saying to the apostles: As the Father hath sent me, even so send I you. Receive ye the Holy Ghost: whose soever sins ye forgive they are forgiven unto them; and whose soever sins ye retain, they are retained.[3] The apostles authorised other men to share their authority, whom we call bishops; and they in turn appointed other bishops; and so the power has been handed down to the present time. And each bishop has ordained men to share with the bishops in the ministry of absolution and in the other powers of Christ's priesthood, laying his hands upon them after the example of the apostles, and saying such words as these: Receive ye the Holy Ghost for the office and work of a priest in the Church of God, now committed unto thee by the imposition of our hands. Whose sins thou dost forgive, they are forgiven, and whose sins thou dost retain, they are retained. And be thou a faithful dispenser of the word of God and of his holy sacraments, in the name of the Father and of the Son and of the Holy Ghost.[4]

When the penitent has been absolved, there still remains for him to make satisfaction for his sins. This means that he must do all he can to put right what has been wrong. For

[1] Chap. x. 2. [2] 2 Cor. v. 18-20.
[3] John xx. 21-23. [4] See further in Chap. x.

94

example, he must restore what he has stolen, or the value of it; he must tell the truth about anyone of whom he has told lies. Also, he must be ready to suffer willingly whatever punishment may come to him because of his sins. All sin merits punishment, and brings its penalty either in this world or the world to come. We do not escape all penalty for our sins by being pardoned and absolved from their guilt and power. We must do penance. The penance which the priest assigns is often some small thing, some prayer to say or some good deed to do, which may help to deepen the sinner's penitence and to correct his faults. That is sufficient as a token of his willingness to make satisfaction for his offences. But also the penance may be something more difficult, if the priest judges that some severity is necessary for the person's spiritual welfare. In the sacrament of penance the priest is both a spiritual judge and a physician of souls. It is his duty to tell the penitent what satisfaction he must make to God and to men.

Public penance is imposed by the bishop, or by the priest authorised by him, in cases of sin which have caused grave open scandal. Those who have sinned grievously and openly should be openly censured. After the penance has been performed, the penitent is admitted again to holy communion publicly by the authority of the bishop.

The Church urges her children very strongly to seek the sacrament of penance always without delay, if their consciences are burdened by mortal sin. For otherwise they remain in a state of sin, and cannot make a good communion, and are in danger of eternal death. The Church of England, through a desire that confession to a priest shall be entirely voluntary, and to avoid the danger of insincerity that may arise where it is made obligatory, has left the responsibility of deciding about seeking the sacrament of penance to the individual. In other parts of the Church sacramental confession is required, at least once a year, by Church discipline.

Because we all easily fall into lesser sins, and it is hard to pass even one day without fault, it is good for all to go to confession regularly and with considerable frequency once a month or oftener. Sacramental confession is the best preparation for holy communion.[1] The sacrament of penance is not only the refuge of the sinner guilty of mortal sin, but also, when it is made part of our regular spiritual life, it has a special power of its own to purify the character and develop the Christian grace of humility.

Finally, let us consider that our chief motive in seeking this sacrament is not, or should not be, our own benefit, great though that benefit is. We go to holy communion because of our great need of the holy food, but yet with the higher motive of glorifying God by obedience to the command : Do this in remembrance of me. And similarly, we go to confession not only to receive the absolution we greatly need, but also to glorify God in the only way a sinner can glorify God—that is, by the free, open, and loving acknowledgment that God was right and that he was wrong. I acknowledge my faults, that thou, O God, mightest be justified.[2]

IV

The Prodigal Son was in the far country.[3] And at last he came to himself. He recovered the right point of view. He was convicted of sin.

Then he said : I will arise and go unto my father. That was his conversion, when he turned his back to the far country and set his face towards home. It is not enough that we should turn over a new leaf. We must come back to God for pardon and restoration to the state of grace.

And he arose, and came unto his father. No word is told us of the long journey, his toil and weariness, his failing strength, and fainting heart, upon the road, his pain and hunger, his sinking down by the roadside in despair; though such must have been his painful experience. The converted sinner has many a struggle, many a failure it may be, ere the habits formed by sinful indulgence are altered and their power finally broken. We know that in our own experience. But there is no word of it here. He arose, and he came. That is all. For God does not wait for the conquest of self to be complete. In his sight, there is only one

[1] Chap. ix. 6.　　[2] Ps. li. 3. 4.　　[3] Luke xv. 17-32; cf. Chap. ii. 5.

96

step from a true conversion to arrival in the Father's home.

But while he was yet afar off, his father saw him. God's love is waiting for the sinner, expecting his return, while he goes his own way. God allows us to go away from him, for he will not coerce us; but we must not think that our wilfulness makes no difference to God.

The father was moved with compassion, and ran, and fell on his neck, and kissed him. Once we are truly contrite, the riches of our Father's love can be poured out upon us in full and free forgiveness, even before our confession. Yet, if we are truly contrite, how shall we refrain from confessing? Father, I have sinned, and I am no more worthy to be called thy son. Not worthy, no; but thank God, still his son. No sins can unmake us the children of God. But again, it is just the fact that we are God's children that makes our sins so sinful.

And the father said unto the servants, Bring forth the best robe, and put it on him. He is given the outward signs of his restoration to the full privileges of a son in his father's home; not merely allowed to come home on probation, but at once restored to his place of honour. The robe of righteousness which he has cast away is given back to him. And it is given back not by the hands of the Father himself, but under his authority by the servants in priestly absolution.

Let us eat, and be merry. The Father and the servants and the penitent sinner are united in the joy of the holy Eucharist. There is joy in the presence of the angels of God over one sinner that repenteth.[1] Saints and angels and repentant sinners are together with God in that holy joy.

But the elder brother will not rejoice; he who trusted in himself that he was righteous, and despised his brother.[2] That is the type of the communicant of virtuous life, but of cold and unloving heart. Is not impenitent respectability the greatest and most deadly of all sins? To such comes God's rebuke : Son, thou art ever with me, and all that I have is thine. But it was meet to make merry, and be glad; for this thy brother was dead, and is alive again; and was lost, and is found.

[1] Luke xv. 7.　　　　[2] Luke xviii. 9.

IX

THE SACRAMENT OF THE ALTAR

I

THE Church has one prayer, the Our Father, given to it by our Lord.[1] And the Church has one service, ordained by Christ himself, to be its one great act of worship and sacrifice; in which is provided the sacramental means of continual communion between Christ and his members, that they may share in the benefits of his eternal life and his atoning death.

Many names have been given to the Lord's service. The scriptural titles of it are the Breaking of the Bread,[2] and the Eucharist, or Thanksgiving.[3] It is called the Lord's Supper, in memory of the night of its institution; but this is not a scriptural title, for the Lord's Supper mentioned in the New Testament[4] refers to the social meal that in the earliest days was connected with the sacrament. Also it is called the Liturgy, a Greek word meaning the Worship of God; and Holy Communion, that is Holy Union with Jesus[5]; and the Holy Sacrifice, because it sets forth sacramentally the sacrifice of the death of Christ[6]; and the Holy Mysteries, because only the faithful used to be permitted to be present, and not the unbaptised or those who were living in open sin. The most usual of all its titles has been the Mass, a word of uncertain derivation, which for that reason is perhaps the most useful, as it does not draw the attention particularly to any one aspect of the service.

[1] Chap. xiv. 3. [2] Acts ii. 42. [3] 1 Cor. xiv. 16.
[4] 1 Cor. xi. 20. [5] John vi. 56. [6] 1 Cor. xi. 26.

II

After the miracle of the feeding of the five thousand, our Lord prepared for the institution of the sacrament by teaching the Jews that the Father would give them the true bread out of heaven, of which the manna given to the Israelites in the wilderness was a type. Receiving that bread they would have his eternal life within themselves. That true bread, he said, was himself : I am the bread of life; the bread that I will give is my flesh.[1]

The Jews were offended at this mysterious truth, as unbelievers have been offended ever since, thinking Jesus to be a mere man like themselves. They said : How can this man give us his flesh to eat? But our Lord did not explain away his words. He went on to assert still more strongly the great reality of spiritual life through communion with him, and communion with him through partaking of his flesh and blood. He said : Except ye eat the flesh of the Son of man and drink his blood, ye have not life in yourselves. He that eateth my flesh and drinketh my blood hath eternal life, and I will raise him up at the last day. For my flesh is meat indeed, and my blood is drink indeed. He that eateth my flesh and drinketh my blood abideth in me, and I in him. As the living Father sent me, and I live because of the Father, so he that eateth me, he also shall live because of me.

Then many even of his disciples said : This is a hard saying : who can hear it? And they went back, and walked no more with him, because they could not explain to themselves how Jesus could be the sustenance of men, or how his flesh could be their spiritual food. But the faithful were not offended. They accepted his teaching, although it was so wonderful, as the Catholic Church has accepted it ever since, knowing that it was the teaching of God Incarnate, who has power to bring to pass that which he says.

In an upper room in Jerusalem, at the time of the Jewish feast of Passover, the night before he suffered, our Lord took

[1] John vi. 22-65.

unleavened bread, and when he had given thanks, he brake it, and gave it to his disciples, saying: Take, eat; this is my body which is given for you. And he took a cup of wine mingled with water, and said: This is my blood of the new covenant, which is shed for you and for many for the remission of sins. Do this in remembrance of me.[1]

Thus he ordained, and commanded us to continue, the sacrament of his body and blood. He made the partaking of it binding upon all Christians. Take eat . . . Do this. The duty of taking part in the Lord's service and of receiving holy communion is as plain as the duty of saying the Lord's Prayer. Either rests upon the command of our Lord. But it was more than a command. It was his appeal to our thankfulness and love; for he said not only, Do this, but, Do this in remembrance of me.

Our Lord's words did not fall upon deaf ears. From the earliest days the holy communion has been the chief act of worship in the Christian Church. The first Christians continued steadfastly in the breaking of the bread.[2] The only public service of the Church mentioned in the New Testament is the holy communion.[3] And we know from history that since that time the Church has regarded it as the one necessary Christian service. The universal rule has been, the Lord's Service on the Lord's Day. Our chief way in which to keep Sunday holy is by devout attendance at holy Mass.

III

Let us observe carefully the words of Jesus Christ, for they are the words of Almighty God. He did not say: This represents my body, or, This is a symbol of my body; but, This is my body. Nor did he say: Take this bread, and it will become my body to those who receive it with faith; nor, Take this bread, and the act of taking it will help you to spiritual communion with me. The plain meaning of his words is: This bread which I hold in my almighty hands is

---

[1] Matt. xxvi. 26-28; Mark xiv. 22-24; Luke xxii. 19, 20; 1 Cor. xi. 23-25.
[2] Acts ii. 42.   [3] Acts xx. 11; 1 Cor. xi. 17.

my body by virtue of my creative word; therefore take it, and eat it. This is the only way in which the Catholic Church has understood our Lord's words, ever since St. Paul taught: The cup of blessing which we bless, is it not a participation in the blood of Christ? The bread which we break, is it not a participation in the body of Christ? Whosoever shall eat the bread and drink the cup of the Lord unworthily, shall be guilty of the body and blood of the Lord; for he eateth and drinketh judgment unto himself, if he discern not the body.[1]

We cannot explain *how* the bread and wine become his body and blood, any more than we can explain how the divine and human were made one in the Babe of Bethlehem. We cannot explain the mystery of the real presence of God-made-man, either at Bethlehem or on the altar. But we dare not, on that account, explain it away.

> Christ took the bread, and brake it;
> His was the word that spake it;
> And what that word doth make it,
> That I believe, and take it.

The Babe was the sign and means of God-with-man, because the Babe was God. The consecrated bread and wine are the sign and means of the presence of Jesus Christ with us in his body and blood, because by consecration the bread and wine are made one thing with his precious body and blood. The visible means are exalted into the heavenly sphere, and become one with the divine reality, and the body and blood are verily and indeed given, taken, and received.[2]

When the priest, obeying Christ's command, and exercising the powers of Christ's priesthood, has consecrated the bread and wine, after Christ's example, that which is on the altar is the true body and blood of our risen Lord, the body which he took of the blessed Virgin Mary, and the blood which he shed for our redemption. In this way he who has ascended to his glory is still present here, God with us; and more than with us, God in us and we in him.

[1] 1 Cor. x. 16; xi. 29.   [2] Article of Religion, xxviii.

101

This presence is a reality. It is not a mere matter of the imagination that has reality only within our minds. It is not that we think about him until we feel him present. The consecration is a reality, apart from any contribution from our devotion: no mere memorial act, but a continuation of the Incarnation. And the reality is not brought about by our faith, though it is only those who have faith that can benefit by receiving it. It is brought about by God's creative word and the power of the Holy Spirit. What was true at the conception of the Son of God by Mary is true at the consecration of the bread and wine. The Holy Ghost comes down upon the earthly elements, and the power of the Most High overshadows them,[1] and that which is present is holy, the Son of God in his body and blood. The blessed sacrament is the body and blood of Christ while it is being given to us, as well as when we have received it. It is the body and blood on the altar, as well as in the heart of the faithful communicant.

The Catholic Church believes, then, that after the consecration, and apart from reception, the sacred body and the precious blood of Jesus Christ are really present in the blessed sacrament under the forms of the bread and the wine. And where Christ's body or Christ's blood is, there is the whole Christ himself, our Lord and our God, in his glorified humanity and his eternal divinity.

This presence of Christ, because it is real, is spiritual. The body of Christ is given to us, not as it was when he died on the Cross, but as it is. His body exists now, not under earthly, but under heavenly and spiritual conditions, risen and living and glorified. If we could see it with our eyes, we should see that which the angels in heaven see and worship. He ascended that we might have even a better gift than his earthly presence with us. He gives himself to us that we may be with him where he is.[2]

And as Christ thus deigns to give himself to us, we must adore him in the blessed sacrament with true spiritual worship, lifting up our hearts, and glorifying him with angels and archangels and with all the company of heaven. The

[1] Luke i. 35.　　　　[2] John xiv. 3.

deepest reverence will be joined with the deepest love. Here is set forth beneath the sacred veils our Saviour himself, on whose bosom St. John lay at the last supper, and before whose unveiled glory the same St. John fell at his feet like one dead.[1] Carelessness or irreverence in the presence of the blessed sacrament would be a personal insult to our Lord.

And this reverence will show itself also in outward form. Since we are sacraments, our bodies as well as our souls have their duty of worship; and not less when we worship our Lord in his sacramental presence. The Church has loved to surround the altar, the throne of the blessed sacrament, with all that is best and most beautiful of material things. Rich vestments, music, incense, lights, have their right place as the outward signs of our worship of God who at his Incarnation consecrated material things by uniting them with his divinity. If true worship in the spirit were lacking, all grandeur of material worship would indeed be but a dead and meaningless form : but true spiritual worship, from beings such as we are, would not be complete and perfected if it were divorced from as perfect an outward expression as we are able to give. This is the principle which underlies all the ceremonial of the Church.

And reverence is due from us, both inwardly and outwardly, to the blessed sacrament, not only at the time of consecration and reception, but also at all times. In many churches the blessed sacrament is reserved on the altar, or in some other suitable place, from one Mass to another, according to the ancient custom of the Church, in order that holy communion may be given to the sick and to any others who could not communicate at Mass. When this good custom is observed, the faithful may come to visit Jesus at any time in the blessed sacrament, as the shepherds came to the Babe of Bethlehem, and as during his ministry the Jews crowded to greet Jesus and to receive blessing from him, wherever they heard that he was. The faithful also can join together at stated times to offer homage to their king in his sacramental presence on his altar-throne. Wherever Christ is, under whatever form he manifests

[1] John xiii. 23; Rev. i. 17.

himself to us, he is worthy of our worship, and his presence itself is a benediction upon all who come to him.

This practice of adoration of Jesus in the sacrament is one means of confessing our faith in the reality and permanence of the Incarnation, and is a witness of special value in these days, when the truth of the Incarnation is doubted or denied by many.

IV

We have thought about the Mass in its relation to the Incarnation. We must now consider it in relation to the Atonement.

The sacrament of the altar was ordained by our Lord to be a continual act of remembrance of his sacrificial death. St. Paul says: As often as ye eat this bread and drink this cup, ye do shew forth the Lord's death till he come.[1] The Church shows forth the Lord's death to the world, and to Church-members, and to Almighty God: to the world, bearing witness to Christ crucified, and to the belief that by his death he triumphed over the powers of evil, and won salvation for all men; to the members of the Church, remembering with thankfulness the exceeding great love of Jesus Christ; and to Almighty God, offering to him continually the sacrifice of Christ his Son.

Wherewith shall I come before the Lord?[2] We have seen[3] that it is a deep-rooted instinct of mankind to approach God with some offering, to offer some sacrifice to him. Wherever there has been any idea of a god, even among heathen races, there has also usually been the idea of the necessity of offering sacrifice. The Israelites had this idea most clearly, in proportion to their clearer knowledge of God. Their sacrifices were of three kinds. The Peace Offerings of which part was offered to God by fire and part was partaken of by the worshippers, were intended as the means of communion and fellowship with God. The Burnt Offerings, of which the whole was consumed by fire, testified to the necessity of entire surrender to God. And the Sin Offerings bore witness to the need of offering something to him as a

---

[1] 1 Cor. xi. 26.   [2] Mic. vi. 6.   [3] Chap. iii. 2.

propitiation for sin. The three root ideas were these: that man needs communion with God, that God has the right to all that man can give, and that man in his sinfulness is not acceptable to God without some atoning sacrifice.

These sacrifices were not in themselves worthy of him to whom they were offered, nor were they able to take away sins. (a) They were the offering of a substitute that symbolised the worshipper, but was not the worshipper himself; and, as the prophets taught, and the people's own conscience told them, man must give himself, sacrifice himself, devote himself entirely to God. Again, they were (b) merely material sacrifices. The blood of bulls and goats could not effect a spiritual cleansing;[1] but it is man's spirit that needs cleansing, for there is the root of his sinfulness. The atoning sacrifice must be made in his spirit. And again (c), the offering, to be worthy of God, must be free from sin; and that is just what no human offering in itself can be. Those who offered, priests and people, were sin-stained. The whole ceremony of Jewish sacrifices taught the need of inward cleanness, but they were unable to give it.[2]

But they were a shadowy outline of the good things that were to come.[3] They pointed forward to the one sacrifice that would be worthy of God and would satisfy man's need. Man needed to offer himself to God: but man the sinner could not offer himself acceptably.[4] Therefore the Son of God became man, and in our human nature he offered (a) no substitute, but his own self. (b) His sacrifice was a material sacrifice, the body crucified and the blood shed,[5] but its essence was the surrender of his will to the Father.[6] It was a spiritual sacrifice of obedience and love; the human obedience of the Son of God throughout his life on earth that reached its perfect end in his willing acceptance of death; the love of the Sacred Heart of Jesus in his perfect self-sacrifice. And (c) it was a sinless sacrifice, the offering to God of unblemished human nature in union with God.

The blood of Christ—that is, his life sacrificed in death and given to men, who offered to God (a) himself, (b) through

[1] Heb. x. 4   [2] Heb. x. 1-3, etc.   [3] Heb. x. 1.
[4] Chap. v. 2.   [5] Heb. x. 10.   [6] Heb. x. 9.

eternal spirit, (c) without blemish—is effectual to cleanse
our conscience for the service of God.[1]

Again, there were four acts in every Jewish sacrifice:
(1) the choosing of a victim without blemish and a priest
ceremonially clean; (2) the slaying of the victim and the
shedding of the blood, which represented the surrender of its
life; (3) the offering of the blood or life before God; and
(4) the application to the worshipper of the benefit of the
sacrifice, either by his partaking of the victim, or by his
being sprinkled with the blood.

The sacrifice of Christ fulfilled this type. (1) He was
chosen by God the Father from all eternity; he was the
Lamb slain from the foundation of the world.[2] By his
Incarnation he became both Priest and Victim. He became
man that he might be our Priest,[3] and that thus man should
offer acceptable sacrifice. He became man that he might
be capable of human obedience and suffering and death,
and that thus man might be the sinless victim. As it is
written: Jewish sacrifices thou wouldest not, but a body
didst thou prepare for me. Lo, I come to do thy will, O God.
By which will we have been sanctified, through the offering
of the body of Jesus Christ once for all.[4] (2) He gave himself to death, surrendering his life upon the altar of the
Cross. And (3) as the Jewish high priest, bearing the blood of
the victim, used to enter into the Holy of Holies, which represented the immediate presence of God, so Jesus ascended to
heaven, still both Priest and Victim, our Advocate with the
Father,[5] and the Lamb as it had been slain.[6] The sacrifice
of the Cross continues, and must continue unto the end, where
Christ now is—that is, at the heavenly altar, and at the altars
of his Church on earth. For wherever Christ is, he remains
continually the acceptable Victim and the High Priest of
humanity, offering the one sacrifice with which God is well-
pleased, consecrated humanity that in union with the Son of
God has perfectly fulfilled the true purpose of human life.
Finally (4) the act of sacrifice is completed by communion.

[1] Heb. ix. 14.   [2] Rev. xiii. 8.   [3] Heb. ii. 17; v. 1.
[4] Heb. x. 4-10.   [5] 1 John ii. 1.   [6] Rev. v. 6.

The benefits of the sacrifice are supplied to the faithful by their partaking of Christ in holy communion, by which they are renewed in their union with the one perfect and sinless Victim, and are themselves made part of the acceptable sacrifice offered to God.

As there is only one Priest and one Victim, there is only one Sacrifice, offered in time on the Cross, and in eternity on the throne of God; offered now continually, both in heaven and sacramentally on earth. Wherever Christ is present, however he manifests himself, there is present the one Priest, the one Victim, and the one Sacrifice. The sacrifice of the Cross, the sacrifice in heaven, and the sacrifice of the Mass are all one and the same sacrifice.

We present on our altars first mere bread and wine—the simplest things, lest we should think that in our own power we can do aught worthy of God. But by the power of God, our earthly offerings are exalted and made one thing with the body and blood of Christ. And Christ is present. God puts him in our hands, that we through him and he through us may make the perfect offering of worship and propitiation. Our service is sacrificial because of the real presence of the one sacrifice and the one Priest.

We are not adding anything at Mass to the sacrifice of Calvary; it is sufficient and complete. Nor are we repeating it again and again; it cannot be repeated, for it has never ceased. But, being united with Christ, the Church, the priestly body of the great High Priest, sets forth sacramentally that same sacrifice which is set forth without a sacrament in heaven. Christ is the Priest and Consecrator at every Eucharist.

This is our sacrifice of worship, praise and thanksgiving. This is our bounden duty and service.[1] For there is no higher praise or thanksgiving possible from us to God than to present to his glory his own best gift to us, Jesus Christ his Son.

This is our effectual sacrifice of propitiation for sin, that we with all the whole Church, the living and the departed, may obtain remission of our sins and all other benefits of his passion.[2]

[1] Communion Service.   [2] *Ibid.*

This is our great means of intercession, by which indeed we pray through Jesus Christ our Lord; for our prayers are united with his sacrifice. We wield the mighty power of the Cross, directing all the intensity of the divine love upon those on whose behalf each of us pleads the merits of the atoning sacrifice.

At every Mass our offering is a corporate action, the act of the whole Church in union with Christ, rather than the separate acts of congregations or of individuals. It is the same one sacrifice at every altar. Our power to take part in the one sacrificial act depends upon our union with the Church, and through it with Christ. When we are one with Christ, abiding in him and he in us, we have the power to share with our brethren everywhere in that which he does through them. Hence only the true member of the Church, admitted by baptism and free from mortal sin, can join in the Church's eucharistic sacrifice. But if in union with Christ, the faithful communicants can join in the offering at any Mass, whether they are then receiving the blessed sacrament or not.

Also, it is only in virtue of union with Christ that we can offer ourselves, our souls and bodies, to be a reasonable, holy, and living sacrifice.[1] Christ offers himself, and with himself he offers his body the Church. Apart from him we are not acceptable to God. But when we are in union with him, we are together taken up and sit in the heavenly places with Christ :[2] our worship is exalted and united with the heavenly Eucharist, and we with the whole Church are presented in Christ and by Christ to the glory of God.

v

Christ instituted the sacrament of the altar, not only that we might be able to offer the acceptable sacrifice, but also that we might receive him as our heavenly food. By giving himself to us, Christ takes us, body and soul, into union with himself, sanctifying us, and raising us into the heavenly sphere of his own divine life.

[1] Communion Service.   [2] Eph. ii. 6.

This spiritual union of man with God here in this world is the same kind, though not in degree, as that enjoyed by the saints in the glory of heaven.[1] It far excels that outward association with Jesus which the disciples had before the coming of the Holy Spirit.

We know the union of partnership, based upon mutual interest; the union of friendship, springing from mutual love; the union of holy marriage, consecrated in mutual surrender. Our union with Christ includes all these: mutual interest, love, and surrender; but it is more than these. It is a union of life, a real oneness between him and us, based upon the one life in each. God sees the Church and Christ as being together one, not two. He only looks on us as we are found in him.

Abiding in Christ, we share in what he has done, and in what he is. We share in the merits of his atoning death. We have made atonement, we are justified in the sight of God, we have died, we are raised to newness of life; for he has died to take away our sin, and we are one with him. There is not, there cannot be, any condemnation for them that are in Christ Jesus, any more than for Christ himself. As by our natural birth we are one with all humanity with its defects and demerits, so by the reception of the supernatural life we are one with all humanity redeemed in Christ, and his grace and merits are ours.[2] In Christ is no sin.[3] We are forgiven, because the holiness of Jesus is made ours. We are not only forgiven for his sake (though this is true), but also we are forgiven because in Christ we are seen by God as being already that which we must become, if we continue to abide in Christ—that is, completely at one with God.

Our atonement with God, our at-one-ment, is not, indeed, a completed fact for each one of us, until we are perfectly conformed to the likeness of Christ, and his work done for us is perfected by his work in us. But his work is now being done in us, in this state of salvation into which we have already been brought. When we think of the atonement, we must never separate the thought of the Cross, of God's forgiveness because of Christ's death, from the thought of the

[1] Chap. xix. 6.   [2] Chap. vii. 1.   [3] 1 John iii. 5.

sacraments, God's mercies to us through the life of Christ given to us.

Our union with Christ gives us the power, and therefore lays upon us the obligation, of striving after moral and spiritual likeness to him in our lives and characters. He gives himself to us, that he may be formed in us.[1] We can work out our own salvation,[2] because of the state of salvation in which we are. We live in union with Christ who died and has risen again, that we may be able to live as those who have died to sin and risen again unto righteousness.[3] We live in union with the one sacrifice, that we may be in this life living sacrifices unto God,[4] following after the example of Christ's self-surrender and obedience, devoted entirely to the glory of God. We are in union with him who is at God's right hand, that we may live the heavenly life on earth.

The sanctifying grace of Christ, sinless and perfect, flows into our souls. The grace that came by Jesus Christ comes to each of us. Of his fulness we all receive.[5] He that abideth in Christ, and Christ in him, the same beareth much fruit.[6] While we abide in him and his life is the continual source of our spiritual life, every good deed that we do, every virtue we possess, every grace of character that we gain, are nothing else than the natural development resulting from the Christ-life in us, the fruits of the spirit of Jesus. Our good works are not our works only, but rather the works of Christ in us, and that is why they are pleasing to God. By grace have we been saved through faith, and that not of ourselves : it is the gift of God : not of works, that no man should glory. For we are his workmanship, created in Christ Jesus for good works.[7]

We are like trees planted by the waterside : we shall bring forth fruit in the due season of gradual spiritual growth.[8] There is no need for impatience, and no place for pride. Of ourselves we cannot acquire one grace, one virtue. We abide in him; we resist by his grace the temptations of our

---

[1] Gal. iv. 19.   [2] Phil. ii. 12.   [3] Col. iii. 1-5.
[4] Rom. xii. 1.   [5] John i. 16.   [6] John xv. 5.
[7] Eph. ii. 8-10.   [8] Ps. i. 3.

lower nature, because sin would separate us from the source of grace, and because sin is truly as unnatural in us who are in Christ as it would be in Christ himself.[1] And in his good time he will work his perfect work in us.

This possession of eternal life by spiritual union with Christ, begun by baptism, maintained by holy communion, and producing in us, by consent of our wills, its proper fruit of holiness, is the state of salvation necessary for our souls' life and health now and eternally. It is the state in which we are now abiding, and in which we may daily advance. To communicate is an act: but union is a state, not limited to the moments when we communicate sacramentally. It is a state whose permanence can be broken only by sin. Each good act of sacramental communion renews and deepens in us the power of living in continual spiritual union with our Lord; and also, the truer our union is with him, the greater is our power of deriving blessing from each sacramental communion.

And our bodies also, as well as our souls, are united with Christ, and with each good act of holy communion the union is deepened. The blessed sacrament meets all the needs of our twofold nature. By it our bodies are made clean by his body:[2] they are refreshed and sanctified, in preparation for a happy resurrection and glorious immortality. By a good communion both our bodies and our souls are preserved unto eternal life.[3] Indeed, we know not of any guarantee to us of a joyful resurrection to glory, save that which is given to us by reception of the blessed sacrament: He that eateth my flesh and drinketh my blood hath eternal life, and I will raise him up at the last day.[4]

VI

Those who live in continual spiritual union with the Lord are always prepared for sacramental communion. Living in the presence-chamber, they are always ready for the coming

[1] 1 John iii. 6. [2] Communion Service. [3] *Ibid.*
[4] John vi. 54. Chap. xx. 3. On holy communion as the sacrament of unity, see Chap. xi. 1.

of the king. Yet they will not wish to approach the altar without some special preparation. Indeed, some special preparation for each communion is required of all, in accordance with the opportunities and needs of each. It is the more necessary, in proportion as the life in union with Christ has not been realised and sacramental communion has been infrequent.

The three things necessary on our side for a good communion are repentance, faith, and charity.

Repentance. We come to God, not because we are good, but because we are weak and sinful. We come as sinners; but as sinners who have turned away from our sins, and by repentance sought God's forgiveness. Unrepented sin renders us incapable of making a good communion. To communicate while in a state of sin can only increase our condemnation. Therefore we must judge ourselves, that we be not judged of the Lord.[1]

Faith. We must believe in God's mercies that are given to us in the sacrament through Christ's death, desiring and expecting to obtain renewal of spiritual life by holy communion.

Charity. We must endeavour to forsake our self-love, and to love God with our whole heart, and all men for his sake. Love incarnate shuns the unloving heart. To be in charity with all men is not easy. It means particularly that we have made amends to any whom we have wronged in thought, word, or deed; and that we are willing to forgive those who have wronged us, if they seek our forgiveness; and that we have put from us all thoughts of revenge. It does not mean that we must have equal feelings of affection towards all alike.

The necessary preparation for holy communion is to make sure by self-examination and prayer that our repentance, faith, and charity are sincere, and that we are in that state of grace in which we ought at all times to be living.[2] If so, we shall not indeed be worthy to receive, for no preparation can make us worthy of so great a gift; but we shall be so prepared as not to receive to our condemnation.

[1] 1 Cor. xi. 31. [2] Church Catechism.

112

Our bodies also need to be prepared by fasting. The rule of the church, established from early times in honour of the sacrament, is that no food or drink should be taken on any day before the holy food, the fast being observed strictly from the midnight previous. Therefore it is desirable that holy communion should be received as early as possible in the day. In cases where it seems impossible to observe this rule of fasting communion, the faithful communicant should consult his parish priest. It is not binding on those who are suffering from serious illness.

Holy communion is usually given in the English Church both in the body and the blood in accordance with our Lord's institution. The same is the custom also in the East. For the sake of reverence, the blessed sacrament is reserved in the West usually only in one kind, and those who are given communion apart from Mass receive the Lord's body only. Communion in the body or in the precious blood only is a full communion; for where either is, there Christ is wholly present. Roman Catholic custom withholds the cup from the laity even at Mass.

The bread used for consecration is unleavened, according to the usual Western custom; because our Lord used unleavened bread, as ordered for the Jews in the time of the Passover feast[1], but this custom is not observed in the East.

The Church invites to the Lord's table all who are baptised and confirmed or ready to be confirmed, and who have the right dispositions. Those who respond to the grace of the sacrament are able to make communion profitably with increasing frequency as their spiritual life advances. Very many communicate every Sunday, and many every day. The more frequently and regularly we are able to communicate, the more blessed are we. Daily communion is a privilege within the reach of all who are trying to live habitually in repentance, faith, and charity. But the only rule that can be laid down is that every Christian should communicate as often as he is able to do so

[1] Exod. xii. 18.

profitably to his soul's health. On the other hand, he who lets a whole year go by without communicating is regarded as having cut himself off from living membership of Christ and the Church.

Attendance at Mass on Sundays and principal feast-days is a duty. Attendance on other days is a devout practice. If one is not yet ready for daily communion, one can at least join in the worship and in the offering of the holy sacrifice. This practice is found to tend towards increased frequency of sacramental communion.

Those who are at any time prevented from being present at Mass can make an act of spiritual communion, wherever they happen to be, by lifting up their hearts in union with that which is done at the altar, dwelling with devout thoughts on the love of Christ crucified, and seeking the renewal of their spiritual union with him.

There is no reason why children should be withheld from attending Mass. Indeed, to bring them to Mass is one obvious way of fulfilling our Lord's command : Suffer the little chidren to come unto me.[1] If children are rightly instructed, the Mass is the easiest of all Church services for them to understand.

The holy Eucharist is God's highest favour and benefit to us while in our pilgrimage here on earth. It is right and seemly, therefore, that we should return thanks to God always after holy communion, both by fervent prayer at the time, and also by carrying with us into our daily life the remembrance of God's goodness to us in the sacrament, seeking continually the enjoyment of his presence with us, and so living that men may take knowledge of us that we have been with Jesus.[2] Let the peace of Christ rule in your hearts, to the which also ye were called in one body, and be ye thankful.[3]

Thus our life becomes more and more a life that is hid with Christ in God,[4] as we endeavour by God's grace to continue in that holy fellowship, and do all such good works

[1] Mark x. 14.
[2] Acts iv. 13.
[3] Col. iii. 15.
[4] Col. iii. 3.

as God has prepared for us to walk in[1]; guarding against those sins that would hide Christ from us; connecting all our prayers and praises with the holy Eucharist, making every intercession through Jesus Christ a continuation of the pleading of the holy sacrifice, and our every thought of God a continuation of our holy communion.

And so the blessed sacrament will become for us the centre of the spiritual life, and the divine presence in us our continual support and stay, Christ in us making us more and more like to himself; until he come again and we see him as he is.[2] Then we shall behold him, our Saviour King, in his unveiled beauty, and commune with him face to face. Then, purified, sanctified, glorified, with the angelic host and all the company of the redeemed in heaven, we shall worship and serve the Lamb upon the throne in perfect satisfaction and unending joy.

[1] Communion Service.   [2] 1 John iii. 2.

X

HOLY ORDER

I

Our Lord has established an organised ministry in his Church.

He appointed the apostles first to be his representatives. He said to them: Whosoever receiveth you receiveth me; and whosoever receiveth me receiveth him that sent me;[1] and, As the Father hath sent me, even so send I you.[2]

The apostles were the appointed rulers and leaders, the official teachers and legislators, in Christ's Church on earth.[3] Therefore they were the centre of unity in the Church from the beginning. The first believers continued steadfastly in the apostles' fellowship;[4] and those who had fellowship with the apostles had fellowship with Jesus Christ.[5]

The apostles were the ministers of Christ and stewards of the mysteries of God.[6] They were the agents through whom the spiritual functions entrusted to the whole body were exercised. They were empowered to minister the holy sacraments, as well as to be the witnesses of the resurrection.[7] They received power and authority to preach and to baptise, when he said to them: Go ye, and make disciples of all the nations, baptising them;[8] and to offer the holy sacrifice, when he said: Do this in remembrance of me;[9] and to absolve sinners, when he breathed on them, and said: Receive ye the Holy Ghost; whose soever sins ye forgive they are forgiven.[10]

[1] Matt. x. 40.   [2] John xx. 21.   [3] Chap. iv. 5.
[4] Acts ii. 42.   [5] 1 John i. 3.   [6] 1 Cor. iv. 1.
[7] Acts i. 8.   [8] Matt. xxviii. 16, 19.
[9] Luke xxii. 19; 1 Cor. xi. 24.   [10] John xx. 23.

116

At first all the spiritual functions of the Church seem to have been performed by the apostles themselves. But before very long, as the Church began to grow, we see them admitting others to a share in their sacramental powers, and in their authority as teachers and administrators. Seven men were ordained to attend to the charitable work of the Church in Jerusalem.[1] This was the beginning of the order of deacons, or servants; although the functions of deacons in later days became different from those of these seven. Then we read that baptism was administered by others than the apostles.[2] It was necessary that those who went about preaching the word should be allowed to complete their work by baptising their converts. And when the Church was planted in any place, the apostles ordained elders to minister in each local congregation.[3] They also shared in the government of the Church; for we read that the decree of the first council was sent out in the name of the apostles and elders.[4] These elders were the first priests of the Catholic Church. The word Priest means Elder. They seem to have been of the same order as those who are called bishops or overseers in the Pastoral Epistles.[5]

Next we see that the apostles authorised some of the elders to ordain others. Thus St. Paul wrote to St. Titus :[6] For this cause left I thee in Crete, that thou shouldest set in order the things that were wanting, and appoint elders in every city, as I gave thee charge. These men who received power from the apostles to rule and to ordain were the first bishops of the Church, in the present sense of the term. And when the apostles passed away, the order of bishops continued, and has continued to the present time, as the successors of the apostles, exercising their power and authority, which is the power and authority of Jesus Christ himself, left by him to his Church.

---

[1] Acts vi. 6. [2] Acts viii. 16.
[3] Acts xi. 30; xiv. 23; xx. 17; 1 Tim. v. 17.
[4] Acts xv. 2, 6, 23; xxi. 18.
[5] 1 Tim. iii. 1-7; v. 17-20; Titus i. 7-9; and cf. Acts xx. 17, 28.
[6] Titus i. 5.

Thus, within the lifetime of the apostles we see the functions of the ministry of the Church already being performed by three orders : bishops, priests, and deacons; and we see the principles established of the passing on of authority from one to another, which has been maintained ever since. The manner, also, of ordination has always been the same, the laying on of hands with prayer by the apostles or bishops, in conjunction sometimes with the elders or priests.[1]

We read also of the other ministers, through whom the abundant life of the Church was active in the first days : prophets, teachers, workers of miracles, healers, speakers with tongues, and others, who were empowered by special gifts of the Holy Spirit.[2] These gifts appear to have been distinct from those which were conveyed by the apostolic laying on of hands. They were found both in apostles,[3] and in those who were not ordained ministers.[4] Although we hear of them but seldom after the first age of the Church, there is no reason to suppose that these gifts have ceased to be given.

II

Wherever the Catholic Church is established in any part of the world, there are the three orders of bishops, priests, and deacons. Of these, the priesthood is the chief and central ministry of the Church, because the whole ministry depends upon the priesthood of Christ.

The priest of the Christian Church, unlike the Jewish priests, are not priests individually and in their own right. They are men who have received power and authority to exercise on earth the functions of a priesthood, the priesthood which belongs to Christ alone. Christ is the one priest.[5] First he was priest in himself alone, receiving power for his office from the Holy Spirit; the one priest, just as he was in himself the whole Church.[6] Then, throughout the ages, Christ with his mystical body united to him

---

[1] Acts vi. 6; 1 Tim. iv. 14; 2 Tim. i. 6.   [2] 1 Cor. xii. 28.
[3] 1 Cor. xiv. 18.   [4] Acts xxi. 9.
[5] Heb. iv. 14; vii. 23-viii. 1.   [6] Chap. vi. 2.

is the Priest and the Church.[1] And, in every age, certain men have been set apart by the Church, and have received power from the Holy Spirit, to act as its agents in the performance of its priestly functions. Therefore a priest's official acts are not, strictly speaking, his acts. They are the acts of the Church done through him; they are the acts of Christ. If Christ did not remain our High Priest, blessing, absolving, sacrificing, ruling, the Church could have no priestly functions, and there could be no true priesthood on earth.[2]

The bishops, though greater in authority and honour than the priests, and essential as centres of unity, are still only priests with the additional powers of ordaining and ruling. The deacons are the servants of the priests.

By the common custom of the Church priesthood is conferred only on those who have already been made deacons, and episcopal power is given only to some of those who have been previously ordained priests. The powers of priesthood, once they are conferred on any man, remain with him permanently. Even if for some offence he may be deprived of permission to exercise his priestly powers, he remains always a priest. Similarly, a bishop always retains his episcopal power, though, according to the universal rule that there shall be only one bishop as pastor of each flock, he has not the right to act as bishop in another bishop's sphere without his permission.

By universal custom from the beginning of the Church to the present day only men are admitted to the sacred ministry of the Church. Our Lord accepted the ministry of women in his service,[3] but he ordained only men to the apostolate. And this appears very significant, when we bear in mind that it was through our Lord's teaching that the status of women has been raised.[4] The Church has always followed his example, and we doubt not that in so doing it has acted according to his mind and will. The Jewish priesthood, to which the Christian priesthood succeeded, was held by men

[1] 1 Pet. ii. 5, 9; Rev. i. 6.   [2] Heb. vii. 11-28.
[3] Luke viii. 3.   [4] Chap. xviii. 2.

only; and the Church, even when it came into contact with
the Greek world, with its many priestesses of heathen cults,
remained faithful to the Jewish custom sanctioned by our
Lord's example, although in many other respects it was
willing to adopt Greek ideas. The Church has always
employed the ministry of women in many directions, and
particularly that of widows first,[1] and later that of virgins or
deaconesses set apart for the direct service of God and the
Church; but it has never approved of women taking any
prominent part as teachers in the ordinary public services,[2]
nor has it ever admitted them to any of the orders of the
sacred ministry.

For many centuries the law of the Church has required
that the sacred ministers shall not marry after they have
been ordained; but this law is relaxed at present in some
parts of the Church.[3]

III

To enter the sacred ministry, a man must first be inwardly
moved by the Holy Spirit, inspiring him with this good
desire. No man takes this honour unto himself, but he
that is called by God.[4] Every lad may, however, hope that
he will be called by God to the honourable burden of the
priesthood. It is the will of God that his people in every
place shall be shepherded and nourished with the holy
sacraments. But, alas! in many places Christ's sheep are
scattered abroad without shepherds.[5] The Church's work
is sadly hindered at the present time for lack of a sufficient
number of ordained ministers. It is not that God does not
call. It is that his sons do not hear, or that their parents
will not let them obey. God calls usually in early youth.
The period of wordly inexperience is the period of the
most important of life's decisions. Therefore anyone who
feels the aspiration springing in his heart need not hesitate
because of his youthfulness; but he should approach his
parish priest to see if a way for his training may be found.
Eli perceived that God had called the child Samuel.[6] Let

---

[1] 1 Tim. v. 9.   [2] 1 Cor. xiv. 34.   [3] Chap. xviii. 7.
[4] Heb. v. 4.   [5] Matt. ix. 36-38.   [6] Sam. iii. 8-10.

parents foster the vocation of their sons, guiding them not by worldly but by spiritual wisdom, that they may be able to say: Speak, Lord, for thy servant heareth.

Secondly, it is necessary that the candidate be chosen and called to his office by the Church; for, in one aspect of his office, he is to be the representative of the members of the Church. This choosing or calling has been done in various ways at different times. The call to diaconate and to priesthood is given by a bishop, after he has examined the candidate, and consulted with his clergy. A bishop is elected in some places by the votes of the priests, or of the priests and laity; in other places by the king, acting on behalf of the other members of the Church; in other places, again, by a bishop of higher rank or by a group of bishops.

But neither the inward impulse nor the outward call, however it may be given, avails to make a man bishop, priest, or deacon. He is not only to be the representative of the congregation, but the representative also of Christ. He must receive his power not from men, but through men from Jesus Christ. Ordination by the laying on of the hands of the bishop, the successor of the apostles, is necessary. And ordination is much more than appointment or authorisation. It is a sacrament, conveying grace by the power of the Holy Spirit for the fulfilment of the function to which the person is ordained.

A bishop is made by being ordained or consecrated by other bishops. By their agency in the sacrament of holy order, our Lord Jesus Christ gives to him those gifts of the Holy Ghost which he first gave to the apostles. The bishops lay their hands upon his head, saying such words as these: Receive the Holy Ghost for the office and work of a bishop in the Church of God, now committeed unto thee by the imposition of our hands.

Every bishop rightly consecrated can trace his spiritual lineage back to the apostles. At every period of the Church we see the greatest care taken that there should be no link missing in the chain of succession; or, to put it more aptly, no mesh broken in the net, for the succession, through the fact that several bishops assist at each consecration, has the strength of a net in widespread intermingling meshes.

The special functions of a bishop, above his priestly powers, are to be the ruler of the Church in his diocese, and to maintain discipline, enforcing the laws of the Church, and administering its spiritual affairs by his sole authority after consultation with his priests; to be the spiritual father and pastor of all the members of the Church in his diocese, providing them with the sacramental means of grace, and guarding them from error in faith or morals; to give the gifts of the Holy Ghost by the sacraments of confirmation and holy order; to cut off unrepentant sinners from holy communion, and those who persist in holding false doctrines; and again to restore them, when they are converted and have done penance; and to consecrate churches to the service of God, and other things according to the rules of the Church, especially holy oils for anointing.

A priest is made by being ordained by a bishop, with the words : Receive the Holy Ghost for the office and work of a priest in the Church of God. He is thereby given both authority and power to act as the pastor of the people, ruling and guiding and caring for them, in the place to which he is appointed, under the bishop; to teach them the faith and morals of the Catholic Church, of which he is an official teacher; to bestow the Church's blessing upon them; to be the minister of the sacraments to the people, and also to guard the sacraments from those who are unworthy. Especially he has power and authority to give absolution to repentant sinners; to anoint the sick and dying; and to offer the holy sacrifice of the Mass on behalf of his people, consecrating the bread and wine to be the true body and blood of Christ, and feeding the faithful with the holy food.

A deacon, ordained by a bishop, is a minister to assist the priest, no longer now only in secular matters (which are administered mainly by lay officials), but in spiritual things, especially assisting him at Mass. In earlier times the diaconate was often a permanent state, and many deacons did not advance to any higher order of the ministry. But now usually only those are made deacons whom it is intended to promote after a short time to the priesthood.

Below the diaconate, the Church has added the order of subdeacons, whose special duty is to take care of the holy vessels of the altar, and to assist the priest at Mass with the deacon. There are also other grades of the ministry, not regarded as sacred : acolytes, readers, exorcists, door-keepers. But these minor orders do not exist in all parts of the Church, their duties being performed by laymen.

Patriarchs, archbishops, and metropolitans are bishops of higher rank and honour than other bishops; and deans, archdeacons, vicars-general, canons, and prebendaries are priests holding particular posts of honour and responsibility.

It is the duty of all loyal members of the Church to reverence the sacred ministry, and to respect the office, even if the holder of it be unworthy. They must heed the godly admonitions given by their priest, and his instruction in Church doctrine. It is written for the laity: Obey them that have the rule over you, and submit to them; for they watch in behalf of souls, as they that shall give account.[1] On the other hand, it is written for the clergy : Take heed to the ministry which thou hast received, that thou fulfil it.[2]

It is the duty of the laity to assist in the work of the Church, as their circumstances may permit, under the direction of the priest. In the service of God and of man, the priest may not act without the laity, nor the laity without the priest. The Church consists of both priests and layfolk, and every good work undertaken by the Church should be the work of all the members, each in his proper place.

Also, it is the duty of the laity to provide a living wage for the maintenance of their clergy, that they may be able to devote themselves without anxiety to their spiritual work; as St Paul teaches :[3] If we have sown unto you spiritual things, is it a great matter if we shall reap your carnal things? The Lord ordained that they who proclaim the gospel should live of the gospel.

[1] Heb. xiii. 17.   [2] Col. iv. 17.   [3] 1 Cor. ix. 1-14.

IV

The fundamental need of everyone is the grace of God, which is the life of Jesus Christ our risen Lord. The grace or life is given to us in the sacraments.[1]

It is therefore necessary not only that everyone should receive the sacraments with a right disposition, but also that he be assured that the sacraments to which he approaches are valid—that is, are to be relied upon as genuine.

Baptism is valid, if performed with water, with the invocation of the blessed Trinity, no matter who the baptiser may be. The Church has allowed that any man or woman may administer the sacrament of admittance into life.

But the Church has not regarded the sacrament of holy communion or that of penance as valid, unless the officiant be an ordained priest. For the maintenance, or for the restoration of the sacramental life, Christians are dependent upon a valid priesthood. The guarantee of the reality of these sacraments does not lie in the receiver's feelings, which can never give him reliable assurance, but in his knowledge that power has been given to the priest.

And the sacramental powers of the priest do not depend upon the ability or virtue in himself, but are those which have been conveyed to him by God at his ordination. They belong to the office, not to the man. The worthiness of the priest, if any priest could be worthy of so great functions, can add nothing to the value of the sacramental acts which he does; nor can his unworthiness deprive them of their value; for the work is not his, but Christ's. To be an effective preacher or evangelist or pastor does require personal gifts of knowledge, eloquence, earnestness, love; but to effect the particularly priestly acts of consecrating, offering the holy sacrifice, and absolving, the priest contributes of his own only a voice, an outward action, and the intention of performing the Church's work. Catholic teaching about priesthood asserts great things of the office, but it makes of little account the personality of the priest himself. He is but the earthen vessel of the sacramental grace of God.[2]

[1] Chap. vi.   [2] 2 Cor. iv. 7.

124

The true reception of spiritual life, and the maintenance of it in us, are assured to us through valid sacraments; and the validity of the sacraments through valid priesthood; and the validity of the priesthood through valid ordination by a bishop who has received his power to ordain in direct and unbroken line from the apostles and from Christ.

Therefore a first requisite in every part of the Church is to have a valid episcopate. Where there are no true bishops, there can be no true priesthood, no real presence of the body and blood of Jesus in the holy Eucharist, no real setting forth on earth of the availing sacrifice, no ministry of sacramental reconciliation of penitent sinners, no sacramental maintaining or restoring of the eternal life. Where there are no bishops, there is no Church.

Again, the bishops, as the successors of the apostles, are the divinely appointed rulers of the Church on earth. Loyal membership of the Church has always been held to involve obedience and subordination to the bishop. Rebellion against his lawful authority is rebellion against Christ himself. Separation from the successors of the apostles involves separation from the Apostolic Church.

And again, the bishops are together the guardians of the faith of the Church. On them, as on the apostles at the first, rests the chief responsibility of protecting the people from error and false doctrine. They are the trustees of the faith handed down from the beginning. The separation of any body of Christians from them has been found by experience to entail sooner or later the penalty of falling out of the central stream of Catholic truth, and losing the proportion of the faith. The beliefs of such bodies tend to become partial, and one-sided, and in the end contrary to revealed religion.[1]

Therefore it is essential for the existence and for the well-being of the Church in every place to have bishops duly consecrated in the apostolic succession.[2]

---

[1] Chaps. xi. 3; xii. 2.
[2] On the validity of Anglican Orders, see Chap. xi. 4.

XI

THE UNITY OF THE CHURCH

I

ONE, holy, Catholic, and Apostolic Church.[1]

There is one Church, one mystical body of Christ, which is the shrine of the one life of Christ bestowed upon each member.[2] There can be only one Church, as there is only one Christ and one Priest.[3]

The one Church is that which Christ established in himself first, and then in the apostles united with him, and finally in the multitude of members added to the Church and to Christ out of every nation.[4]

Because there is the one life in Christ and in the Church, and all who are admitted into the Church are made members of Christ, it follows that they are also members one of another.[5] There is spiritual union between Christ and each of his members, and therefore there is spiritual union between one member and all the others, both those who are still living in this world and those who have departed.

It is the will of God that the Church should be one undivided body throughout the whole world;[6] one in belief, in obedience, in work, in worship, and in brotherliness; one on earth, as it is in heaven. Christ established the Church to be Catholic—that is, universal—to embrace within itself all the nations as his chosen people, in place of the Jewish nation only.[7] The Church possesses all that is necessary for the salvation of everybody who desires salvation, without distinction of rank, or colour, or sex. It is Christ's will

---

[1] Nicene Creed.   [2] Chap. vi. 2.   [3] Chap. x. 2.
[4] Acts ii. 47.   [5] Eph. iv. 25.   [6] John xvii. 11.
[7] 1 Pet. ii. 5, 9; Eph. ii. 19, 20.

that this Catholic Church should be the new brotherhood of
man, and that thereby should be healed the enmity between
man and man, between class and class, between nation and
nation, which has become natural to mankind since the Fall.
Each should be at one with all, because at one with him.
It is his will that within the Church the barriers should be
broken down which have been created by human pride and
selfishness.

This is the practical significance of baptism, as St Paul
taught. In the spirit were we all baptised into one body.
There can be neither Jew nor Greek, there can be neither
bond nor free, there can be no male and female; for ye are all
one man in Christ Jesus. Ye have put off the old man with
his doings, and have put on the new man, which is being
renewed unto knowledge after the image of him that created
him : where there cannot be Greek and Jew, circumcision
and uncircumcision, barbarian, Scythian, bondman, freeman :
but Christ is all, and in all.[1]

Again, since the blessed sacrament of the altar is the means
of maintaining the union made at baptism between Christ
and each of his members, it is also the means of maintaining
union between one member and another. The Eucharist
is a social sacrament. The one bread given to each, and
the one cup shared by all, are the symbols of unity. Partaking of the one bread, we are renewed in our living membership of Christ and the Church. We who are many are one
body, for we all partake of the one bread.[2]

At the Lord's table we enjoy communion through him
with all other souls that are in him. We unite with the
heavenly worship of the saints in heaven,[3] who without
sacraments are living in him and he in them. And we are
united with the souls of all the faithful departed.[4]

And, in spite of the divisions which exist in the Church on
earth, all who at any altar partake of the one Christ are
united spiritually with all other faithful communicants.
As the one baptism admits not merely to a section of the
Church, but to membership of the whole body so at every

[1] 1 Cor. xii. 13; Gal. iii. 28; Col. iii. 10, 11.
[2] Cor. x. 17.   [3] Chap. xix. 6.   [4] Chap. xix. 4.

altar the members of all the divided parts of the Church have holy communion with their one Lord, and receive anew of the one life, and therefore are in living union with one another.[1]

And, not least, we are united in Christian charity with all other communicants, of every race and colour and class. The Church recognises, and can allow, no inequalities of Christian privilege amongst those whom, all alike, God deigns to favour with the same gift of his life. He who kneels beside me at the altar, and who receives with me the blessed sacrament, is my brother in Christ. And if I fail to acknowledge him as such, and to act towards him as such, I show that I have not understood what holy communion means.

II

But, alas! we have to acknowledge that this understanding of holy communion, and this charity among communicants, are feeble in many, and in some entirely lacking. Man's sin and self-will have again and again thwarted the purpose of God, renewing the barriers and prolonging the separations. Give diligence, said St Paul, to keep the unity of the spirit in the bond of peace; there is one body, and one spirit, even as ye were called in one hope of your calling, one Lord, one faith, one baptism, one God and Father of all.[2] But his injunction has been little heeded. Our Lord's prayer yet awaits its perfect fulfilment : Holy Father, keep them in thy name which thou hast given me, that they may be one, even as we are : neither for these only do I pray, but for them also that believe on me through their word; that they may be one, even as thou, Father, art in me, and I in thee, that they may be one in us : that the world may believe that thou didst send me.[3]

Not only has the spirit of brotherliness that should exist among all the members of the Church been marred through sin; but also the visible brotherhood, the one Church, has itself been broken and rent asunder. It is unseemly and sinful that those who share in the inward unity of life have

---

[1] Chap. ix. 5. [2] Eph. iv. 3-5. [3] John xvii. 11, 20, 21.

128

become separated in outward organisation, and that strifes and dissensions have come and still remain within the Church on earth. It is grievous that the Church ordained by Christ to be the new brotherhood of mankind, and the means whereby human divisions should be healed, has itself become divided. It is still more grievous that many who profess themselves disciples of Jesus have turned from the one faith handed down from the beginning[1] and have forsaken the Catholic Church, to which they belong each one by his baptism.

All this is a great evil. The Church is weakened in its work of witness to God and of ministry to the world. Divided Christendom speaks with discordant voices. Multitudes lack the grace of God, which the Church, if it were united, would be able to give to them. Many are without the truth of God : and many, bewildered by rival teachings, have even ceased to believe that any truth has been revealed by God to men. The world does not believe, because the Church is not at one within itself.[2]

The recognition that disunion is evil is the first step towards reunion. At every Mass we pray that the time may come when all they that confess God's holy name may agree in the truth of his holy word and live in unity and godly love.[3] There is great need for such a prayer, and for the desire for reunion which it expresses. And the continual prayer of the Church is without doubt bringing the end we desire. But true union cannot be brought about simply by closing our eyes to the real differences in belief and organisation which unhappily exist. For example, to join with others outwardly in holy communion, before the separations are healed, cannot re-establish genuine union. Such action would be but an empty token of a unitedness which does not yet exist. We pray for peace; but to act as if there were already peace, while as yet there is no peace, but only the desire for it, would not amend the broken walls of the Church, but would only daub the breaches with un-tempered mortar.[4] We may not ignore the differences of

---

[1] Jude 3.
[2] John xvii. 21.
[3] Communion Service.
[4] Ezek. xiii. 10.

belief and of obedience, through our zeal for mutual charity.
The differences are not trivial or negligible; they are serious
and of long standing.

III

It is a cause of great concern and grief to every loyal
Catholic that there exist, in every part of the world, numerous
organisations apart from the one Apostolic Church that has
its centre of unity in the order of bishops. It is a
grief to us because, while we recognise in those which are
separate from the Church much that is not only good but
very good, we realise that their separation is not in accordance with the mind of Christ, and that they are losing much
of the fulness of Catholic belief and of sacramental life.

These organisations are called Protestant, because they
came into existence as protests, not only against various
abuses that were then found in the part of the Church from
which they broke away, but also against belief and practices
that belong rightly to the whole Catholic Church.

They are separated from the centre of unity, having fallen
away from the apostolic succession of the bishops in the
Church. Therefore the organisations are not branches of
the Catholic Church. But, in most cases, their members
have been validly baptised, and are therefore members of
the Church, although they are living separate from it.

Not having bishops, they have not the sacrament of
confirmation, nor the sacrament of ordination. Lacking
bishops, they lack also priests. They have ministers, pastors,
preachers, and they believe their ministries to be divinely
sanctioned: but they have not, and they would repudiate
the idea of having, a sacrificing priesthood. They have not
the true sacrament of the altar; they are able only to receive
bread and wine in memory of our Lord's death, seeking by
the help of that memorial act to lift up their hearts into
spiritual communion with him. And not having the sacrament of penance, they have but their own feelings by which
to judge of the reality of their forgiveness.

Most Protestants regard the Bible as the word of God; but
they often fail to understand it rightly, because they rely

upon their own private interpretation of it, rather than upon the guidance of the Church. Others are inclined to regard the Bible, and even the revelation of truth given by Jesus Christ, as open to question and capable of amendment. Many of them object to any creeds or definite statements of doctrine : they follow the teaching of their founders in the main, but as time goes on they tend more and more to leave each individual free to believe just what seems to him to be true, regarding any obligation of faith as contrary to Christian liberty. Being apart from the Church, they have ceased to value it as the guardian of the Christian faith.[1] The decisions which from time to time in past ages the Church has made in matters of belief do not seem to them to be final, each generation being free to reopen questions which the Catholic Church regards as settled for all time. Hence many Protestant bodies show great variations of belief among their members, and between one generation and another. In some cases the body has abandoned belief in the particular doctrine, to lay stress upon which it separated from the Catholic Church.

In discipline and morals, although some Protestant bodies are strict in their control of their members, there is a similar tendency to regard each man as a law to himself, his own conscience and his interpretation of Scripture being his only guides.

Having lost the true idea of membership in the one visible body, which is the channel of grace and truth to all its members together, they tend to regard religion as being solely a matter for each person separately. The Church, in their notion of it, is the sum total of individuals who are separately united to God, with or without sacraments, by personal faith in Christ. They think that the Church is invisible, its members being known only to God; and that the visible organisation and ministry are not of divine arrangement.

In the judgment of the Church, such Protestant denominations are termed schismatical and heretical. They are schismatical (from a word which means separation) because

[1] Chaps. xii., xiii.

in their organisation they have separated themselves, and remain separate, from the visible Catholic Church; and heretical (from a word meaning choice) because in their belief they have chosen to hold doctrines which the Church has not held, and to deny doctrines which the Church has universally held.

The degree of guilt in schism or heresy depends upon the degree in which each person is responsible. Those only are fully responsible who through deliberate intention and with full knowledge have become or remain schismatical or heretical. We believe that very few are guilty in this sense. And certainly, while Catholics must censure the heresy or schism (for such censure is but the negative side of the confession of the true faith in the one visible Church), yet it is not for them to censure the individuals, nor to apportion blame. That is God's function, not ours. Enough for us to hold fast that which we have received,[1] lest we also go astray; and to remember that to whomsoever much is given, of him shall much be required.[2]

God is able to give to members of schismatical or heretical bodies the grace of the sacraments apart from the sacraments. We believe that he does give them rich blessings, since in most cases it is not through wilfulness that they are living without the sacraments of the Church. They have been brought up in ignorance of the whole of Catholic truth, and they believe and practice what they have been taught. It is not surprising that, not knowing how great are the privileges God has prepared for them in the Catholic Church, they cling to that which they have learnt, and in which they have found spiritual benefit. No man having drunk old wine desireth new, for he saith the old is good.[3] It is not their fault that they do not know that what is old to them in their experience is really a new departure from the Christian faith, and that what would be new for them to adopt is in reality as old as the Christian Church itself.

Further, though we believe that schism from the Church, or the holding of heretical opinion condemned by the whole Church, can never, under any circumstances, be according

---

[1] Rev. iii. 11.   [2] Luke xii. 48.   [3] Luke v. 39.

132

to the will of God, still we cannot but acknowledge that the Church itself in past ages has not been without blame in this matter. For example, many of the English schismatical sects were helped into their schism by the unsympathetic treatment which their leaders received from the Church in England, while yet they had not broken their membership; and many of the heresies now taught in England found adherents at the start because they brought into prominence various parts of the truth which at the time were obscured in the Church's teaching. The promise that the Church will be guided into all the truth[1] was given to the Church as a whole; there is no divine promise that every part of it will be faithful always in proclaiming the whole truth and nothing but the truth. And, indeed, the Church leaders in England, in fact if not in will, were sometimes more heretical, in an opposite direction, than the sect which opposed them. That does not justify the schism, for the maintenance of union is necessary for the holding fast of the truth.[2] In many cases, the particular belief which a sect cherished was at first no heresy at all, but was a true part of the faith; and it became heresy only by too great stress being laid upon it, out of proportion to the rest of the faith, through the sect becoming separated from the Church and therefore losing touch with the teaching of the whole body.

Catholics are bound to fight for the true faith : but not to fight with people who have not known it. They must wage war against error, but they must not be intolerate towards individuals. They are not permitted to join with Protestants in their services, especially in their Lord's Supper, for to do so involves denial of the Catholic truth about the Mass and the condoning of schism. But there are many activities in which Catholics can and should unite with Protestants, in the promotion of public morals, and in charitable works and social life. And, further, living in peace and charity with them, they will try, by intercession for them, and by loving explanation, and by their own faithfulness to what they have received, to bring them back into the unity of the Catholic Church.

[1] John xvi. 13.   [2] John viii. 31, 32.

IV

Besides schisms from the Church, there are schisms within it. The members of the family of God on earth have become separated into distinct divisions within the one household. The three divisions with which we are concerned are now commonly known as the Roman Catholic Church, comprising those bishops and people throughout the world who give allegiance to the Pope, the Bishop of Rome; the Orthodox Eastern Church, chiefly in Eastern Europe and the North of Asia; and the comparatively small group consisting of the Church of England, with the bishops and people of those dioceses throughout the world which are in communion with the English bishops.

The one Catholic Church came to be divided into these three divisions by sad and momentous quarrels. First there came a schism between the East and the West, between Constantinople and Rome, in the eleventh century; and in the sixteenth century there came another, between England and the rest of the Western Church in communion with Rome.

Into the unhappy history of these old quarrels we have not space to enter. In every family quarrel there are faults on both sides. The causes which made the separations are not the same as those which maintain them at the present time. Each divided part has lived its own life in separation, without even any very earnest desire for reunion until recent years; and each, in consequence of its aloofness from the others, has been harmfully affected in its beliefs and teaching and in its power to witness for God among mankind.

What is important for us to realise is that they are not really three Churches, though they are often loosely spoken of as such. Christ is one, and the Catholic Church, his mystical body, can be only one, the one Church which was founded by Jesus Christ and organised by his apostles.

Each of the divisions is a living part of the one Church, because each has true bishops who draw their powers in unbroken succession from the apostles, and therefore each has true priests and valid sacraments and real sacramental life. They differ from each other on certain points; but not on the most important points of faith or practice, for each maintains its fidelity to the true Christian faith which has been handed down in the Church ever since the apostles first began to teach it—the faith which is summed up in the Apostles' and the Nicene Creeds. They each believe that the one Church is the treasury of grace and truth, of divine life and light, for men; that it has power to convey the grace to its members by sacraments, and authority to declare the truth, both as regards faith and morals, without error, by its united voice.

The English Church since its separation has been tainted with Protestant spirit. Being isolated, it suffered from the schism more than did the larger and central part of the Church. Many of its bishops and priests have taught heretical doctrines. But that state of affairs is now happily beginning to pass away. And even at the commencement of that movement which we call the Reformation, the Church of England sinned more through exaggerated national feeling than through any desire or will to break away from Catholic unity. While in its political opposition to the Pope it was led into association with Protestant bodies on the Continent, and was wrongly influenced by them in many ways, it yet differed stoutly from them by clinging to the order of bishops, holding that the loss of bishops, which the Protestants accepted without regret, would put England outside the Catholic Church. And, amid much error commonly held by many of its members, and willingness to risk much in order to include as many as possible in its membership, it has always avoided committing itself to heresy in its Prayer Book and other authoritative formularies.

The main point of difference that at the present time remains between the English Church and Rome, as also between the Eastern Church and Rome, is the claim made by the Roman Church that the Pope is in himself, apart from the other bishops, the Vicar of Christ, in the sense not only that he, as the successor of St Peter, is the chief bishop of Christendom—which we readily admit—but also that

135

the authority of the bishops to act as bishops comes to them from Christ solely through the Pope; that only those bishops who accept his jurisdiction are true and proper bishops of the Church; and that to be separated from communion with the Holy See of Rome means to be separated from the Catholic Church. This claim appears to us to go beyond the teaching of the whole Church while it was still undivided; and also beyond the evidence of Holy Scripture, in which, as we have been accustomed to interpret it, our Lord is shown as giving his authority to all the apostles collectively, recognising St Peter only as chief and first among them, not as his sole representative above them.[1]

The separation between the English Church and the East has been maintained chiefly because of ignorance on both sides. Eastern and Western minds view the faith from different angles, and hence some of our statements of doctrine have seemed to them to point to greater differences from them in belief than is really the case. But also they naturally are suspicious of the remains of Protestant leaven in the English Church. And, on our side, it is chiefly that Protestantism, which, in the minds of some, hinders the desire for reunion with the East.

The Eastern Church used to be doubtful about the validity of Anglican orders; but its doubt is being laid to rest, now that it has received full information of the facts. The Roman Catholic Church still persists in asserting that we have not valid orders, on the ground either that the succession was broken at the Reformation, or that the intention of ordination in the English Church is to appoint Protestant ministers, and not to ordain Catholic bishops, priests, and deacons. This attitude of the Roman Catholics has caused the English Church to look very carefully into history, and to make sure that the succession was maintained without a break during the period of the Reformation. Those who are interested in the question can consult some of the many books on the subject. As regards the intention of the

[1] *Cf.* Matt. xvi. 19 with Matt. xviii. 18 and John xx. 21; Luke xxii. 31, 32 with Luke xxii. 28, 30; Matt. xvi. 18 with Eph. ii. 20 and Rev. xxi. 14.

Church of England, it is sufficient to quote the preface to the
Ordination Services in the Book of Common Prayer:

"It is evident unto all men diligently reading Holy
Scripture and ancient Authors, that from the Apostles' time
there have been these Orders of Ministers in Christ's
Church: Bishops, Priests, and Deacons. Which offices were
evermore had in such reverend estimation, that no man might
presume to execute any of them, except he were first called,
tried, examined, and known to have such qualities as are
requisite for the same; and also by publick Prayer, with
Imposition of Hands, were approved and admitted thereto
by lawful authority. And therefore, to the intent that these
Orders may be continued, and reverently used and esteemed,
in the Church of England; No man shall be accounted or
taken to be a lawful Bishop, Priest, or Deacon in the Church
of England, or suffered to execute any of the said functions,
except he be called, tried, examined, and admitted thereunto, according to the Form hereafter following, or hath had
formerly Episcopal Consecration or Ordination."

v

One holy, Catholic, and Apostolic Church. These are
the four marks of the Church: unity, holiness, catholicity,
apostolicity. In each part of the divided Church these four
marks remain, although, because of the divisions, they are
less perfect than they ought to be.

Each part is apostolic, in that it proclaims the faith which
the apostles held, and maintains the organisation which has
been handed down through all the generations from the
apostles; although the whole is not apostolic, by reason of
rebellions against apostolic authority, and strifes and separations within the family, such as the apostles knew of, even
in their day, but never approved.[1]

The Church, again, is Catholic, universal, in that it is
intended and qualified to be the way of salvation, the channel
of truth and grace, for all nations. Yet it is still only imper-

[1] 1 Cor. 11; Gal. i. 6, etc.

fectly Catholic. Each nation has, indeed, its own special contribution to make to the enrichment of the Catholic Church; but in each part of the Church, because of the divisions, national or local points of view tend to become unduly prominent, and sometimes even to cause men to lose sight of what is truly Catholic and universal. There is something of the sectarian spirit in each part of the divided Church. Each endeavours to fulfil the Church's Catholic mission independently of the rest. Each in its isolation from the others is inclined to think itself the whole of the Church. Each is unable to grasp that full comprehension of the one Catholic faith which would be gained, if, as of old, all parts of the Church could make its free and equal contribution to the forming of the Church's mind.[1]

The Church is holy : holy in its origin, its nature, and its purpose. It is the abode of the Spirit of God, entrance into which cleanses men from sin, and communion in which fortifies them against sin; whose members, by virtue of their membership, are separated from the world that knows not God, and are endued with the holiness which is God himself. But this ideal of holiness is but faintly realised in the individual members. The name of God is blasphemed among the unbelievers,[2] because the Church's witness to righteousness is obscured through its divisions, and because its discipline over its members in many places is lax, and their conduct and character not such as the obligations of their membership are known to require.

The holiness, the catholicity, the apostolicity, of the Church are yet very far from being perfect. Nay, when we look back to the earlier ages of the Church we may doubt whether the Church in each of its parts has not even fallen back. And this need not surprise us, if it be so; for God's promises are to the Church as a whole, to the Church undivided, and not to any one part of it, nor to all its parts separately. Disunion has brought its inevitable penalty.

But as we do not despair when we recognise that the Church, as we see it, is faulty and imperfect in its holiness,

[1] Chap. xii. 1.
[2] Rom. ii. 24; 1 Tim. vi. 1; Titus ii. 5.

its catholicity, and its apostolicity, so we need not think
all is lost because the oneness of the Church is defective.
The disunion within the Church is one great cause of the
Church's other defects. But the Church has been in times
past more divided within itself even than now. And perhaps
never before has there been so clear a recognition in each
part of the sinfulness of disunion, or so genuine a desire to
heal it.

In seeking the reunion of the Church, let us bear in mind
that it is only the outward union of the Church that is
broken, and needs to be restored. We have no need to seek
to create the unity of the Church, for it has not been lost,
and cannot be lost. There is one Christ and one Church,
and there will always be one Church, however great may be
the outward divisions that need to be made up, and however
many there be who have forsaken it. It is one Church
here on earth, and, still more, it is one and the same Church
beyond this life, where the dissensions of this sinful world
cannot avail to frustrate our Lord's will, that they may be
one in Us.[1]

The Church is one. Its unity should be a trinity: one
way, one truth, one life.[2] First, the Church is one through
oneness of life, the one life of Christ in all its parts and in all
its incorporated members. This unity, and it is the most
important, is not broken. Next, this unity of life should
be manifested in unity of truth, the whole Church united
receiving and reflecting the one faith, the one full light of
God's revelation. This unity, as we have seen above, has not
been completely lost, but it has undoubtedly been marred;
for so long as schisms persist within the Church, it cannot
speak with the authority or the inspiration of an undivided
whole. Thirdly, there should be the unity of one way of
organisation and of obedience. Here and here only the
unity has been lost, in several antagonistic organisations
that are out of communion with each other, split asunder
each from each, although each is built upon the one
foundation.

[1] John xvii.   [2] John xiv. 6.

139

Since each of the divided sections within the Church preserves within itself the sacramental union with Christ by which comes the life, and has therefore interior union in the one body; and since the agreements of belief between them are much greater than their differences; the outward separations between them are more grievous and less reasonable than the separation between any one of them and those denominations which have abandoned essentials of Catholic unity. Thank God, we of the English Church are at last beginning to recognise this, and to desire that, as the mists of ignorance and self-will clear away, the old-standing quarrels may come to an end. God is not a God of confusion, but of peace.[1] Since we have one life, and in order that we may have one faith, shall we not seek to restore ere long the one way, that is, the visible Church united throughout the world under one head?

Jesus Christ said to St Peter: Thou art Peter, and upon this rock I will build my Church;[2] and, When once thou art converted, strengthen thy brethren.[3] Our Lord in Holy Scripture is shown as placing St. Peter as the chief and leader of the apostles, the first among his brethren. The history of the Catholic Church through the ages shows us Rome, the see of Peter, as the centre of the Church's organisation, and the Bishop of Rome as the primate of the Church's episcopate. If we of the English Church cannot conscientiously grant him greater honour than this, can we, dare we, grant him less, when we look at the history of the Church, and see in it the working out of God's providence and the indication of his will? We English are the more bound to desire reunion with Rome, since it was to the missionary zeal of Rome that we mainly owed our Christianity, and it was to the spiritual primacy of Rome that our fathers of old were willing to submit, to their great benefit.

The Church cannot be an organised whole on earth without a visible head as its chief authority and the centre of its administration. Who is there, except the Bishop of Rome, who claims to be, or has any justification from the Church's tradition to claim to be, that head? Who would refuse

[1] 1 Cor. xiv. 33.   [2] Matt. xvi. 18.   [3] Luke xxii. 32.

submission to his jurisdiction, if he on his side were known to stand in just the same relation to other bishops as St Peter stood to the other apostles? There is clear proof of the primacy of Peter and of the see of Rome—as clear as there is of any other fact or doctrine of the Catholic Church. But we doubt whether there is sufficiently clear justification for the modern claims of the papacy. And it is the denial of these claims by about half of Christendom that remains at the present time the greatest obstacle to the outward manifestation of the essential unity of the Catholic Church.

XII
TRUTH IN THE CHURCH—I.

I

GRACE and truth came by Jesus Christ.[1] In him was life, and the life was the light of men.[2]

We have now considered how life or grace is given to men through Christ and the Church. We pass on to consider the giving of light or truth.

Jesus Christ came as the dayspring from on high, to give light to them that sat in darkness.[3] He came to teach the truth to men, the truth which they were unable to find by themselves, the truth which they needed to know that they might enter into salvation and live to the glory of God.

Jesus Christ showed the truth to men, not only by his words, but also in himself. He whom God sent spoke the words of God :[4] but we should be in possession of the truth, even if he had not given any public teaching, nor any enlightening words to be recorded and handed down for all time. Jesus Christ himself is God in human nature : God given to man in a form which man can understand. While I am in the world, said he, I am the light of the world :[5] and again, I am the way and the truth and the life.[6] No man hath seen God at any time : the only begotten Son hath declared him.[7] He came to be himself the revelation of God : and so truly was he that revelation that he could say, He that hath seen me hath seen the Father.[8]

The revelation of God through and in Christ was final; it was the summing-up and completion of all the earlier and partial revelations of God. God, having of old time

---

1 John i. 17.   2 John i. 4.   3 Luke i. 78.
4 John iii. 34.   5 John ix. 5.   John xiv. 6.
7 John i. 18.   8 John xiv. 9.

142

spoken unto the fathers in the prophets by divers portions and in divers manners, hath at the end of these days spoken unto us in his Son.[1] To that cllimax the Jewish prophets had looked forward :[2] for that clear light of revelation the philosophers had been preparing the minds of thinking men.[3] No new revelation is to be looked for, now that the revelation of God has been given in his Son. No new voice is needed after the Incarnate Word of God.

This final revelation, the faith once for all delivered to the saints,[4] needs to be duly received by men. For a life-giving reception of it, each person needs not only to listen to Christ's message and to know who Christ is; he must have also that will to believe and to obey, to accept and embrace Christ and his gospel, of which all men are capable, being made in the image of God, and which God gives to those who truly seek it, but which it is in the power of man's self-will to refuse. He must have the divine gift of faith.

And, in order to understand the revelation aright, he must be in spiritual union with Jesus Christ. We know, said St John, that the Son of God is come, and hath given us an understanding, that we may know him that is true, and we are in him that is true, even in his Son Jesus Christ.[5] In other words, real knowledge of the truth is bound up with membership in Christ : to have the light we must have the life.

And further, it remains for each person who has received the revelation to advance more and more deeply, with all the power of his soul and mind, into the understanding of the truth, and to grow in the knowledge of Jesus Christ and of God.[6] This growth in spiritual understanding is granted, not to all men of goodwill equally, but to each according to his natural and spiritual capacities.

And as it is with each individual, so it is also with nations, and with generations.

A symphony of Beethoven has an infinity of meaning that cannot be received at a first hearing, nor by any one hearer in its fulness. The divine music of the gospel was given

[1] Heb. i. 1.   [2] 1 Pet. i. 10-12.   [3] Chap. iii. 2.
[4] Jude 3.   [5] John v. 20.   [6] Col. i. 10; 2 Pet. iii. 18.

to the Church: its meaning needed to be gradually unfolded
to the members. That unfolding is the work of the Holy
Spirit, working upon the minds of men. Our Lord said:
The Holy Spirit shall guide you into all the truth; for he
shall take of mine, and shall declare it unto you.[1]

Each individual, each generation, each nation, coming
within the membership of Christ's body, inherits the accu-
mulated understanding of the one faith that was gained by
those who have gone before. This is called the Tradition
of the Church. And each individual, generation, and nation
contributes something to the fuller comprehension of the
faith and to the richness of the tradition.

Each may see wrongly, for each can see only in part.
No mind is able to comprehend the whole. But the mind of
each is corrected and completed by the mind of all. The
test of truth in the Church has been that that is true which
has been held always, everywhere, and by all; that is to say,
any new light must be false, if it contradicts what the Church
has universally received and taught. The Spirit of God in
one individual or generation or nation cannot contradict the
same Spirit in the whole body of Christ.

Thus the Catholic Church from age to age progresses
towards the full understanding of the revelation that has been
given in Christ, and yet never advances outside of what is
contained in that revelation. But even the united mind of
the whole Church cannot attain in this life to the complete
understanding of the mysteries that have been revealed.

Nor has Christ revealed to the Church everything that
we might wish to know. Christianity does not profess to
give the answer to every question. The revelation in
Christ is the true light, but it is light shining in the darkness.[2]
We cannot see further than the light illumines. We see,
and we see truly, but all of us together see only in part; and
we shall see only in part while this world lasts. We wait
for the time when the shadows shall flee away, when in the
unveiled presence of God with perfected power of comprehension we shall know the truth in which we now believe.
Until then there has been revealed to us, and we have each of

[1] John xvi. 13, 14.   [2] John i. 5.

us sufficient power to accept and to understand, just so much
of the divine light as will enable us to plant our feet firmly
on the road that leads us to God. Now we see in a mirror
darkly; but then face to face : now I know in part, but then
shall I know fully, even as also I have been known.[1] But
already we have him who is the way and the truth and the
life.[2] And the light we have in Christ is true, and eternally
true, valid for all eternity.

II

We can imagine that God might have revealed his truth
to the mind and heart of each person individually, and to all
people alike, so that all should know the truth instinctively,
without needing to be taught by others. But God's method
of enlightening men has not been such. His method of
giving us supernatural knowledge has been the same as his
method of giving us natural knowledge; namely, by means
of our fellow-men.

First, the truth was brought to men in Jesus alone, and
was given by him to men under all the limitations of time
and space, and of the human nature which he took at his
Incarnation. The Son came to show himself to men in
human nature, and in himself to show God; but he showed
himself in one land only, and only to one generation. He
came to teach by human words spoken to human ears;
but he taught only in one language, or at most in two. And
he gave his full teaching, not to all of his generation, nor
even to all who came within hearing of his words. He said
to the very few chosen disciples : Unto you it is given to know
the mysteries of the kingdom of heaven, but to the multitude
it is not given.[3] It was not that he wished to make an inner
circle of believers specially illuminated. Christianity knows
no such inner circle, to whom is reserved the key to the
mysteries. He willed to teach a few, in order that they should
teach to others that which they had received.[4] He taught
the Twelve, that the world should be taught by the Twelve.
As they were dependent upon knowing him and hearing his

[1] 1 Cor. xiii. 12.   [2] John xiv. 6.
[3] Matt. xiii. 11.   [4] Matt. v. 14-16; x. 27.

145

words for their enlightenment, so he willed others should be dependent upon them. He willed to use human agency, with all its limitations, for the giving of truth, as for the giving of grace. This is clearly shown by his last charge to the disciples : Make disciples of all the nations . . . baptising them . . . teaching them.[1]

But with that charge there was given also the assurance : Lo, I am with you always.[2] The reception of truth by the apostles, and the passing of it on by them to others, were not to be lifeless and mechanical. There was to be with them the continual presence of the Lord through the power of the Holy Spirit. The truth was not to be a dead deposit : the Spirit of truth was to make it alive and keep it alive. The Spirit of truth, said Christ, abideth in you, and shall be in you. He shall teach you all things, and bring to your remembrance all that I said unto you. He shall bear witness of me, and ye also shall bear witness. He shall guide you into all the truth; for he shall not speak of himself, but what things soever he shall hear, these shall he speak. He shall glorify me for he shall take of mine, and shall declare it unto you.[3] The declaration of truth in Jesus was final : he made known all things that he heard from the Father.[4] The work of the Holy Spirit is not to give a new and further revelation, but to quicken the minds and souls of men to receive and understand the revelation given once for all in Jesus. But, if it were not for the work of the Spirit, we should have no guarantee of the preservation of the living truth in incorruption. Men by themselves could not have held the faith incorrupt; but God the Holy Spirit lives and works in the Catholic Church.

Thus, then, the Catholic Church, constituted first in the apostles, and quickened by the Holy Spirit, was by Christ's appointment made the pillar and the ground of the truth.[5] The apostles were the first trustees of the truth, as well as of the grace of God, for the Church. They were commissioned to bring others to the knowledge of the truth by their

---

[1] Matt. xxviii. 19, 20.   [2] *Ibid.*
[3] John xiv. 17, 26; xv. 26, 27; xvi. 13, 14.
[4] John xv. 15.   [5] 1 Tim. iii. 15.

teaching. As God sent Christ into the world, even so Christ sent the apostles, that men should believe on him through their word.[1]

And we know from the New Testament how fully the apostles fulfilled their commission. The gospels record all that Jesus began both to do and to teach;[2] and the Acts of the Apostles record all that Jesus by the power of the Holy Spirit continued to do and teach through the agency of the apostles. I shrank not, said St Paul, from declaring unto you the whole counsel of God.[3] We are witnesses, said St Peter and the others, and so is the Holy Ghost.[4] And again St Peter said: I delivered unto you that which also I received, how that Christ died for our sins, and that he hath been raised; so we preach, and so ye believed.[5]

And again, within New Testament times, we see those who received the tradition of the faith from the apostles becoming in their turn the trustees of it for others. Thus St Paul wrote to St Timothy: The things which thou hast heard from me among many witnesses, the same commit thou to faithful men, who shall be able to teach others also;[6] and, Hold the pattern of sound words, which thou hast heard from me, in faith and love which is in Christ Jesus. The good deposit which was committed unto thee guard through the Holy Ghost who dwelleth in us.[7]

If any man would enter the Church, the first step thereto must be the receiving of the faith. If any man would remain in the fellowship of the Church, he must abide faithful to the apostles' teaching and fellowship.[8] The members of the Church were warned to guard jealously the faith which they had received. There were many rival teachings: even within the Church many individuals were led astray, and were ready to lead others astray. The test of every teaching was only this: does it agree with the teaching given in and by Christ, and held by the whole body of the Church? St Paul wrote: There is one Lord, one faith, one baptism.[9]

[1] John xvii. 18, 20. [2] Acts i. 1. [3] Acts xx. 27.
[4] Acts v. 32. [5] 1 Cor. xv. 3, 11. [6] 2 Tim. ii. 2.
[7] 2 Tim. i. 13, 14. [8] Acts ii. 42. [9] Eph. iv. 5.

147

Try your own selves, whether ye be in the faith,[1] Watch ye, stand fast in the faith.[2] Stand fast in one spirit, with one soul striving for the faith of the gospel, and in nothing affrighted by the adversaries.[3] Continue in the faith, grounded and steadfast.[4]

And mark the other side of the picture : Some have made shipwreck concerning the faith.[5] Take heed lest there shall be anyone that maketh spoil of you, after the tradition of men, and not after Christ.[6] Turn away from the profane babblings and oppositions of the knowledge which is falsely called knowledge; which some professing have erred concerning the faith.[7] If any man preacheth unto you any gospel other than that which ye received, let him be accursed.[8] Mark them which are causing the divisions, contrary to the doctrine which ye learned; and turn away from them.[9] Our Lord had said : Beware of false prophets, which come to you in sheep's clothing, but inwardly they are ravening wolves;[10] and St Paul was mindful of his warning, when he said to the elders of Ephesus : Take heed to yourselves, and to all the flock, in the which the Holy Ghost hath made you overseers, to feed the Church of God; for I know that after my departing grievous wolves shall enter in among you, not sparing the flock; and from among yourselves shall men arise, speaking perverse things, to draw away disciples after them.[11]

It is unnecessary to pursue this subject through the history of the Church. Wherever we look, we find the experience of the apostolic age repeated. We see the one faith of the whole body of the Church as the light shining in the darkness of the world, suffering continual attacks from the surrounding darkness, but never overwhelmed by it.[12] We see the false lights abiding but for a time, and then being absorbed again into the darkness from which they sprang; each one, when brought into contrast with the true light, being by that contrast shown to be false.

[1] 2 Cor. xiii. 5.   [2] 1 Cor. xvi. 13.   [3] Phil. i. 27.
[4] Col. i. 23.   [5] 1 Tim. i. 19.   [6] Col. ii. 8.
[7] 1 Tim. vi. 20, 21.   [8] Gal. i. 9.   [9] Rom. xvi. 17.
[10] Matt. vii. 15.   [11] Acts xx. 28, 29.   [12] John i. 5.

Enough has been said to show how the tradition of the faith has been handed down in the Church from generation to generation to the present day. We are Christians and Catholics, because those who have gone before us were faithful stewards of the mysteries of God.[1] Other men laboured, and we have entered into their labours. We have reaped, because they sowed.[2] And in our turn we are called to the stewardship : we hold the faith in trust, to give it to those who will come after us, and to those also who, whether in England or in heathen lands, are now sitting in the darkness.[3]

III

The duty of the faithful Christian is to learn the faith, and when he has learnt it, to believe it. He promises at his baptism to believe all the articles of the Christian faith, as well as to renounce the devil, and to keep God's holy will and commandments. Therefore he may not believe what he likes, any more than he may do what he likes. Being free, and having divine grace, we are responsible for our beliefs as well as for our actions. Those who say, It does not matter what a man believes, so long as he lives a good life, forget that all actions are the outcome of beliefs, and that God gave us that revelation of truth which was necessary for us that we might live rightly.[4]

Belief means, first, the will to believe, the submission of our wills to receive the faith, and the whole of the faith, in a docile spirit. Without such submission it is impossible to learn any truth, whether religious or secular. We must learn like little children, before we can think like men. It is not our part to pick and choose among the doctrines of the Church, embracing some and rejecting others, according as they seem to suit us or not. Still less is it our part to work out a system of belief, each one for himself, out of his own brain, as if no revelation of the truth had been given by God. Nor is it possible to do so. If it had been possible for man to find out supernatural truth by himself, God need

[1] 1 Cor. iv. 1.   [2] John iv. 36.
[3] Luke i. 79.   [4] Chap. i. 2.

not have given a revelation. Yet many try to do so, thereby really putting themselves in the position of the pagan thinkers before Christ came. And some object to one part or another of Church doctrine, because they have not learnt the whole of the faith, in the light of which they must understand the part. Others, again, presume to criticise and to attack the faith, in whole or part, before they have really learnt it. This is no more reasonable than it would be to criticise mathematics without having learnt what mathematics have taught. The greatest hindrance to right belief is pride of intellect.

But, secondly, the duty of belief concerns not only the will, but also the understanding. We must exercise our minds on that which we have received. This duty is the more urgent in proportion to the degree of one's mental capacity; but to some extent it is obligatory upon all. We ought to be able to give a reason concerning the hope that is in us.[1] The creeds and other authoritative definitions[2] have not been published to excuse us from thinking, or to relieve us from the necessity of thinking. The faith is to be digested, not merely swallowed. Every clause of the creeds is a kind of notice of No Thoroughfare, not to stop us from walking, but to save us from walking to no purpose. For example : the words, He was buried, and the third day he rose again from the dead, stand for all time, not to stop each new generation from searching into the meaning of the mystery of Christ's resurrection, but as a warning that any merely spiritualistic explanation of it is a false path which can only serve to delay those who are seeking to understand the truth.

Not least at this present time is it necessary for us to examine that which we have received, when the divisions of Christendom have produced many variant teachings, each professing to be the truth. Prove all things, said St Paul, hold fast that which is good.[3] Prove the spirits, said St John, whether they are of God; because many false prophets are gone out into the world.[4] And those are commended

[1] 1 Pet. iii. 15. [2] Chap. xiii. 1.
[3] 1 Thess. v. 21. [4] 1 John iv. 1.

150

who, on being taught by St Paul, received the word with all readiness of mind, examining the Scriptures daily, whether these things were so.[1]

Again, in these days, when in every department of human knowledge great advances are being made, the Church knowing that all truth comes from God, who does not contradict himself, has no desire to debar its members from learning freely all that can be discovered or learnt by the human mind. All it asks is, that they shall remember that this is not the first time that new floods of knowledge have broken in upon men's minds; and that in past times the old divine knowledge has not been upset, but has illuminated and been illuminated by the new learning. Churchmen must not, in the excitement of the new, be ready lightly to cast away the old and the eternal; but rather must search patiently for that sifting of the false from the true in the new knowledge, by its co-ordination with the old, which will lead to the enrichment of the tradition of the faith. It has been so in the past again and again, and the Christian has no doubt but that it will be always.

Thirdly, belief is not complete without corresponding action. Faith without works is dead.[2] Belief in a holy God involves the renouncing of the world, the flesh, and the devil. Belief in Jesus Christ involves conversion, and the confessing of his name. Belief in the atonement involves the duty of accepting the salvation offered in Christ, and the living of a life at one with God. Belief in the Church has little meaning without obedience to its authority and the use of its sacraments. Belief in the sacrament of the altar obliges us to take part in the offering of the holy sacrifice, and to be communicants. Belief in the forgiveness of sins implies that we shall seek forgiveness.

And finally, belief in the doctrines of the Church is dependent from first to last upon the divine gift of faith[3] in God himself revealed to us in Jesus Christ our Lord. By faith we are enabled not only to hold correct beliefs

[1] Acts xvii. 11. [2] Jas. ii. 26.
[3] Chaps. i. 2; vi. 4; xvi. 2.

151

about him, but to believe in him personally, to know him, to love him, to trust him, to take him for our Master, our Saviour, and our Friend. Without this all other belief is naught, and can avail nothing for our salvation. The devils tremble, for they believe without saving faith.[1] And if we have it not, we must seek for it by continual and earnest prayer, for it is the one gift above all others needful. But if we seek it sincerely, we shall find it. God does not refuse the gift of faith to those who seek it. God never gives us good desires, to disappoint them.[2]

---

[1] Jas. ii. 19.   [2] Matt. vii. 7, 8.

XIII

TRUTH IN THE CHURCH—II.

I

THE Church is the treasury of revealed truth. Its first duty is to bear witness[1] to the truth, setting up the standard of right belief and right conduct before men, to be a guide to those who are willing to obey, and a challenge to those who will refuse. The Church, like Christ himself, has come not to judge the world, but to save it.[2] But also Christ said: For judgment am I come into the world.[3] His presence among men offering them grace and truth in himself set up of necessity a judgment and a separation between those who accepted him and those who rejected him.[4] By his presence among them men were forced to declare themselves, according as they came out of darkness into the light or remained in the darkness of a sinful world. This is the condemnation, that light is come into the world, and men loved darkness rather than light.[5] So also the Church, as the light-bearer,[6] has the double duty, not only to save the world, but also by the faithfulness of its witness to set up so plain a standard against the false standards of the world, that those who refuse it shall stand self-convicted. In other words, the Church has a duty towards God, to serve his glory in spirit and in truth, which is greater even than its duty towards men.

There have been times when the Church in various places has allowed itself to be invaded by the spirit of worldliness, and for a time in those places the darkness has overcome the light. And there have been other times, of which the present is one, when the Church has forgotten that its primary

[1] John i. 7; Matt. xxiv. 14; John iii. 11.   [2] John iii. 17.
[3] John ix. 39.   [4] Luke ii. 34, 35.
[5] John ii. 19.   [6] Matt. v. 14; Eph. v. 8; Phil. ii. 15.

duty is to bear witness to the truth, for the glory of God; and
has relaxed the strictness of its message, in the fond desire
of including on easy terms as many as possible within its
fold.   But in so far as the Church has done so, it has failed
in its first purpose as Christ's representative in this world,
the promotion of the glory of Almighty God.   Christ in
his love for men never forgot what was due towards the
Father who had sent him : but the Church is hindered in its
service of God by the presence within it of a multitude of
unconverted   members.   And   when   the   Church   forgets
what is due to God, and seeks to gain adherents on any
terms, it avails to bring them in to a sort of twilight only,
instead of into the clear light and true knowledge of God.
Such half-faith is not the faith that saves.   It can inspire
neither love in those who hold it, nor hate in those who refuse.
Wherever the world does not hate and persecute the Church,
there is reason to suspect that the Church is unfaithful in its
witness.[1]

As the teacher of the truth, the Church has two spheres :
the bearing witness to the truth among those who are outside or half-outside, which includes both missionary work
among non-Christians, and the enlightenment of those many
in Christian lands who are lacking the full faith; and the
instructing and building up of those who are within, that
they may grow in the knowledge of the word which they
have received.   Nor can we say that the one sphere of work
is more important than the other.

Everyone who has received the knowledge of the faith is
thereby made a trustee of it for the benefit of others.   We
cannot but speak of the things which we have seen and
heard.[2]   No one is exempt from the duty of witnessing,
and confessing Christ before men.   All are responsible for
passing on to others, and especially to their children and
dependants, the light that is in them.

But in each place the chief official teacher, on whom rests
the Church's responsibility of witness and of instruction, is
the bishop; and under him the same double duty rests upon
the priests.   Their duty is to give the Church's teaching to

[1] John xv. 18-21.   [2] Acts iv. 20.

154

men, explaining it, and applying it to their hearers' circumstances and capacities. They are to speak the words
of the Church, to hand on to others the tradition of the faith
which they have received, and of which they were empowered
at their ordination to be official teachers. It is not their
duty, and they have no right as teachers in the Church, to
give the people any mere notions or speculations of their own.

It is, therefore, of the first importance that the Church shall
see that in every place the teachers are prepared for their
office by being given an effective training, and chiefly accurate instruction in Church doctrine; so that they may be able
to teach the people from true knowledge, and not out of
error or ignorance. If the blind lead the blind, shall they
not both fall into the ditch?[1]

The Church has many ways both of witnessing and of
instructing. The people used to attach too much importance
to the hearing of sermons, and the clergy now perhaps attach
too little. Certainly the ministry of preaching is, as it has
always been, one of the most necessary parts of the Church's
work. But also much teaching is given by the orderly
services of the Church, the psalms and hymns and prayers.
Every baptism is a reminder to the congregation of the first
principles of Church membership. Every Mass is a showing
forth of the Lord's death before men, as well as before God.
The systematic reading of Holy Scripture throughout the
year is a continual instruction in the message of God to men.
The festivals of the Church and the seasons of the Church's
year bring before men's minds all the great events and truths
of the gospel. Therefore, even without sermons the regular
attender cannot but be reminded of God, and the great
things that God has done for men, and the obligations which
men owe to God.

The recitation of the creeds, again, in Church services is
of great value for instruction, as well as for confession of
faith. The creeds are summaries of some of the main points
of the Christian tradition, which have been put forth by
authority of the Church, and have been approved through
great lengths of time by the Church as standards and tests

[1] Matt. xv. 14.

155

of teaching. The different clauses of the creeds were written in various councils of the Church, not without the guidance of the Holy Spirit who dwells in the Church; and they were the Church's answers to false teachings that arose from time to time, or they were its statements of the faith which it put forth to be accepted by those who sought admission to it by baptism.[1]

When the Church has thus solemnly spoken, and its voice has been widely accepted through a considerable length of time, its utterance is held to be as accurate an expression of truth as human words can give; and any teaching that arises later and contradicts what the Church has said is on that account judged at once to be contrary to truth. The degree of reliance to be placed upon any pronouncement about belief or conduct is in proportion to the degree of its acceptance by the Church at large, whether by a part only or by the whole. The voice of the whole Church is as true as the voice of Christ himself. Christ said to the first official teachers of the Church : He that heareth you, heareth me.[2]

The Church of England refers its teaching to the authority of the universal Church. At the Reformation its intention was not to repudiate any doctrine that had been universally accepted from primitive times; but only to free the apostolic faith from such newer teachings as seemed to be at variance with the true Catholic tradition.[3] Also the English Church appeals to the authority of Holy Scripture. It holds that no doctrine may now be taught by the Church as necessary to salvation which has not been taught by the Church in Holy Scripture, or which is not a plain inference from the principles set forth in Holy Scripture.[4]

In this double reference to authority, the English Church is not different from other parts of the Catholic Church, Western or Eastern. No part of the Church claims the right to set aside the Catholic tradition, or the Catholic writings, or to invent new doctrines that were not contained within the original revelation.

[1] Chap. xii. 3.   [2] Luke x. 16; cf. xii. 1.   [3] Chap. xi. 4.
[4] Articles of Religion VI. XX.; cf. Chap. xiii. 3.

An important point on which the Roman Catholic Church has differed from the rest of Christendom is her definition of the doctrine of papal infallibility; that is, that the Pope is by his office empowered to speak as the teacher of the whole Church defining the Church's doctrines in matters both of faith and of morals; and that when he does so, he is withheld by the Holy Spirit from committing the whole Church to error; and that therefore his pronouncement is to be accepted as being itself a part of the Catholic faith. This claim of infallibility, however, has seemed to the rest of Christendom to lack support from the Catholic tradition, and there has arisen against it a heat of controversy which largely spends its fierceness against infallibility of a kind which Rome has never asserted. The subject needs more careful study than Anglicans in general have yet given to it.

II

One of the chief ways by which the Church has fulfilled its office as teacher has always been its use of Holy Scripture.

The Old Testament[1] was our Lord's Bible, as it was the Bible of the Jews. The first Christians were accustomed to hear the Law and the Prophets read in the synagogues.[2] And when they ceased to attend the synagogues, they continued to read the Old Testament and to sing the psalms in their public and private worship.

The earliest Bible of the Christian Church was the Old Testament, including those books which are called the Apocrypha, that is, those books which were not written in Hebrew, but had been used by the Jews living outside Palestine. The Church made use of the Old Testament, not only in worship, but also for moral and spiritual instruction. They believed that every scripture inspired by God is profitable for teaching, for reproof, for correction, for instruction in righteousness.[3] St Paul taught that it was for the edification of Christians that the history of the Jews had been written: All these things happened unto them

---

[1] Chap. iii. 3.   [2] Luke iv. 17 *ff.*; Acts xiii. 15; Jas. ii. 2.
[3] 2 Tim. iii. 15, 16.

THE KING'S HIGHWAY

by way of example; and they were written for our admoni-tion.[1] Whatsoever things were written aforetime were written for our learning, that through patience and through comfort of the Scriptures we might have hope.[2] We may not now be particularly interested in the details of Jewish history, but we still read it to learn God's judgment upon the actions of men, and to trace the gradual way in which he led the chosen people onwards towards true knowledge of him.

We know that much of the teaching of the Old Testament stands firm for all time—teaching about the one true God, and his will for all men. But we have learnt also that some of its teaching was meant for the Jews only, until Christ should come; and that such parts have now become out of date, since Christ has come and taught the will of God more clearly and fully. The Law was our schoolmaster, to bring us to Christ.[3]

Many of the laws and customs of the Jews, ordered in the Old Testament, are not binding upon Christians, because our Lord has given us new principles which have taken the place of the old. Those only of the old laws and customs are still binding which were confirmed by the teaching of Christ and the Church.[4] For example: the laws of love toward God and man have been confirmed;[5] and those of prayer and fasting and almsgiving have been reasserted and purified from unworthy motives.[6] Many laws, such as those against unrighteous anger, adultery, and false swearing, have been made more stringent, and applied to secret thoughts as well as to outward actions.[7] But, on the other hand, our Lord showed that the many laws about clean and unclean foods are no longer binding:[8] and he annulled the permission of polygamy and divorce given in the Mosaic law, asserting the principle that the twain are one flesh, on which depends all Church legislation about marriage.[9] And the Church soon found that the many laws about sacrifices no longer applied, now that we have the one

[1] 1 Cor. x. 11. [2] Rom. xv. 4. [3] Gal. iii. 24.
[4] Chap. xvii. [5] Matt. xxii. 35-40.
[6] Matt. vi. 1-18; Chap xv. 2. [7] Matt. 17-48.
[8] Mark vii. 1-23. [9] Mark. x. 1-12; Chap. xviii.

158

effectual sacrifice;[1] and that circumcision is not necessary for Christians, because the Church is not merely Jewish but universal.[2]

Especially we have learnt that the chief value of the Old Testament for us Christians is that it can be interpreted in reference to our Lord. St Paul wrote to St Timothy: From a babe thou hast known the sacred writings, which are able to make thee wise unto salvation, through faith which is in Christ Jesus.[3] Faith in Christ is the key to the right interpretation of the Old Testament. We have the guidance of our Lord himself in this way of understanding it. He said to his disciples: All things must needs be fulfilled which are written in the Law of Moses, and in the Prophets, and in the Psalms, concerning me.[4] The Jews had been accustomed to see throughout the Old Testament the promise of the Messiah.[5] The Church differed from them only in applying that principle of interpretation more fully.

Thus, the story of the sacrifice of Isaac[6] is valuable to us chiefly as a picture of the greater sacrifice of a greater Son, Jesus the only-begotten Son of God, whom the Father gave to die for us, and who for our sakes was more truly than Isaac obedient unto death.

The picture of the suffering servant of Jehovah[7] was probably drawn to symbolise the people of God suffering for their faithfulness to him: to us it means Christ, in whom is all humanity obedient to God and sacrificed for the sin of the world. But it has come to mean this to us, only because the inspired Church has so taught us. Of ourselves we ask the question of the Ethiopian eunuch,[8] who on reading, He is led as a lamb to the slaughter, said: I pray thee, of whom speaketh the prophet, of himself, or of some other man? Like Philip, the Church from this passage has preached unto us Jesus. Otherwise our answer to the question, Understandest thou what thou readest? could only be, How can I, except someone shall guide me?

---

[1] Heb. ix. 1; x. 17.   [2] Acts xv. 1: 29. See further, Chap. xvii.
[3] 2 Tim. iii. 15.   [4] Luke xxiv. 44, 45.   [5] Chap. iii. 3.
[6] Gen. xxii.   [7] Isa. liii., etc.   [8] Acts viii. 26-35.

We believe that the Old Testament is the record of men who spake from God, being moved by the Holy Ghost;[1] and that under his inspiration it was written in such a way as to be ready to bear the Christian meaning which the same Holy Ghost was to enable the Church to see in it. The meanings present to the writers' minds, or to those of their Jewish readers, are interesting and profitable for us to know; but they are now for us usually of secondary importance.[2]

III

The New Testament also belongs to the Church, but in a different way. The Old Testament was taken over, and newly interpreted, by the Church; but each book of the New Testament was written for the Church by a member of the Church. Of the many books which were written, some came to be regarded as worthy to be ranked with or above the Old Testament, as truly expressing the Church's mind. Those survived which in the judgment of the whole Church were the fittest to survive.

The New Testament contains four books of the gospel, the good news about Jesus Christ, his birth and death and resurrection, his works and teaching and example. Matthew, Mark, and Luke are written upon one plan, and are closely related to one another. John is independent of the others. Also the New Testament gives us in the Acts of the Apostles the earliest history of the Church, as it began to spread throughout the world. The epistles are letters on doctrine and conduct written to particular congregations or persons, usually by the man who had converted them, and to meet the particular needs or to correct the errors of those to whom they are addressed. The Book of Revelation records a series of visions in which the Church is seen in conflict with the

[1] 2 Pet. i. 21.
[2] For other examples of mystical interpretation of the Old Testament in the New, see John vi. 32, 33; Rom. x. 4-8; 1 Cor. v. 7, 8; x. 1-4; 2 Cor. iii. 7-18; Gal. iii. 6-18; iv. 21—v. 1; Eph. v. 31, 32; Heb. i. 5-14; ii. 5-18; 1 Pet. ii. 1-10; etc. On the mystical interpretation of the Psalter, see Chap. xiv. 2.

world, and in its final glory when the divine judgment shall be made manifest.

The New Testament was never the Church's only medium of teaching. During the first hundred years, the books of the New Testament were either not written, or not widely circulated. The truth was first taught by word of mouth, and that method of teaching has never ceased, the method of Church tradition. The new Testament was written to supplement the Church tradition, and to keep it pure and uniform. The New Testament was the earliest, and remains the permanent, written evidence to Church tradition. Without it Church teaching would have become very various and uncertain. We see this plainly in the preface to St Luke's gospel : Foreasmuch as many have taken in hand to draw up a narrative concerning those matters which have been fulfilled among us, even as they delivered them unto us, who from the beginning were eye-witnesses and ministers of the word, it seemed good to me also, having traced the course of all things accurately from the first, to write unto thee in order, most excellent Theophilus, that thou mightest know the certainty concerning the things wherein thou wast taught by word of mouth.[1]

But, on the other hand, without the guide of Church teaching, the New Testament would have been of very little avail for imparting the truth. It is not a complete or orderly handbook of Church doctrine, nor was it ever intended to be such. Every new and strange teaching that has ever arisen among Christians has claimed to be supported by the New Testament. Sects holding doctrines mutually contradictory has equally appealed to it. It is necessary to read the New Testament with the Church's mind and with Church tradition as our guide; not simply relying on one's own private interpretation or inspiration. In a word, the New Testament is the book of the family of the Catholic Church : it belongs to the family, and the family alone knows how to understand it.

All the doctrines and laws of the Catholic Church can be proved and established by the witness of the New Testament :

[1] Luke i. 1-4.

161

although not nearly all are explicitly stated therein. The Church taught the doctrines, and gave us the laws. The same Church wrote the New Testament. In both ways of teaching the Church has been under the guidance of the Holy Spirit. And so the voice of the Church and the voice of Holy Scripture are always in agreement with each other. We may be sure at once, when we read the New Testament, that any interpretation of a passage contrary to the teaching of the Church cannot be the right interpretation; and also we may be sure that anything that is taught as the doctrine of the Church cannot really be the Church's teaching, if it is contrary to the plain meaning of Scripture.

We do not accept and believe Christian doctrine on the direct authority of Holy Scripture. Rather, we accept and believe it on the authority of Christ and his Church, and the witness of Holy Scripture is the guarantee to us that what we are taught in the Church is the true Church teaching.

We should be thankful to Almighty God that in this two-fold way we are kept in the way of truth: and we should always bear in mind that neither the Church without the Bible, nor the Bible without the Church, is a guide upon which we can confidently rely.

Much error has arisen through the ignorance of the Bible that is common in all parts of the Church. Much harm, also, has arisen from the giving of the Scriptures in the mother-tongue to those who, for want of knowledge of the Church tradition, read them by the light of private inter-pretation only.

IV

Closely connected with the office of the Church as teacher is its authority to enforce its teaching by laws governing conduct.

The Church is the kingdom of God on earth. It has not only a king, but also officers and a constitution, laws and customs. It has a spiritual kingdom, and its laws are spiritual. Civil government is not directly within its province;[1] but its laws of necessity affect civil life, since

---

[1] But see 1 Cor. vi.; Matt. xviii. 15-18.

the kingdom though not of this world is yet a kingdom in this world.

It is the duty of the citizens of the kingdom to give ready obedience to its laws, to respect its established customs, not lightly to differ from what has been generally approved, and to expect to find their personal advantage in subordination to the authority of the Church under which God has placed them.[1]

Christ is the king, and he was the first legislator in the Church. He said: All authority is given unto me in heaven and on earth.[2] He laid down the lines of the constitution by ordaining, instructing, and commissioning the apostles. He settled the plan of campaign: All authority is given unto me . . . Go ye, therefore, and make disciples of all the nations.[3] Ye shall be my witnesses, both in Jerusalem, and in all Judaea, and in Samaria, and unto the uttermost part of the earth.[4] And he established the ruling principles, and some of the sacraments, of the Church; but he himself enacted only a few definite laws.

His own work by himself was only a beginning. Most of the sacraments and rites of the Church, and nearly all its laws and regulations, yet remained to be established. All the filling up of the lines he laid down was left to the Church, which was not separate from him, but was his Body, filled with his Spirit. He committed his authority to the apostles, that they should carry out the plan of campaign, and develop the constitution by the orders of the sacred ministry,[5] and apply the ruling principles to the circumstances of the converts.

Christ authorised St Peter first, and then all the apostles, to act as legislators with divine authority, saying: What things soever ye shall bind (that is, forbid) on earth shall be bound in heaven; and what things soever ye shall loose (that is, allow) on earth shall be loosed in heaven.[6]

The Church was fully conscious of its authority and of the presence of the Holy Spirit guiding its decisions. Thus,

[1] Article of Religion, XXXIV.   [2] Matt. xxviii. 18.
[3] *Ibid.*   [4] Acts. i. 8.   [5] Chap. x.
[6] Matt. xvi. 19; xviii. 18.

the decision of the first council of the Church, at Jerusalem, which settled for ever that the Church is Catholic, and that converts need not become Jews in order to be Christians, was published in these words:[1] It seemed good to the Holy Ghost, and to us having come to one accord . . . And the matter being thus settled, nothing but obedience remained for all who would be accounted loyal members of the Church. The messengers of the council delivered to the congregations the decrees for to keep which had been ordained of the apostles and elders that were at Jerusalem. So the churches were strengthened in the faith, and increased in number daily.[2]

We read of this principle of Church authority being applied to the regulation of worship: The spirits of the prophets are subject to the prophets; for God is not a God of confusion, but of peace, as in all churches of the saints. Let all things be done decently and in order.[3] Even such an apparently small matter as the veiling of women at worship was settled by reference to general Church custom.[4] And such a great matter as the observance of Sunday we owe not to any recorded command of Christ, but to Church order.[5]

The authority of the Church has been exercised in many different ways, and by various agents; but the principle of it has been uniform. That principle is that in the Catholic Church the whole has authority over the part, and the part over the individual member. And the authority is divine. Christ rules the whole Church, and rules the parts of it through the whole. Christ rules and guides each individual through the Body of which he has made him a member. This principle has been maintained throughout the ages, and it is one of the characteristics of the Catholic Church. Church discipline has been one of the greatest means by which not only the morals of the Church have been kept pure, but also its faith, for faith and morals are very closely connected.

The weight of authority varies according to the degree in

[1] Acts xv. 25-28.   [2] Acts xvi. 4, 5.   [3] 1 Cor. xvi. 32-33.
[4] 1 Cor. xi. 16.   [5] Chap. xvii. 4.

which any law or custom has been established. That which has been from the beginning, that which has been universally received, is binding upon all. That which is a temporary or a local bye-law is binding only for a time, or upon those on whom it was imposed. But the nature of the authority is always the same : it is always dependent upon that divine authority which our Lord gave to his Church. The English Church, like every other part of the Catholic Church, has authority to make bye-laws; but not such as contradict rules universally accepted by the whole Church and permanently established. Examples of universal laws are those of Sunday worship, and of observing certain feasts such as Easter, Christmas, and Ascension. Example of English bye-laws are those of communicating at least three times in the year, and of keeping a great number of days in the year as days of abstinence.

The authority to make laws implies the right to dispense from their obligation. The authority that made the law can dispense from it. Those laws which have been laid down explicitly by God himself are not dispensable by the Church : for example, monogamy. Those which have been established by the consent of the whole Church can be dispensed only by the whole Church. Those which have been made by a part of the Church only are readily dispensable. But in no case may dispensation be granted without due cause, that is, it may not be granted simply to please the person or persons concerned, without some definite reason which justifies them being regarded as exceptions.

I believe in the Church. The phrase has little meaning, unless it includes : And therefore I will obey the authority of the Church. But members are sometimes disloyal and rebellious, for submission to authority is grievous to human pride of independence. And such rebellion has been one of the commonest causes of schism.

The Church has power to punish those who wilfully refuse obedience, with spiritual penalties, and in the last resort even to excommunicate them. Authority is no authority if it cannot assert itself against the rebellious.

165

The individual member who chooses to violate the laws of the Church, or of any part of the Church, has no reasonable ground of complaint if he is deprived of the benefits of membership; for it is only on the promise of obedience that anyone is made a member.

The power of excommunication was given to the Church by our Lord, when he said: Whose sins soever ye retain, they are retained.[1] And from the beginning the Church exercised its power.[2]

[1] John xx. 23.
[2] Acts v. 1-11; viii. 18-24; 1 Cor. v. 1-5, 11; 2 Cor. ii. 5-11; 2 Thess. iii. 6; 1 Tim. i. 20; Titus iii. 10, 11.

XIV

PRAYER—I.

I

PRAYER is the effort of the soul to enter into communion
with God, lifting up towards him the understanding, the
feelings, and the will.

Prayer is not peculiar to Christians. The Jews were
taught that their prayers were pleasing to God unless they
were offered with a disobedient and rebellious heart.[1]
Also those who were not within the covenant could offer
acceptable prayer. Cornelius, who was neither Christian
nor Jew, was told that his prayers and alms had gone up for
a memorial before God.[2] There is no reason to doubt that
the prayers of Moslems, and even of heathen, although
misdirected through false beliefs, reach him whom they
ignorantly worship.[3] Wherever there is any conception of
a supreme being, or of any personal being higher than man,
the instinct of man is to seek some way of approach to him;
and God, who gives the instinct, accepts any expression of
it that is well-intended and sincere, however faulty or mis-
guided or superstitious it may be, accepting each one according to that which he hath, not according to that which he
hath not.[4]

Prayer is natural: Christian prayer is also supernatural.
Prayer is the expression of a natural human instinct; but
the prayer of Christians moves on a different plane from
that of non-Christians. The prayer of a non-Christian is
separate and individualistic; that of a Christian is part of the
spiritual movement of the whole Body of Christ towards

[1] Ps. l., etc.
[2] Acts x. 4.
[3] John iv. 22; Acts xvii. 23.
[4] 2 Cor. viii. 12.

God. Human nature in Christ is placed on the high road of prayer, the high road of direct access to God.[1] The Church, united with Christ and living by his life, draws nigh to God corporately through Christ. The Church prays through Christ and in Christ; and Christ, who on earth prayed in his own person alone, now prayers in and with the Church. And in that whole action of prayer of Christ and the Church the prayers of each member are a part. All Christian prayer depends upon the fact, and is in truth part of the fact, that Christ now appeareth before the face of God on our behalf.[2] Because he is still both the high priest of humanity and the acceptable sacrifice of God, the Church which is united with him can draw near to God through that high priest and in the power of that availing sacrifice.[3]

Therefore, if we would understand the true character of Christian prayer, and its special acceptability and power with God, we must fix our minds first on Christ's prayer where he is at the right hand of God, and the permanence of his sacrifice in heaven; and next we must see the whole Church moving in prayer towards God as one body in union with Christ. The prayers of individual Christians can never really be individual or separate. They are but individual expressions of that one energy of the Church. Their acceptability and power do not lie in any energy of their own; but depend upon the reality of the union of each Christian with the whole body, that is, with Christ. The prayer of a Christian is effectual because it is thus energised.[4]

Three consequences follow from this. First, Christian prayer finds its most characteristic expression in the prayers of the saints in heaven, that is, in the part of the Body of Christ where union with Christ is perfected, and sin can no longer enter as a separating force. The saints' contemplation of the beatific vision of God is perfect Christian prayer.[5]

Secondly, the most characteristic prayer of Christians on earth is the holy sacrifice of the Mass, because we have in it the real presence of Christ the one Priest and Victim, and

[1] Heb. x. 19-22.   [2] Heb. ix. 24.   [3] Chap. ix. 4.
[4] Jas. v. 16.   [5] Chaps. xiv. 5; xix. 6.

because holy communion is the means of our union with Christ and his Church and with the Church's continual worship of God through Christ. No praise or supplication of any Christian, even if privately offered, can ever be independent of, or really separate from, the perpetual fact of the offering of the holy sacrifice; and there can be no aspiration of a praying Christian that is not already contained within the universal scope of that sacrifice. The personal praises and supplications of Christians are only the working out of the details of that one act of worship which is done corporately by the whole Church at every Mass.

Thirdly, as Christian worship is corporate in its essence, the united prayers and praises of a congregation are a more characteristic expression of it than are private devotions. Hence Christians may not forsake the assembling of themselves together for worship, as the manner of some is.[1] The worshipping congregation is the whole worshipping Church in miniature.

II

From the beginning the Church has had two ways of worship. There was the holy sacrifice, which took the place and fulfilled the type of the old Jewish sacrifices. Of this we have already thought.[2]

The other way of worship has been the divine office, that is, the divine duty, what is due to God. This was rendered to God, in praise and meditation and supplication, by the orderly recitation of the Psalter and the reading of Holy Scripture. The divine office, which grew out of the Jewish synagogue-worship, came to be regarded as the daily duty of the Church, and was divided into various numbers of offices in different places.

In the Western part of the Church there were established seven daily offices, in accordance with the words: Seven times a day will I praise thee.[3] Lauds was sung before dawn; Prime, Terce, Sext, Nones were intended for the first, third, sixth, and ninth hours; Vespers was the evening worship; and Compline, the night-prayers, completed the

[1] Heb. x. 25.   [2] Chap. ix.   [3] Ps. cxix. 164.

daily round. These offices were of obligation upon the clergy, but were shared in to a greater or less degree by the laity. Part of the night-time also was given to the night-office, called Nocturns or Mattins; even as it is written: At midnight will I rise and give thanks unto thee.[1]

In the Church of England since the Reformation the obligation has been reduced to two daily offices: Morning Prayer, which represented the older Mattins and Lauds; and Evening Prayer, which combined parts of Vespers and Compline. The language was changed from Latin to English, for the greater edification of the laity; and Holy Scripture was read more extensively than in the older offices.

In these daily offices, whether many or few, the main feature always has been the recitation of the Psalter in its entirety, either daily, or weekly, or once a month.

The Psalter is the Church's hymn-book. The Jews had used the psalms in their worship. Christ used them. The Church, therefore, adopted them from the beginning:[2] claiming them as its own, and marking the Christian sense in which it understood them by the addition of the doxology: Glory be to the Father, and to the Son, and to the Holy Ghost; as it was in the beginning, is now, and ever shall be, world without end. Amen.

Those Christians who know their Psalter well, and understand it, have little need of any other hymn-book. The production of many hymns, mostly of a personal sort suitable only for private use, marks a falling away from the sounder idea of corporate worship. It has arisen partly from the fact that the right interpretation and use of the Psalter have been to a great extent forgotten. Protestantism has always a tendency to depreciate the Psalter, to omit parts of it, and to substitute for it metrical versions or other hymns.

The key to the interpretation of the Church's hymn-book is that it is intended primarily for united use. The word "I" in the Psalter does not mean the person who is reciting the words. It denotes our Lord himself, or the Church united with him; and if it is applicable to the individual

[1] Ps. cxix. 62.   [2] Acts iv. 23-28.

worshipper, it applies to him only as a member of Christ and the Church. The worshippers are meant to use the words, not to express their own personal sentiments, but in order to enter into the mind of Christ and his Church. For example : such words as, I have refrained my feet from every evil way, that I may keep thy word,[1] are not an assertion of one's own self-righteousness, but of Christ's righteousness. The whole of Psalm cxix. is a meditation on the perfect human nature and character of Christ. The Church cantemplates him, while it repeats words which could be absolutely true only as spoken by Christ, and which, when spoken by the members of the Church, are true of them only in so far as they are in union with Christ and conformed by his grace to his likeness.

In the same way, the penitential psalms[2] have their full meaning, not as the expression of the repentance of David or of any other repentant sinner, but as the words of him who bore for all men the burden of sin, and in union with whom alone men can truly repent.

The historical psalms[3] are used in Church worship, not simply as records of the events of Jewish history, but because that history is regarded as typical of the history of the Catholic Church throughout the ages : privileged, sinning, forgiven, punished. When we sing of Israel, Jacob, Sion, we mean the Church.[4]

Again, the imprecatory, or cursing, psalms[5] are by no means used by Christians as the expression of their own desire for God's vengeance upon their personal enemies. It is not likely that even the Jews in their worship so understood these psalms. Certainly to the instructed Christian they are lyrics of the passion of Christ, and of the vengeance of eternal righteousness upon wilful evil. They speak to us of Christ and Christ's enemies in every age. They lead us to look at his enemies from the point of view of the Cross, and

---

[1] Ps. cxix. 101.
[2] Pss. vi., xxxii., xxxviii., li., cii., cxxx., cxliii.
[3] Pss. xliv., lxxviii., xcv., cv., cvi., cxxxvi., etc.
[4] Pss. xlviii. 2; lxxxv. 1; cxiv. 1, etc.
[5] Pss. lv., lxix., lxxxiii., cix., etc.

show us the mystery of sin in its utmost malignity, and of
sin's penalty in the just judgment of the God who died for
love of sinners.

Thus the whole Psalter is full of Christ and the Church.
A gospel could be compiled from the psalms. Indeed, if
we put together only those phrases which are directly applied
to Christ in the New Testament, we get a fairly complete
picture of him :

Christ is the Lord who in the beginning laid the foundation of the earth, and the heavens are the works of his hands.[1]
He is the Son of God.[2] God prepared for him a body,[3] and
made him a little lower than the angels.[4] He is the anointed
Messiah,[5] and David's Lord.[6] He was the blessed one who
came in the name of the Lord.[7]

He declared God's name unto men, his brethren.[8] He
opened his mouth in parables.[9] God gave his angels
charge concerning Christ.[10] God perfected his praise out of
the mouths of babes and sucklings;[11] but the reproaches
of them that reproached God fell upon him.[12] Judas, who
ate Christ's bread, lifted up his heel against him.[13] Therefore the habitation of Judas was made desolate, and another
took his office.[14] They parted Christ's garments among
them, and upon his vesture did they cast lots.[15] They gave
him gall and vinegar.[16] He said, My God, my God, why
hast thou forsaken me?[17] and, Into thy hands I commit my
spirit.[18]

But he beheld the Lord always before him. God was on
his right hand, that he should not be moved. Therefore his
heart was glad, his flesh also rested in hope. God did not
leave Christ's soul in hell, nor give his holy one to see corruption.[19] He was the Priest and Victim, and had come into
the world to do the will of God, who had no pleasure in
Jewish sacrifices for sin.[20] And he is a priest for ever, after

[1] Heb. i. 10.   [2] Heb. i. 5; v. 5.   [3] Heb. x. 5.
[4] Heb. ii. 7.   [5] Heb. i. 9.   [6] Matt. xxii. 24.
[7] Matt. xxiii. 39.   [8] Heb. ii. 12.   [9] Matt. xiii. 35.
[10] Luke iv. 10.   [11] Matt. xxi. 16.   [12] Rom. xv. 3.
[13] John xiii. 18.   [14] Acts i. 20.   [15] John xix. 24.
[16] Matt. xxvii. 34.   [17] Matt. xxvii. 46.   [18] Luke xxiii. 46.
[19] Acts ii. 25-28; xiii. 35   [20] Heb. x. 5-7.

the order of Melchisedek.[1] He was the stone which the builders rejected, but God made him the chief corner-stone of the Church.[2] God said to the risen Christ, Thou art my Son, this day have I begotten thee;[3] sit thou on my right hand.[4]

Christ's throne is for ever and ever, and the sceptre of uprightness is the sceptre of his kingdom. He loved righteousness and hated iniquity. Therefore God anointed him with the oil of gladness above his fellows.[5] God crowned him in his human nature with glory and honour, and put all things in subjection under his feet.[6] So, when Christ ascended on high, he led captivity captive, and gave gifts unto men.[7]

The sound of the Christian believers has gone out into all the earth, and their words unto the ends of the world.[8] The eyes of the Jews were darkened, that they should not see;[9] but the Gentiles praised the Lord, and all the peoples praised him.[10] For Christ's sake Christians have been killed, and accounted as sheep for the slaughter:[11] but it is they that shall enter unto God's rest.[12] Why did the nations rage, and the peoples imagine vain things, against the Lord and against his anointed one?[13] God shall put all enemies under his feet.[14]

The works of creation shall perish, but Christ continueth. They all shall wax old as doth a garment. Christ shall roll them up, and they shall be changed. But he is ever the same, and his years shall not fail.[15]

This brief explanation of the Church's mind in the use of the Psalter may serve as a guide to its interpretation, for those who are willing to adapt their minds to the Church's mind. It is unfortunate that many, for lack of knowledge of this method of interpretation, persist in endeavouring to fit the words of the psalms only to themselves personally,

---

[1] Heb. v. 6.
[2] Matt. xxi. 42; Acts iv. 11; Eph. ii. 20; 1 Pet. ii. 7.
[3] Acts xiii. 33; Rom. i. 4.   [4] Acts ii. 34.
[5] Heb. i. 8, 9.   [6] Heb. ii. 7, 8.   [7] Eph. iv. 8.
[8] Rom. x. 6.   [9] Rom. xi. 9, 10.   [10] Rom. xv. 11.
[11] Rom. viii. 36.   [12] Heb. iv. 3.   [13] Acts iv. 25, 26.
[14] 1 Cor. xv. 25.   [15] Heb. i. 11, 12.

an endeavour which means that they have no use for those parts which do not fit their experience or temperament, and at best endure the recitation of the whole Psalter for the sake of particular verses which appeal to them personally.

The principle here stated applies to the whole of the divine office. Always the words spoken by the congregation are the words of Christ or of the Church in union with him, which the congregation corporately repeat. A congregation is not a conglomeration of people praying privately and individually; it is a part of the Church exercising its share in the Godward attitude of the whole Church in Christ. This consideration alone can deliver many of the Church's prayers from the charge of unreality. Thus, when we say, We have erred and strayed from thy ways like lost sheep, or, The memory of our sins is grievous unto us, and the burden of them is intolerable, we are not necessarily putting into words the sentiment of which at the moment each of us is conscious; but rather we are expressing together with the whole Church the only attitude of mind in which the Church can approach the holy God. The We does not mean I : and the individual worshipper who does mean I when he says We, and thinks only of his own particular sins, may be making a good act of personal contrition, but has for the time let slip the idea of corporate worship. Similarly, when he says, We praise thee, O God; we acknowledge thee to be the Lord, he is not making an act of personal faith, but stating the faith of the whole body of the Church. The first person singular rarely appears in the Church's forms of prayer. The most notable case is in the creeds : I believe in one God; and in this case the Eastern use of We believe is better than that of the Western Church.

III

There is one prayer only accepted by the Church as having been given to it by Christ himself : the Our Father.

St Luke quotes it in a brief form,[1] and prefaces it by a direct command of Christ to his disciples to use it in their

---

[1] Luke xi. 2-4.

prayers : When ye pray, say, Father, hallowed be thy name, Thy kingdom come. Give us day by day our daily bread. And forgive us our sins; for we ourselves also forgive every one that is indebted to us. And bring us not into temptation.

St Matthew gives the Lord's Prayer in the extended form,[1] which had become, and which remains, the form accepted and used by the Church. Father becomes Our Father who art in heaven. Thy will be done, is added, probably from our Lord's prayer in Gethsemane.[2] The words, As in heaven so on earth, are added, which are intended probably to refer to each of the preceding clauses : Hallowed be thy name on earth as it is in heaven; Thy kingdom come on earth as it is in heaven; Thy will be done on earth as it is in heaven.

The daily bread is doubtless to be understood as a petition for the supply of both temporal and spiritual needs : sufficient food for the body and sufficient grace for the soul.[3] Similarly the words, Bring us not into temptation, or, into trial, probably refer both to material and to spiritual trials, and are usually interpreted as meaning, Suffer us not to be overwhelmed by any trial too great for us to bear.[4] St Matthew adds, And deliver us from evil, or, from the evil one.[5] The doxology, For thine is the kingdom, and the power, and the glory, for ever and ever, Amen, does not occur in the true text of either gospel. It is an addition by the Church to the Lord's Prayer.

The Church Catechism gives a good commentary on the Lord's Prayer, as it is commonly understood and used :

Our Father who art in heaven: I desire my Lord God, our heavenly Father, who is the giver of all goodness, to send his grace unto me and to all people; *Hallowed be thy name:* that we may worship him : *Thy kingdom come:* serve him; *Thy will be done:* and obey him; *On earth as it is in heaven:* as we ought to do. *Give us this day our daily bread:* And I pray unto God that he will send us all things that be needful both for our souls and bodies; *Forgive us*

---

[1] Matt. vi. 9-13.   [2] Matt. xxvi. 42.
[3] Matt. vii. 9-11; John vi. 33-35.
[4] 1 Cor. x. 13.   [5] John xvii. 15.

our trespasses: and that he will be merciful unto us, and forgive us our sins; *And lead us not into temptation:* and that it will please him to save and defend us in all dangers ghostly and bodily; *But deliver us from evil*: and that he will keep us from all sins and wickedness, and from our ghostly enemy, and from everlasting death. And this I trust that he will do of his mercy and goodness, through our Lord Jesus Christ. And therefore I say *Amen,* so be it.

St Matthew states that our Lord gave the prayer to be the model of all Christian prayer: After this manner pray ye. The Church, therefore, not only uses the Lord's Prayer in every service and rite, but also regards it as containing certain principles of prayer which should be applied to the making of all prayers. These principles are: First, in all prayer the thought of God should come before the thought of ourselves. We pray to our heavenly Father for the making holy of his name, the coming of his kingdom, and the fulfilment of his will, before we pray for our own needs. We say the word Thy three times before we come to the word Us. Secondly, the Christian may not approach the common Father of all, except as a member of the family. He may not think of himself alone. The words are Our and Us: not My and Me.

From these principles, three rules of prayer emerge, which may be stated briefly thus: In Christian prayer, whether public or private, think most of God, think much of others, think least of self. We may put these rules in another form: There are four acts of prayer, and the letters of the words Acts may serve to remind us of them. Thus, A adoration, C confession, T thanksgiving, S supplication. There is no prayer that is not the exercise of one or more of these acts. In adoration we are thinking almost entirely of God alone. In thanksgiving we are thinking of others as well as of ourselves, and merging both thoughts in that of the beneficent goodness of God. In confession of sinfulness and unworthiness we should try to feel with Christ the burden of the sin of the whole world, and especially the sin of the family of God; and we cannot repent rightly unless we combine the thought of God's holiness and outraged love with that of human error and sin, and realise God's great worthiness even more deeply than our own unworthiness. In supplication, when we bring our needs before the throne of grace, we may not shut out the thought of our brothers' needs. We must love our brothers in Christ as we love ourselves : human selfishness may not enter into Christian prayer. And all our suppliant petitions will be based on trust in our heavenly Father, or at least imply our submission to his holy will.

These four acts of prayers appear in equal proportion at Mass and in all the public prayers of the Church. In private prayer, however, there is a natural but faulty tendency towards self-centredness, so that in the minds of many prayer is regarded as consisting almost entirely of personal confession and personal supplication, while adoration, thanksgiving, and intercession for others hardly appear.

IV

It cannot be denied that there are many intellectual difficulties connected with prayer; but it is worth while to observe that they concern only prayers of supplication, and are oppressive burdens only to those who limit prayer to the asking of things.

It is hard to understand what need there is for supplication or what power our supplications can have with God. Since God knows all things, and knows our necessities before we ask him,[1] and since he is revealed to us as a loving Father,[2] the mind cannot but ask, What need is there for us to state our needs to him? Again, since all things are ordained by the will of God, to whom past and future are eternally present, the mind asks, How can our prayers be supposed in any way to affect the issue?

The answer to this problem is not given in Christian revelation. We may indeed consider that there is no necessary conflict or contradiction between our belief in divine predestination and our belief in the value of supplication. Prayer itself lies within the scope of God's ordaining

[1] Matt. vi. 8.   [2] Matt. vii. 11.

will as much as any other fact. We can readily think that, if God's will determines what is to come to pass, his will may also determine that it shall come to pass in answer to the prayer which he enables us to make. In prayer it is not really we who begin. It is not that we ask, and God responds. Rather, God moves us to pray, and we respond to his inspiration.

Again, prayer must not be regarded as an energy brought to bear upon God from outside him, as if human prayer apart from God were trying to coerce his will. All Christian prayer, as we have seen, is part of the prayer of the body of Christ. It is made in Christ and through Christ by the power of the Holy Spirit, abiding in the Church and in each member. It is made in faith, which is itself the gift of God; and it is made according to God's will. Only in so far as we abide in Christ, and his words abide in us, are we able to ask whatsoever we will, and it shall be done unto us.[1] And again Christ said : Whatsoever ye shall ask in my name (that is, as Christians), that will I do, that the Father may be glorified in the Son.[2] Of ourselves we know not how to pray as we ought, but the Spirit himself maketh intercession for us, and God knoweth what is the mind of the Spirit because he maketh intercession for the saints (that is, for Christians) according to the will of God.[3] Thus prayer is seen as being an energy not apart from God, but within the blessed Trinity and in union with God Incarnate. It is one thing with the mystery of the availing sacrifice of him who is able to save to the uttermost them that draw near to God through him, seeing he ever liveth to make interecssion for them.[4]

Such answers, of course, do not amount to a complete solution of the intellectual difficulties about prayer. The plain man, however, is content to follow the example of Christ himself, whose whole ministry was full of prayer and supplication.[5] He is content to obey the explicit commands

---

[1] John xv. 7.   [2] John xiv. 13.
[3] Rom. viii. 26, 27.   [4] Heb. vii. 25.
[5] Luke iii. 21; Mark i. 35; Luke v. 16; ix. 29; xi. 1; xxii. 32; John xvii.; Matt. xxvi. 39-44; Luke xxii. 44; Heb. v. 7; John xii. 27, 28; Luke xxiii. 34.

PRAYER — I

of Christ, commended to him by the amplest promises:
Hitherto have ye asked nothing in my name: ask, and ye
shall receive, that your joy may be fulfilled.[1] Ask, and it shall
be given unto you. Everyone that asketh receiveth.[2] All
things whatsover ye shall ask in prayer, believing, ye shall
receive;[3] or, still more forcibly, All things whatsoever ye
pray and ask for, believe that ye have received them, and ye
shall have them.[4] The Christian understands these sayings
not as asserting the immediate and direct effect of every
faithful petition in bringing about a particular result, but
rather as the emphatic statement that there is no subject,
not even the removing of mountains, so great as to lie outside
the scope of the power of prayer.

Relying on these promises, as the apostles did, the Christian
follows their example,[5] and their admonitions. In nothing is
he anxious, but in everything by prayer and supplication
with thanksgiving he makes his requests known to God.[6]
He does not think, as some of little faith have taught, that
his prayers have no real efficacy, serving only to help him
to bring his will into line with God's will. Rather, like the
apostles,[7] he looks for definite results as the consequences of
his prayers, and particularly of the united prayers of the
Church.

Whatever the Christian desires before God he asks for.
He cannot do otherwise. Every desire of the Christian's
heart, who lives in union with God, even if it be not formu-
lated in words, is prayer in the sight of him who knoweth
the heart.

And in his practical experience of prayer the Christian is
not disappointed. The problem of supplicatory prayer is
not solved for his intellect, but he finds that it has faded
away in the light of experience. This problem, like many
other problems of Christianity, is a stumbling-block only to
those who approach it with the intellect alone, apart from

---

[1] John xvi. 24-26.   [2] Matt. vii. 7-11.   [3] Matt. xxi. 22.
[4] Mark xi. 24; cf. Matt. ix. 38; xxiv. 20; xxvi. 41; Mark ix. 29;
Luke xviii. 1; John xv. 16; xvi. 23.
[5] Phil. i. 4; Col. i. 9; 1 Thess. i. 2.   [6] Phil. iv. 6.
[7] Acts i. 24; ix. 40; xii. 5, etc.

179

practical experience. Those who make the venture of faith find that their faith is justified.

Christ and the Church boldly propose this proof from experience to those who are perplexed and doubtful: Come and ye shall see.[1] And almost the last word written in the New Testament on prayer is the testimony of the Church's experience: This is the boldness which we have toward him, that, if we ask anything according to his will, he heareth us: and if we know that he heareth us, whatsoever we ask, we know that we have the petitions which we have asked of him.[2]

v

We do not pray alone. There is with us the whole Church, striving and suffering here on earth, waiting in expectant rest in the intermediate state, triumphant and glorified in heaven. Each of us is a living member of the Church: that which we do in Christ we do in living union with one another.

As at Mass, so always, our adoration and thanksgiving is united with the more perfect worship of heaven, with the angels and archangels, and with the whole company of the saints: for already we are come unto Mount Zion, and unto the city of the living God, the heavenly Jerusalem, and to innumerable hosts of angels, to the general assembly and church of the firstborn who are enrolled in heaven, and to the spirits of just men made perfect.[3] We believe in the communion of the saints, and that there can be no communion without the reality of union and the possibility of communication.

As in the sacrament of penance, so always, our confession of sin is not only to God Almighty, but also to blessed Mary, blessed Michael the archangel, blessed John the Baptist, the holy apostles Peter and Paul, and to all the saints, and to our brethren on earth; for we have offended against the saints and angels and against the Church on earth, as well as against God.

And similarly, our supplications are united with the prayers and intercessions of the worshipping angels who minister

[1] John i. 39.   [2] 1 John v. 14, 15.   [3] Heb. xii. 22, 23.

to us, and with the prayers of all the saints upon the golden altar before the throne.[1]

It is lawful and right for Christians on earth to pray to God that they may benefit by the good prayers of the whole company in heaven. This has been the universally accepted custom of the Catholic Church from early times; and it has passed, since the fourth century, into direct petition to the saints and angels to pray for us. There is no difference in principle between praying God that we may be aided by the prayers of the saints, and in the presence of God asking the saints to aid us by their prayers. The same result is gained by saying, May blessed Mary pray for us, and by saying, Holy Mary, pray for us sinners now and in the hour of our death.

The invocation of saints and of angels is a Catholic custom. It is the outcome of the instinct of Christians to join with others in prayer. It is natural for us to ask those who are living here on earth to pray for us, and especially those who are better than ourselves, whom we believe to be living closer to God, and whose prayers are less hindered than ours. It is still more natural to ask the departed to pray for us, and specially those whom we believe to be in heaven, in that perfected union with God which can no longer be marred or weakened by any sin. If the power of prayer depends, as we have seen, upon union with Christ, who can pray more powerfully than the saints? Similarly, it is natural to ask the holy angels to pray for us, who always behold the face of our Father in heaven.[2]

There is no argument against such invocation that would not apply equally against asking for the intercessions of good people on earth; except such as arises from the doubt in the minds of some as to whether the saints and angels can hear our requests. But there is no doubt on this point in the mind of the Catholic Church, which has taught us in holy Scripture that the angels are our guardians and know our affairs, and also assures us that we are compassed about with a great cloud of witnesses,[3] who themselves in their lives bore witness to Christ, and fought the good fight,

[1] Rev. viii. 3.   [2] Matt. xviii. 10.   [3] Heb. xii. 1.

and kept the faith, and finished their course.[1] These, who
surround us, like the spectators in the arena, watch us in our
witnessing to Christ and in the struggles of our Christian
course. They, who have experienced what we in our turn
have to endure, sympathise with our trials, and rejoice in our
victory. There is joy in heaven over one sinner that
repenteth,[2] joy among the saints, and joy among the holy
angels who guard us and never cease from prayer.

The intercessions of these holy ones do not take away from
the uniqueness of Christ's office as our Intercessor[3] and
Advocate with the Father.[4] Their prayers, like ours on
earth, are made through Jesus Christ our Lord. They pray
in union with Christ sacrificed. But they are suppliants
and we are suppliants, in a sense in which Christ is not.
They and we are before the throne of God, but he is on
the throne. His presence there is his intercession. The
sacrifice whose merits we and the saints and the angels
plead is within God.

---

[1] 2 Tim. iv. 7.   [2] Luke xv. 7.
[3] Heb. vii. 25; 1 John ii. 1.
[4] On the saints, see also Chap. xix. 6.

XV

PRAYER—II.

I

PRAYER, whether public or private, is a duty to be done, a lesson to be learnt, and a life to be lived.

Prayer, in its several parts of adoration, thanksgiving, confession, and supplication, is a duty. It is due from the child to his Father, from the creature to his Creator

It is not the mere indulgence of our inclination, nor merely the expression of our natural instinct. Often the duty of prayer rests upon us at times when the desire to pray is not present. And it may well be that prayer made at the call of duty, when it seems difficult for us to pray because we are not aided by inclination, is more acceptable to God than prayer made at other times, when from the ease and pleasure we experience in prayer the element of self-sacrifice may be lacking. Anyway, our feelings, whether they prompt us to pleasure in prayer or to distaste of praying, matter very little. What does matter is our will, whether we will to do our best to perform our duty in prayer towards God and our neighbour, even if the best possible from us at the time seems but a poor and cold thing. In other words, our response to the grace of God is faith working through love and wrought through love;[1] and love is shown chiefly by obedience: This is the love of God, that we keep his commandments.[2]

Again, we know that the profit we derive from the habit of prayer is great, although we are not always conscious of deriving benefit from every particular act of prayer. But the seeking of profit for ourselves is not the right motive for

[1] Gal. v. 6.   [2] 1 John v. 3.

prayer. The highest motive in prayer, as in all else that we do, is the glory of God.[1] We are to pray for his sake rather than for our own sakes.

The true Christian does not pray because he wants to pray, but because he ought to pray. He does not pray in order to get good for himself by prayer, but in order to give glory to God : and, since God will remain no man's debtor, the more the Christian gives to God his due, and thinks more of God than of himself, the more does he himself profit by his prayer.

What exactly is each person's duty of prayer, in frequency, kind, and manner, varies according to the age and circumstances and temperament and spiritual capacity of each. He learns it partly through the general precepts of the Church, partly by personal guidance and inspiration from the Holy Spirit.

Prayer is a lesson to be learnt : and therefore, like most lessons, it is difficult to learn, and it may be distasteful at the outset. To hold communion with God, to speak the language of heaven, cannot be easy. Although prayer is a natural instinct, there is in us the faulty inclination that is at variance with our better nature.

As in other lessons, so in this, some start with more ability and aptitude than others. We are not all given the same natural power or the same supernatural grace to attain to equal proficiency. This is not an excuse for slackness, as if the power to pray were only a gift from God passively received. There are many who, because they have only one poor talent of prayer, bury it, and make no good use of it. Rather, we ought to set ourselves to cultivate whatever power of prayer we have received, that we may gain other talents also.[2]

To learn the lesson of prayer, we need to bring effort, attention, judgment, and persevering practice. What God requires of us is not necessarily quick progress or great success. Our success is not dependent upon our efforts only. But God does ask of us faithfulness of effort, according to the capacity of each, in response to the grace he gives.

[1] 1 Cor. x. 31.   [2] Matt. xxv. 17.

And faithfulness of effort implies attention—that is, the will to attend seriously to what we are doing as to the work which God has given us to do.[1] This attention of will is quite different from attentiveness of mind. Wandering thoughts, for example, are not more sinful in prayer than in any other work : in no case are they sinful unless they are wilfully sought or encouraged. But to engage in prayer, or in any other work that lies in our path of duty, perfunctorily and carelessly is always sinful.

Again, perseverance is needed. That which at first is difficult can become easier only by continual practice. And we may not cease learning the lesson of prayer : always we must be seeking to advance.

Not least, there is needed judgment and consideration. We should at times set ourselves to scrutinise our habits of praying, their time and manner, their substance and their quality, so that our effort to advance in prayerfulness may be well directed. We cannot hope to advance in the learning to pray unless we bring our thought to bear upon the matter. A schoolchild does not always remain in the first standard : but many Christians never advance from the first standard in the school of prayer; and the result is that their devotional life ceases to be in a true relation to their developed mind and wider experience, and therefore their prayers become unreal.

Although we cannot all attain to the greatest heights, our hope and desire must ever be to climb higher. If our ideal be not continually advancing, our attainment will always be lower than it might be. But still, as in all lessons, it is better for us to begin with that which is easy : to set ourselves easy tasks in prayer, and learn to fulfil them well, before we attempt the more difficult. For example, to learn the prayer of supplication before we set ourselves to the higher task of adoration or thanksgiving; and to learn to pray for others, by praying at first for our own immediate circle, those who are naturally near and dear to us, for whom we are specially bound to pray, before we extend the scope of our intercessions. We must learn to walk before we can

[1] John xvii. 4.

fly. We must learn to perform rightly the minimum duty of prayer before we can hope to be able to soar into the heights. But the Christian whose effort and intention is faithful in that which is least will find before long that the Holy Spirit has promoted him to higher things, and that he is being led on to habits and practices of prayer which at the outset he would have regarded as utterly beyond his reach.

Prayer is a life to be lived. He is living the life of prayer who has learnt to live always in the presence of God, and whose conscious communion with God is rarely, and his subconscious communion never, broken. This is not so completely difficult as it may appear. The beginning of it is to learn to approach God at frequent set times of prayer, and to lift up the heart to him continually in brief acts of prayer in the midst of one's daily occupations. There are very many Christians who thus fulfil the apostolic injunction to pray without ceasing.[1]

Another way in which we can live the life of prayer is to learn, whatever we do, to do it heartily, as to the Lord and not unto men,[2] accepting our daily duties in the world as given to us by God to be done as our service to him personally.[3] Whatsoever ye do, in word or in deed, do all in the name of the Lord Jesus.[4] Whether ye eat or drink, or whatsoever ye do, do all to the glory of God.[5] He whose intention is so to live his daily life makes of his whole life a prayer, even though the thought of God be not in the forefront of his consciousness perpetually, and indeed cannot be. He will doubtless offer each begun and each completed work to God; but in the performance of it his service to God requires the concentration of all his faculties upon the work in hand. This concentration on work is prayer, just as concentration on prayer in set times of prayer is work. Thus each part of life's activities, or of life's sufferings, may be sanctified, being done and endured for God and in God; and each smallest and most ordinary task may be made a Te Deum in the sight of God. We can pray by the labour of our

[1] 1 Thess. v. 17.   [2] Col. iii. 23.   [3] Eph. vi. 7.
[4] Col. iii. 17.   [5] 1 Cor. x. 31.

brains, or by the sweat of our hands, as truly as by the strivings of our souls, and so continually live the life of prayer. But a warning must be added, that if we neglect prayer in the ordinary sense of the term, we soon lose the Godward intention in our work, and it ceases to be prayer.

II

Our Lord has joined fasting and almsgiving with prayer, under the title of Righteousness.[1] Fasting and almsgiving, like prayer, are each a duty to be done, a lesson to be learnt, and a life to be lived.

Fasting disciplines the body, which, if undisciplined, will hinder the soul from prayer. Almsgiving corrects the natural tendency of self-centredness which spoils prayer. Fasting is the outward sign and expression of the prayer of penitence : almsgiving of the prayer of thanksgiving.

The duty of fasting or abstinence in some form is obligatory upon all Christians, because of our Lord's word[2] and the custom of the Church from the earliest times.[3] In different ages and places the Church has laid down different rules for the fulfilment of the duty. The faithful Christian is bound by the Catholic principle of obedience to observe whatever rules are put upon him by lawful authority. The rules of widest acceptance have been to observe the fast of Lent on the forty weekdays before Easter, to abstain from flesh-meat on Fridays in memory of the Lord's death, and to abstain from all food and drink before receiving holy communion.[4]

Beyond these particular obligations, every Christian is bound to practise due self-control and self-denial at all times in eating and drinking and other bodily pleasures.[5] All things are lawful for me, said St Paul, but I will not be brought under the power of any.[6]

A Christian is not ordinarily bound to any abstinence that is really harmful to his health; but he is not justified in any case if he breaks the Church's rules on his own

[1] Matt. vi. 1-18.
[2] Matt. vi. 16; Mark ii. 20.
[3] Acts xiii. 3; xiv. 23.
[4] Chap. ix. 6.
[5] 1 Cor. vii. 5; 1 Pet. iii. 7.
[6] 1 Cor. vi. 12.

motion, without having received dispensation from Church authority.

The duty of almsgiving also rests upon the word of Christ[1] and the practice and teaching of the Church.[2] The payment of church dues, for the necessary maintenance of the services of the Church, is enjoined in the New Testament.[3] It would seem a matter of simple honesty that those who receive the benefit of Church services and ministration should pay for their upkeep. But the duty of almsgiving goes beyond this. The Christian will also make voluntary offerings; both for the poor and needy,[4] and for the worship of God, as our Lord taught.[5] Voluntary offerings can be made by acts of service as well as by gifts of money.

What amount each person should give in charity, over and above his obligatory church-dues, is a matter on which the Church has laid down no rules. Let each man do according as he hath purposed in his heart, not grudgingly or of necessity, for God loveth a cheerful giver.[6] The Jewish law of giving the tenth part of the harvest[7] does not apply to Christians. The tithe was almost the whole of the taxation in the Jewish state, and its place has been taken in modern States to a great extent by the civil taxes. But any Christian is at liberty to make the Jewish standard his own. The Church makes no regulation, but also it prescribes no limit, except that a Christian may not give to others, nor to the Church itself, that which is necessary for those who are dependent upon him.[8]

A Christian is entitled only to necessary maintenance, his food and raiment, with which he should be content.[9] He is not the owner of his money, but only the steward, to use it for the glory of God and the welfare of men. The love of money is a root of all kinds of evil.[10] It is a great hindrance

---

[1] Matt. vi. 2; Mark xii. 41-44; Luke xii. 33, 34.
[2] Acts iv. 32; 1 Cor. ix.; 2 Cor. ix. 6, 7; Gal. vi. 10; 1 Tim. vi. 17-19; Heb. xiii. 16; 1 John iii. 17.
[3] Gal. vi. 6, 7; Matt. xvii. 24-27; *cf.* Exod. xxx. 12.
[4] Ps. xli. 1. [5] Mark xiv. 3-9. [6] 2 Cor. ix. 7.
[7] Deut. xiv. 22. [8] Mark vii. 9-13; 1 Tim. v. 8.
[9] 1 Tim. vi. 8-10. [10] *Ibid.*

to salvation;[1] and therefore needs to be mortified. Give alms: make for yourselves a treasure in the heavens that faileth not: For where your treasure is, there will your heart be also.[2] He that hath pity upon the poor lendeth to the Lord;[3] and whatever is done to the least of Christ's brethren, is done unto himself.[4] The widow was commended who gave all she had.[5]

Such is the teaching of Christ and the Church.[6] The obvious conclusion is that the utmost which a Christian gives away, up to or beyond what seem to him the limits of capacity and prudence, is not too much. But Christians have so far fallen from such a standard, that it would be well if they could now be induced to give even the obligatory minimum.

Almsgiving and fasting, like prayer, are to be done with a worthy motive; not for the sake of gaining reputation among men,[7] nor seeking to establish a claim upon God by one's good deeds;[8] but simply as the outward expression of an obedient and thankful and loving heart.

III

We began the preceding chapter with the consideration that all Christian prayer is corporate in its essence, the prayer of the body of Christ in union with him; and that private prayer is never really separate from that, but is the personal direction by one member of the perpetual energy of the whole body towards God. This consideration needs to be borne in mind in what remains to be said of private prayer.

The Church has, and each member has, the power and privilege of free access to God through Christ.[9] Upon the individual, therefore, as upon the Church, rests the duty of prayer; and he can and ought to fulfil it by himself as well as in the congregation.

[1] Mark x. 25.
[2] Luke xii. 33, 34.
[3] Prov. xix. 17.
[4] Matt. xxv. 40.
[5] Mark xii. 33, 34.
[6] See also Chap. xvi. 1; xvii. 8.
[7] Matt. vi. 1.
[8] Matt. xx. 1-16.
[9] Heb. x. 19-22.

Public prayer needs to be normally in set forms of words and ceremonial, to which each member subordinates himself, that one may not hinder another. United prayer must be orderly; there can be no union without discipline. The regulation of public worship in each congregation rests with the priest under the bishop.

Although the keeping or omitting of a ceremony, considered in itself, is but a small thing, yet the wilful and contemptuous transgression and breaking of a common order and discipline is no small offence before God. Let all things be done among you, said St Paul, in a seemly and due order :[1] the appointment of the which order pertaineth not to private men; therefore no man ought to take in hand, nor presume to appoint or alter any publick or common order in Christ's Church, except he be lawfully called and authorised thereunto.[2]

But in private prayer there is no need for such order. Indeed, it is not desirable that any Christian should allow his private prayers to become merely the recitation of set forms such as the Our Father, the Hail Mary, and the Creed, valuable though these are in private as in public. In addition to these, there is ample room for free and variable prayer, according to one's daily circumstances and dispositions. Each day brings its own needs for the special direction of our adoration and thanksgiving and confession and supplication. If in congregational worship it is right to adapt ourselves to the forms and the spirit of the united prayer, in private it is better to fit our prayers to our own personal desires and needs. But there is a strangely contradictory tendency in us, in public to insist upon giving personal application to the common prayer, and in private to pray by constructing set services for a congregation of one.

In private prayer be easy and free. It is possible to be easy and free with God our Father, without becoming free and easy. Though kneeling is normally the most fitting and helpful posture, it is not the only one consistent with reverence. Though each of the four acts of prayer should

---

[1] 1 Cor. xiv. 40.　　　[2] P.-B. Preface on Ceremonies.

enter into our prayers, the proportions of these and their
order may vary from day to day. Though it is good to have
rules for our guidance as to the length of time, and the
number of times, to be assigned to definite prayer, yet these
rules should not be coercive on the conscience. We should
desire to pray so long and so frequently as our circumstances
and our capacity permit; but these change from day to day.
Christian experience, however, shows it is good to hold ourselves bound as a minimum to pray every morning and
night : in the morning anticipating the coming day, seeking
the special graces we shall need, and directing our intention
to do all for God's glory; and at night reviewing the day
past, with a view to particular confession and thanksgiving
and intercession.

Secondly, in private prayer be natural and real. Say
what is in your heart, rather than what you know ought to
be there. In speaking with an intimate friend, we speak
naturally; not continually stopping to consider properties
of speech. If you feel nothing, tell God so, or in silence
wait upon him. I am so feeble that I cannot speak,[1] is
sometimes our sincerest prayer. If you can thank God only
for the pleasure or successes of the day, do not force yourself
to thank him also for the sorrows or the failures or the
sufferings. If you do not feel full contrition for sin, do the
best you can to be contrite, and leave it at that; it is of no
avail to utter words of contrition that are unreal. Sometimes the best act of sorrow for sin that we can make is to
ask for the sorrow which we know we lack. If we enter
into prayer with our souls beset by unfaith or by unchari-
tableness, from which we seem unable to escape, then our best
prayer is to lay our state before God, trusting him to understand his own children; and we shall find that he will not
leave us long in that state.

Thirdly, in private prayer be definite and slow. Let
every word be the expression of a real thought. Pause
frequently, especially when repeating well-known forms,
that you may not lose touch with God. Such definite
prayer is of greater value than long-continued prayer. Be

[1] Ps. lxxvii. 4.

not rash with thy mouth; let not thine heart be hasty to utter anything before God. God is in heaven, and thou upon earth; therefore let thy words be few.[1] Hastiness in prayer can seldom be without insincerity and irreverence.

IV

Another field of private devotion is the reading of holy Scripture, or the meditation upon some mystery of the faith with a view to prayer. Such devotional meditation is of very great value, as thereby alone the character of our Lord and the truths of his revelation become of power to us individually, and are brought into relation with our lives. It is not the truth we have been taught, but the truth we have inwardly received, that becomes part of us. Another fruit of meditation is that we gain thereby topics for conversation with God in prayer.

A useful method of Bible reading or meditation is comprised in the five words: Prepare, picture, ponder, pray, promise.

Prepare, by fixing your mind on the presence of God, endeavouring to banish alien thoughts, and asking the guidance of the Holy Spirit. A wise man said: Before prayer, prepare thy soul, and be not like a man that tempeth God.[2]

Picture: try not merely to read, but also to use the imagination and the memory to make your subject vivid to your mind.

Ponder: ask yourself such questions as, What does this mean? What does this teach about our Lord? What does this mean to me? What is the plain lesson I can learn from this? We do not need to search for abstruse or difficult thoughts, but to grasp clearly the plain meanings. We do not meditate in order to learn new truths, though we should not reject any new light that may be given us. Our main business in meditation is to ponder the old truths, which we already know, in such a way that the power of them may enter into us. Meditation, thus understood, is a very simple matter.

[1] Eccles v. 2.   [2] Ecclus., xviii. 22.

192

Pray : our thoughts then lead us on to the making of such acts of prayer—words of faith, hope, love, contrition, thanksgiving, adoration, aspiration, trust, sympathy with Christ, etc.—as our subject suggests to us under the inspiration of the Holy Spirit. This mental prayer is the principal part of the whole exercise; and the more we can make the pondering in the form of prayer, the better our exercise will be. For example, if our subject be the manger at Bethlehem, and our first thought be, Christ became poor for our sakes, it is best to make that thought itself a prayer : Lord Jesus, thou didst become poor for our sake; so that our every thought is not only about him, but also directed towards him. And we should bear in mind that prayer is conversation with God; and conversation implies listening as well as speaking. I will hearken what the Lord God will say concerning me.[1] Speak Lord, for thy servant heareth.[2]

Promise : frequently in our thoughts or prayer some good resolution will be forcibly suggested to our minds, by which we can more closely conform ourselves and our lives to the truth that has come home to us. If so, we can make a promise to God to that effect, as the fruit of meditation, asking for his grace to help us. Simple promises relating to that day only are the safest. Large or difficult resolutions should not be made without grave consideration and serious conviction that they are God's will for us. If no other resolution occurs to us, it is good to promise to recall the subject of the meditation at some definite time or times during the day, so that the influence of our prayer may be prolonged. All promises made to God in prayer should become subjects of self-examination at night.

Those who seriously enter upon this exercise of prayer, though they may seem to have poor success and little fruit from day to day, will find great profit even from the effort towards meditation and mental prayer. Even the effort to think of God, and to think most of God, and of ourselves only as we are in the sight of God, is acceptable and efficacious prayer. The fruit of this habit of prayer is nothing less than the quickening of our apprehension of God and the

[1] Ps. lxxxv. 8. [2] 1 Sam. iii. 10.

things of God, and a consequent alteration of our whole outlook on religion and on life.

If the practice of interior prayer is continued, the common experience is to find that the intellectual pondering is less and less needed. The picture or the subject leads us directly to communion with God, without any or with very few particular considerations. Even a particular subject becomes unnecessary; our realisation of God's presence is itself sufficient to maintain us in interior prayer. This higher form of prayer is such as is expressed in the words: When thou saidst, Seek ye my face; my heart said unto thee: Thy face, Lord, will I seek.[1] O God, thou art my God, early will I seek thee. My soul thirsteth for thee, my flesh longeth after thee, in a dry and weary land, where no water is. So have I looked upon thee in the sanctuary, to see thy power and thy glory; for thy loving-kindness is better than life.[2] The whole exercise then consists of direct prayer and direct communing with God, to which at first we set ourselves by the deliberate direction of our wills, and into which later we are led without our conscious choice or co-operation.

Beyond this second stage there lies the highest state of prayer, which is called contemplation, when the interior realisation of God suffices the soul for communion with him without any conscious acts of prayer. This in its fulness is the experience only of mature and holy souls, long practised in the way of prayer; and the road to it lies through many mortifications, trials, and temptations. It is the highest form of personal prayer possible for human beings in this world, for it is the same in kind, though not in degree, as that contemplation of God and that communion with him which the angels and the saints enjoy in heaven. But it is this, and nothing less than this, that God has destined eternally for all whom he has made and redeemed and sanctified; it is for this end that he has created us, to see him as he is, and to live for ever in the joy of his unveiled presence.

[1] Ps. xxvii. 8.   [2] Ps. lxiii. 1-3.

Many there be that say, Who will show us any good?
Lord, lift thou up the light of thy countenance upon us.[1]
As for me, I shall behold thy presence in righteousness;
and when I awake up after thy likeness, I shall be satisfied
with it.[2]

[1] Ps. iv. 6.   [2] Ps. xvii. 15.

XVI

CHRISTIAN CHARACTER

1

THE four qualities or virtues which form the foundation of the Christian character are wisdom, fortitude, temperance, and justice.[1]

Wisdom is that common sense without which no strong or stable character can be formed. He who is deficient in it is a fool, at the mercy of every passing whim. He is unable to make right judgments either about himself or about others.

Fortitude is the courage and strength of will which enables a person to give effect to his judgments. Without it he would be dominated by his surroundings and by his inherited tendencies; he would be a coward, unable to stand firm against opposition, or to endure the blows of misfortune, or to suffer pain.

Temperance denotes that power of self-control by which a man can rise superior to his lower nature, resisting his fleshly temptations, and whatever else is contrary to his principles. He who has little power of self-control is a weakling, and is not master of himself.

Justice is the quality without which a man cannot really share in social life with his fellow-men, for it is the faculty of recognising the rights of others and the will to deal fairly by them.

These qualities, like all human qualities, are the gift of God the Creator, from whom comes every good gift.[2] No one who is possessed of reason is without some share in them; but they are present in each of us in different degrees. No one starts his life possessing them all in their fulness: few, if any, ever come to the perfection of them all. But

---

[1] Wisdom viii. 7.   [2] Jas. i. 17.

each of us, by prayer and the use of the sacraments, by
faithfulness of effort in response to grace, is able to attain
to some development of them.

These qualities are the foundation of the Christian
character in the sense that it is only in so far as any Christian
has them that he is a capable and responsible human being,
true to the image of God in which he has been made. Never-
theless, they are not in themselves Christian virtues. They
are natural to mankind, and they are the foundation of
character in all men, heathens as well as Christians. Pagan
philosophers have written of their value and of how they
may be cultivated. They are Christian only if they are
the fruit of grace received through Christ, and if the motive
for their cultivation is Christian.

Similarly, conscience is not necessarily Christian.
Heathens as well as Christians are guided by conscience,
and rebuked by it when they act counter to it.[1] Conscience
is the recognition of some standard of conduct which a man
has learnt to respect. It is the sense of right as distinct
from wrong; and it exists in all men, though they differ
widely as to what they regard as right and what as wrong.
A Christian is bound to obey his conscience : he is bound not
to do what he feels to be wrong, but to live true to the
highest he sees. But he needs to educate his conscience by
the law of God and the teaching of Christ and the Church.
It is only in so far as he has really learnt the Christian
standard of conduct that he can rely on his conscience not
to lead him astray.

II

The virtues of faith, hope, and charity are essentially
Christian and supernatural. The words denote the three
gifts of God by which the people of God have been enabled
to receive and respond to the divine grace and truth vouch-
safed to them, partially under the old covenant, and fully
under the new. A heathen can in a dim way believe in
God, and have hope in him, and be charitable; but we should
not say he possessed faith or hope or charity.

[1] Rom. ii. 15.

Christian faith is the gift of God by which we are enabled in our personal experience to know God revealed to us in our Lord Jesus Christ. Faith is the power to grasp the unseen realities.[1] It is the first requisite for a Christian life: the righteous shall live by faith.[2]

A man of faith is regarded by God as having already attained righteousness,[3] for by the power of faith given to him he takes to himself the fruits of the union with God into which he has been brought, and on which the attainment of personal righteousness depends.

We are saved, and we are being sanctified, through being united with Christ; and the means to that union are the sacraments on God's side and faith on ours. Hence we are saved by faith, not by our own works. Thus St Paul's desire was to be found in Christ, not having a righteousness of his own, but that which is through faith in Christ, the righteousness which is of God by faith.[4] Our works and characters can never be really righteous in themselves. They are righteous in God's sight only in so far as they are the result of the grace of Christ received by faith. Works which are not so done in faith—that is, done through Christ's grace and for God's glory—may make us respectable in the eyes of men; but they are not pleasing to God, being acts that are merely human and tainted by the universal faultiness of human nature.

We cannot be saved by our own works. Christianity is by no means the same as civilisation or culture. We and our civilisation and our culture need to be saved by Christ. The purpose of Christ towards us is not that he shall make us decent living, respectable, self-respecting. We might become such through our own efforts. His purpose is to save us from ourselves, by uniting us with himself. And then, when we are joined to him by sacraments, and take him to ourselves by faith, we in him and he in us can bring forth the true Christian virtues which are not natural but supernatural, the fruit of the supernatural life of Christ in us. It is of no use to fasten paper roses on a rose-tree;

[1] Chap. vi. 4. [3] Rom. i. 17.
[2] Rom. iv. 5. [4] Phil. iii. 9.

the only rose worth having is that which is produced by the life in the tree. And similarly the only virtues worth having are those which we have not made by our own efforts, but which spring from the Christ-life within us. And so Christ says: He that abideth in me and I in him, the same beareth much fruit; for apart from me ye can do nothing.[1]

Salvation is by faith, not by good works apart from faith: by the works of the law there shall no flesh be justified.[2] But faith is manifested in good works: as works without faith are dead,[3] so also faith that does not show itself in good works is but a dead faith.[4] Faith is the root of all belief in God,[5] and of all true obedience towards God.[6] By faith we can draw near to God;[7] by faith we can endure, as seeing him who is invisible;[8] by faith only can we pray effectually.[9]

In fact, the word faith sums up the whole relation of a Christian towards God; and the result of receiving and growing in the gift of faith is that a man's whole life and character, his thoughts and actions, his aims and purposes, his endurance and his sufferings, are directed Godwards. Faith implies a God-centred life.

Christian hope is dependent upon faith, for faith is the assurance of things hoped for, the proving of things not seen.[10] Hope is a characteristic of the faithful Christian. The heathens have no hope, being without God in the world;[11] but God has begotten us Christians again unto a living hope by the resurrection of Jesus Christ from the dead.[12] Through the resurrection of Christ and our union with him, we have the hope of resurrection,[13] of salvation,[14] of eternal life,[15] of being like Christ and seeing him as he is,[6] of perfected righteousness.[17] Yes, Christ himself, with whom we are made one in the power of his risen life, is our hope[18] both

---

[1] John xv. 5. [2] Rom. iii. 20. [3] Heb. vi. 1.
[4] Jas. ii. 26. [5] Heb. xi. 6. [6] Heb. xi. 8.
[7] Heb. x. 22. [8] Heb. xi. 27. [9] Luke xvii. 5.
[10] Heb. xi. 1. [11] Eph. ii. 12. [12] 1 Pet. i. 3.
[13] Acts xxiv. 15; 1 Cor. xv. 19; 1 Thess. iv. 13.
[14] 1 Thess. v. 8. [15] Titus iii. 7. [16] 1 John iii. 3.
[17] Gal. v. 5. [18] 1 Tim. i. 1.

in this world and in the world to come. Christ in us is our hope of glory.[1]

Hope, then, is the gift of God which enables faithful Christians to rely with confidence upon God, being sure that he will give them through Christ grace in this life and glory hereafter. They only can have hope who believe in God's mercy and his promises and his power. The effect of hope is that the Christian is not downcast by the trials and afflictions of this life, or by the apparent triumph of evil in this present world; but is enabled to serve God whom he knows by faith, and to have patience in his service, knowing that this life is not the whole of life.[2] Christian hope involves the other-worldly outlook on life, and inspires Christians to give diligence to make their calling and election sure.[3] It was in the power of faithful hope that St Paul wrote of himself: I press on, if so be that I may apprehend that for which also I was apprehended by Christ Jesus; forgetting those things which are behind, and stretching forward to the things which are before, I press on towards the goal, unto the prize of the high calling of God in Christ Jesus.[4] And every faithful Christian can lay hold of the hope that is set before us, which we have as an anchor of the soul both sure and steadfast, and entering into that which is within the veil, whither as a forerunner Jesus entered for us.[5]

The virtue of charity, or Chrstian love, is the gift of God by which the Christian is enabled to respond to God's love bestowed upon him. It is the proper outcome, the super-natural expression, of faith and hope. By it he can love God whom he knows by faith and serves in hope. Without love his knowledge of God would lack intimacy, and his service would be slavish or selfish. The effect of receiving this gift of supernatural love is that we desire and strive to love God with entire devotion and complete surrender of mind and heart and soul; and to bring our love of people and

---

[1] Col. i, 27.
[2] Rom. viii. 24, 25; 1 Thess. i. 3.
[3] 2 Pet. i. 10.
[4] Phil. iii. 9-15.
[5] Heb. vi. 19.

things within our love to God, so that they shall not be rivals to him, but shall be loved by us in subordination to his will and for his sake.

It is of the essence of love that it be mutual. Love is not complete until it meets with a response. When we love God, we are but returning to him the love which he has bestowed upon us. Love is of God, for God is love. Herein is love, not that we loved God but that he loved us. We love him, because he first loved us.[1]

And it is of the essence of love that it shall confer benefit upon the beloved. It is not an idle feeling, but tends to proceed forth actively, bestowing blessing. God so loved that he gave.[2] Jesus so loved that he came, and died, and gives himself to us.

And the perfection of love is shown in self-sacrifice: the good shepherd giveth his life for the sheep.[3]

Christians are to return to God this love which springs from him; and to return it, not only in feelings, but by self-sacrificing actions, conferring benefit upon him, that so love may be fulfilled. But God in high heaven lacks nothing. He needs no benefit that we can bestow upon him. Jesus is no longer within reach of human ministrations.[4] How, then, can we do good to him? The answer is that he accepts as done to him whatever we do for the least of his brethren—that is, for any who are in need of our sympathy and help.[5] They are his representatives, to receive from us the practical expression of the love we owe to him. If God so loved us, we also ought to love—whom? God? Yes, certainly; but how? We ought to love one another. If a man love not his brother, how can he love God? This commandment have we from him, that he who loveth God love his brother also.[6] And so, in our Lord's words, by this shall all men know that we are his disciples, if we have love one to another.[7]

Hence it is that brotherly love is one of the main marks of true Christianity.[8] And this brotherly love knows no

---

[1] John iv. 7-19.   [2] John iii. 16.   [3] John x. 11.
[4] Luke viii. 3.   [5] Matt. xxv. 40.
[6] 1 John iv. 11-21.   [7] John xiii. 35.
[8] Rom. xii. 10; 1 Thess. iv. 9; Heb. vi. 10; xiii. 1; 1 Pet. i. 22

limits of natural likings, or of race or class or colour. It embraces, in its practical beneficence, all whom God has made, all for whom Christ died.[1] It embraces many whom we are unable to like.

Supernatural Christian love has the effect of enabling us to rise superior to natural feelings, and it sanctifies and exalts our natural relationships. It is meant to be the purifying influence of home-life, of marriage, of patriotism, and of all our relations with our fellow-men. But note that, according to New Testament teaching, the main sphere for the exercise of Christian charity is the family of the Church. The brothers so often alluded to in the epistles[2] are the members of the new brotherhood of mankind made by Christ. A general philanthropy is not a true fulfilment of Christian charity, unless first we love, and show love to, the brotherhood.

St Paul treats of charity as including many Christian virtues. He sums up under this term the main points of the Christian character, depicting that unselfishness which is displayed in all those who are truly conformed to the likeness of Christ. Charity suffereth long and is kind; charity envieth not; charity vaunteth not itself, is not puffed up, doth not behave itself unseemly, seeketh not its own, is not provoked, taketh not account of evil; rejoiceth not in unrighteousness, but rejoiceth with the truth; beareth all things, believeth all things, endureth all things.[3] He who can thus practise charity has indeed begun to learn the spirit of Christ.

Now abideth faith, hope, charity, these three; and the greatest of these is charity.[4] For faith will end in the unveiled knowledge of God; hope will pass into the enjoyment of perfected communion with him; but charity—love of God and love of our brothers—will abide eternally.

---

[1] Rom. xiv. 15; 1 Cor. viii. 11.
[2] Rom. xii. 10; 1 Cor. viii. 12; 1 Thess. iv. 9; Heb. xiii. 1; 1 Pet. ii. 17; 1 John iii. 14, 16; Chap. xi. 1.
[3] 1 Cor. xiii. 4-7.   [4] 1 Cor. xiii. 12.

III

In order to set forth the Christian character in still clearer light, let us consider briefly certain classifications which are stated in the New Testament, or are commonly used in Church teaching.

The seven corporal works of mercy are: To feed the hungry; to give drink to the thirsty; to clothe the naked and to supply the wants of the needy; to show hospitality to travellers and strangers,[1] especially to those who come in the name of Christ; to aid the sick; to show sympathy with prisoners, and the outcasts and down-trodden, and especially those who are persecuted for Christ's sake;[2] and to bury the dead who die in the Lord. Most of these are taken from our Lord's own teaching.[3] They are instances of ways in which Christians may follow the example of him who went about doing good.[4]

The seven spiritual works of mercy are: To convert sinners from the error of their ways;[5] to teach the ignorant; to advise those who are in doubt or perplexity; to comfort mourners and all who are sad; to bear with patience persecutions and troubles brought upon us by others;[6] to forgive those who have wronged us;[7] and to pray for others, both the living and the dead. He who does these is treading even more closely in the footsteps of Christ, whom we see in the gospels converting Matthew[8] and Zacchæus,[9] teaching the ignorant multitude[10] and the woman of Samaria,[11] advising the young ruler who was seeking the way of perfection,[12] comforting Martha and Mary,[13] enduring the contradiction of sinners against himself,[14] and praying for the forgiveness of the soldiers who crucified him.[15]

Christians can perform the corporal works of mercy by supporting the various organisations of charitable relief, such

[1] Heb. xiii. 2. [2] Heb. x. 34; xiii. 3. [3] Matt. xxv. 35 ff.
[4] Acts x. 38. [5] Jas. v. 19, 20.
[6] Matt. v. 38-42; 1 Pet. ii. 19-25. [7] Luke xvii. 3, 4.
[8] Matt. ix. 9. [9] Luke xix. 1-10. [10] Mark x. 1.
[11] John iv. 7-26. [12] Mark x. 17-21. [13] John xi. 21-28.
[14] Heb. xii. 3. [15] Luke xxiii. 34.

as hospitals, convalescent homes, orphanages, asylums for the aged, homes of refuge for the fallen, prisoners' aid societies, etc.; and the spiritual works by supporting secular schools, and church education, and all the work of the Church at home and abroad. But modern organisation should not be regarded as doing away with the need of direct personal service.

The seven root-sins, from which all other sins spring which spoil the Christian character, are: Pride or self-will, the sin of Satan; avarice or covetousness, especially the love of money, which is the false god of this world;[1] lust or impurity, the rebellion of the flesh; envy or jealously, the sin of self-love; gluttony, or intemperance, the sin of self-indulgence; unrighteous anger and hatred, the violation of charity; sloth or discontented depression, which is rebellion against God's will. The virtues which are the opposites to these evil tendencies are: To pride, humility before God and men;[2] to avarice, generosity;[3] to lust, purity and the pure love of Jesus;[4] to envy, brotherly love;[5] to gluttony, self-control and the spirit of mortification;[6] to anger, the meekness and gentleness of Christ;[7] and sloth, cheerful diligence.[8]

There are seven characteristics which have distinguished the Church from the world, and by which each member may test the spirit of his membership. They are:

1. The whole-hearted hatred of sin, as being offensive to the holiness of God and an outrage against his love. This hatred of sin does not involve hatred of sinners: God hates the sin, but loves the sinner. It manifests itself in persistent and determined effort to root out evil, whether in the Christian himself, or in the Church, or in the world around him. The Christian lives in a state of unending war.[9]

2. Bravery in the confession of Christ and bearing witness to the Catholic faith, not merely by spoken words, but also

---

[1] Matt. vi. 24; Col. iii. 5.   [2] Luke xviii. 9-14.
[3] Luke xix. 1-10.   [4] Luke vii. 36-50.   [5] 1 John iii. 10-12.
[6] 1 Cor. ix. 27.   [7] 2 Cor. x. 1.   [8] Matt. xxv. 14-30.
[9] Rom. xii. 9; Eph. vi. 10 ff.; 1 Tim. vi. 12; 2 Tim. iv. 7.

and chiefly by living true to Christian and Catholic principles in his daily life in the world. Everyone who shall confess me before men, said Christ, him shall the Son of man also confess before the angels of God; but he that denieth me in the presence of men shall be denied in the presence of the angels of God.[1]

3. The spirit of self-abnegation and willingness to bear the Cross. Christ's call is : If any man would come after me, let him deny his own self, and take up his cross, and follow me.[2] This is, in Christ's philosophy of life, the practical answer to the problem of pain. The Son of God, out of his divine love for us, willed to take into his own human experience that burden of human suffering which is inexplicable to us.[3] Christ suffered for us, leaving us an example.[4] The disciple of Christ is called not only to endure patiently such troubles of life as come upon all men whether Christian or not; but, much more than that, to take up the cross—that is, to be eager to accept sufferings that he might avoid, if he were not a Christian. He can make the best of his life, not by trying to escape tribulations, but by choosing and embracing them, after the example of his Master and in union with him. And so only can the pain of the world cease to be for him a crushing burden and a source of intolerable perplexity.

4. Active enthusiasm for the will of God. The prayer, Thy will be done, is not merely a cry of resignation, although resignation is a rare Christian virtue. It is a suitable prayer on the lips of the dying; but it is much more suitable as the prayer of first communicants. He who prays this prayer with real meaning pledges himself to strive mightily by God's help for the fulfilment of God's purposes in himself and in the world.

5. Zeal for the extension of the Church : Thy kingdom come. The Church is a militant power, an extending realm. Continual growth has been its characteristic from the beginning.[5] A chief sign of the healthiness of the Church, in each place, has always been missionary zeal for the

---

[1] Luke xii. 9.　　[2] Matt. xvi. 24.　　[3] Chap. ii. 1.
[4] 1 Pet. ii. 21.　　[5] Matt. xiii. 31-33.

spreading of the faith and for the conversion of sinners and unbelievers. Christ goes forth conquering and to conquer,[1] and the Church, when it is faithful to him, takes the field with him.

6. Love of the brotherhood of the Church, which should show itself in unselfish and humble service one of another.[2] The only pre-eminence lawful to the Christian is that which is thus manifested. Whosoever would be first among you shall be your servant, even as the Son of man came not to be ministered unto, but to minister.[3]

7. Gladness of heart,[4] that can persist in spite of worldly troubles and afflictions; the joy that no man can take away,[5] because its source is union with Christ in his risen life. This gladness of Christianity stands in marked contrast with the gloom of the heathen world.[6] It is that joy which began on the first Easter Day; then were the disciples glad, when they saw the Lord.[7] It is the joy which is known only by those who hold nothing back from completeness of surrender to Christ.

IV

In the eight beatitudes of the sermon on the mount, our Lord has given us his own description of the character he desires to see in the members of his kingdom. It is a character that is in marked contrast with the spirit of the world.

It would seem that St Luke[8] gives his words more nearly as they were spoken, while St Matthew[9] supplies a fuller form and an inspired commentary.

1. Blessed are ye poor, for yours is the kingdom of God. Blessed are the poor in spirit, for theirs is the kingdom of heaven. Blessed are they who in their spiritual life realise their need of God. The secret treasures of the kingdom are for those who can humble themselves to receive them.[10]

2. Blessed are ye that weep now, for ye shall laugh.

---

[1] Rev. vi. 2. [2] Gal. v. 13.
[3] Matt. xx. 27, 28; cf. John xiii. 12-17. [4] Phil. iv. 5.
[5] John xvi. 22. [6] Heb. ii. 15. [7] John xx. 20.
[8] Luke vi. 20-23. [9] Matt. v. 3-10. [10] Matt. xviii. 3, 4.

Blessed are they that mourn, for they shall be comforted. This is explained by our Lord's saying to his apostles: Ye now have sorrow, but I will see you again, and your heart shall rejoice, and your joy no man taketh away from you. In the world ye shall have tribulation, but be of good cheer; I have overcome the world.[1]

3. Blessed are the meek, for they shall inherit the earth. Blessed are they in whom is reproduced the meekness of Christ.[2] They are worthy to be members of Christ's kingdom who accept suffering for Christ's sake, and in the spirit of Christ. The true rewards even of this life are not to be won by self-assertion.

4. Blessed are ye that hunger now, for ye shall be filled. Blessed are they that hunger and thirst after righteousness, for they shall be filled—filled with that righteousness of Christ which they desire, which man cannot gain, but must receive.

5. Blessed are the merciful, for they shall obtain mercy. Blessed are those who are merciful even as their Father in heaven is merciful.[3]

6. Blessed are the pure in heart, for they shall see God. Blessed are not only those who are pure from fleshly sins, but also all those whose allegiance is undivided, who seek God only with singleness of heart. They shall find him whom they seek.

7. Blessed are the peace-makers,[4] for they shall be called sons of God. That is, in the broadest sense, blessed are those who are on the side of Christ, to establish his peace in the world. And that peace is established only by war—war against all sin and evil and all the enemies of Christ. Such peace-makers, indeed, merit to be called sons of God, like Christ himself.

8. Blessed are they that have been persecuted for righteousness' sake, for theirs is the kingdom of heaven. Blessed are they who in the bitter school of the world's tribulation,[5] and by their glad acceptance of the cross have been faithful, and have triumphed even in apparent defeat. Blessed is the man that endureth trial, for when he hath been approved, he

[1] John xvi. 22, 33. [2] Matt. xi. 29; 2 Cor. x. 1. [3] Luke vi. 36.
[4] Jas. iii. 18. [5] Rev. vii. 14.

207

shall receive the crown of life, which the Lord hath promised to them that love him.[1]

The Church covers the same ground as does this teaching of our Lord's, when it enumerates twelve Christian characteristics, naming them the twelve fruits of the Spirit:[2] love, joy, peace, long-suffering, kindness, goodness, endurance, gentleness, faithfulness, humility, temperance, purity. The first blessedness is humility; the second joy; the third, long-suffering; the fourth, goodness; the fifth, gentleness and kindness; the sixth, temperance and purity; the seventh, peace; the eighth, endurance and faithfulness. And all the beatitudes are included in love.

Beyond and above all particular statements of Christian virtues there stands the character and example of Christ himself. In him we see the perfection of human nature in union with God. He is the standard of life, the ideal of humanity. Sacramental grace is given to us that we may follow the example of our Saviour Christ[3] in outward act, daily proceeding in all virtue and godliness of living; and also that we may daily mortify all our corrupt affections, and, through the mysterious working of his life in us, may be made like unto him,[4] that Christ may be formed in us.[5]

---

[1] Jas. i. 12.   [2] Gal. v. 22.   [3] Baptismal Service.
[4] 1 John iii. 2.   [5] Gal. iv. 19.

XVII

CHRISTIAN DUTY

THIS is the love of God, that we keep his commandments.[1]
Love is shown by obedience; obedience is the outward and
visible sign of inward and spiritual love. Love is not real
unless it constrains us to fulfil the will of the beloved.

But if love is valueless without obedience, obedience is
valueless without love. Mere conformity to laws from
fear of penalties is slavish. The letter killeth, but the
spirit giveth life.[2] Compliance with the letter of the law is
unworthy of the sons of God, unless it springs from the spirit
of willing obedience. Christian obedience is personal service
of God our Father.

Actions are in themselves neither good nor bad. Their
goodness or badness depends upon the will and purpose and
motive of the doer of them.

When we consider our duty towards God and men, we
are wont to think chiefly of the ten commandments which are
written at the beginning of the laws of Moses.[3] These are
binding upon us, not because they are written in the Old
Testament,[4] but because they are commended to us by the
Church as a summary of Christian moral law. In so com-
mending them, the Church has followed the example of our
Lord, who himself re-enacted several of them in his teaching.[5]
They are to us Christian laws, not Mosaic laws; and they
are to be understood by us, not in their Jewish meanings,
but according to the Christian interpretation given to them
by our Lord and the Church.

The main differences of interpretation are: First, the
Mosaic commandments forbade what is wrong. They said:

[1] 1 John v. 3. [2] 2 Cor. iii. 6. [3] Exod. xx
[4] Chap. xiii. 2. [5] Matt. v. 17-48.

Thou shalt not. The Christian commandments order what is right: Thou shalt; setting before us positive virtues as high ideals at which to aim. For example, Thou shalt not kill, becomes for the Christian, Thou shalt be kind. There is no stopping-place in Christian obedience short of perfection: Ye shall be perfect, as your Father in heaven is perfect.[1]

Secondly, the old commandments forbade certain grave sins, such as murder and adultery. As interpreted by the Church, each commandment is understood to forbid also all lesser sins of the same kind. Thus, Thou shalt not kill, forbids all deeds or words or thoughts or unrighteous anger, and all wanton injuries, as well as actual murder.

Thirdly, the old law took cognisance of sinful acts: the new law of desires and intentions as well as acts. The desire to sin, even if unfulfilled, is sinful. Every one that looketh upon a woman to lust after her hath commited adultery with her already in his heart.[2]

With this preface we may proceed to consider the ten commandments separately.

I

Thou shalt have none other gods but me. *Thou shalt obey the one true God in all things.*

The Church Catechism explains this commandment thus: My duty towards God is to believe in him, to fear him, and to love him, with all my heart, with all my mind, with all my soul, and with all my strength;[3] using words which were cited by our Lord as the first and great commandment. Indeed, all commandments are covered by these words, for every obedience, in belief or worship or life, is but a way of loving God with all our powers, and having him alone as God. This commandment, then, is the law of obedience to God.

[1] Matt. v. 48.   [2] Matt. v. 28; *cf.* Mark vii. 21-23.
[3] Deut. vi. 4, 5; Matt. xxii. 37.

II

Thou shalt not make to thyself any graven image, or likeness of anything: thou shalt not worship it. *Thou shalt worship the true God.*

The Jewish commandment forbade not only the worship of images, such as the heathen associated with the worship of their false gods; but even the making of any image or likeness, for fear it might be wrongly used. The Catholic Church, on the other hand, realising that God has deigned in the Incarnation and sacraments to use material things as the channels of grace, has felt little fear, either of the making of images or of the use of them by the faithful as instruments of their worship. Imaginary pictures of the invisible God have not been widely used, but images of Christ, and especially of Christ crucified, and of the Saints, have been common both in the East and the West from very early days. Signs of respect and reverence to them have been permitted and encouraged, it being understood that the reverence was really shown not to the image in itself, but to that which it betokened. There is little danger of idolatry in the Catholic Church, since the instinctive desire of men to have a God whom they could see and touch has been satisfied by God sending his own Son in the likeness of sinful flesh.[1]

The meaning of the second commandment, in the mind of the Church, is that it is the law of worship: My duty towards God is to worship him, to give him thanks, to put my whole trust in him, and to call upon him—that is, the duty of adoration, thanksgiving, and faithful supplication; and as we are sinners, we may add, under this commandment, the duty of confessing our sinfulness before God.[2]

III

Thou shalt not take the name of the Lord thy God in vain. *Thou shalt reverence what is holy.*

The name of the Lord is understood to denote God himself, and the revelation of God in Jesus Christ his Word;

[1] Rom. viii. 3.   [2] Chap. xiv. 3.

and then, by a natural extension, all that is associated in our minds with the Christian religion; not only images, but also churches consecrated to God, and altars as the thrones of his Son's sacramental presence, and the Bible as containing his revealed truth. This is the law of reverence : My duty towards God is to honour his holy name and his word.

By this commandment there is forbidden, by contrast, any superstitious use of holy things, by attributing to them power in themselves apart from God, or expecting benefit from them apart from faith and prayer; and also all trafficking with the powers of evil : for example, by witchcraft, or the superstitious use of charms. Also there is forbidden irreverence in worship, and all profaning of holy things, and blasphemies, and vain swearing or the idle use of any holy name.

Our Lord, in saying, Swear not at all,[1] stated what he willed to be the state of things in his kingdom on earth, when brotherly love and truthfulness should be universal, and therefore all oaths would be unnecessary. The Church has not regarded his words as forbidding, under present circumstances, the solemn appeal to God in confirmation of statements, as, for example, in courts of law. That this is a right interpretation is shown by the fact that Christ consented to be put under oath, and by various passages of the New Testament.[2]

IV

Remember that thou keep holy the sabbath day. Six days shalt thou labour, and do all that thou hast to do. But the seventh day is the sabbath of the Lord thy God; in it thou shalt do no manner of work, thou, and thy son and thy daughter, thy servant, and thy cattle. *Thou shalt serve God in working and in rest.* My duty towards God is to serve him truly all the days of my life, week-days as well as Sundays.

Man is to be a worker, like God.[3] The duty of earning

[1] Matt. v. 33-37; Jas. v. 10.
[2] Matt. xxvi. 63, 64; Heb. iii. 18; vi. 13-17; vii. 21; Rom. i. 9; ix. 1.   [3] John v. 17.

our livelihood, whether our livelihood is or is not dependent upon our working, is a duty from which no Christian is exempt who is capable of any work or usefulness. But, in an organised community, work does not mean bodily labour only. The scientist, the brain-worker, and the artist are workers, as much as the craftsman or the manual labourer.

To the Christian work is not a curse; it was never meant to be a curse; man worked before the Fall.[1] But it is a universal law: If any will not work neither let him eat.[2] Time and human faculties are gifts from God, to be used for him. Wilful idleness and the unprofitable use of time and the purposeless use of our faculties are sins. The world is God's vineyard, into which we are daily called to work.[3] All work undertaken according to God's will is holy.

The Christian, like Christ, should be able to say of his life's employment, whatever it has been: I have glorified God on the earth, having accomplished the work which he gave me to do.[4] For the chief way in which any man can glorify God is by showing the greatest efficiency possible for him in his daily occupations. Whatsoever ye do, work heartily, as unto the Lord, is the apostle's injunction both to slaves and free-men.[5] To advance in efficiency in our daily work is as much a duty and to God's glory as to advance in our daily prayers; and indeed, work is prayer, if it be done in this way for God.[6]

If work is the universal duty, it is also the universal right. It is the duty of the State—that is, of the men and women who are the State—to do away with unemployment as being evil in the sight of God and an injustice towards their fellow-men.

Secondly, rest is ordered by God, and, as part of rest, lawful recreations. Rest and recreation, equally with work, are necessary for man's well-being. The Church has had scant sympathy with the Puritanism that saw evil in the cheerfulness of recreation. Is any merry? let him sing psalms, said St. James:[7] but psalm-singing is not the only

<hr>

[1] Gen. ii. 15; iii. 19.   [2] 2 Thess. iii. 10.
[3] Matt. xx. 7.   [4] John xvii. 4.
[5] Col. iii. 17, 23.   [6] Chap. xv. 1.   [7] Jas. v. 13.

way of showing cheerfulness, nor to every Christian is it always the natural way. The Church would say also : Is any merry? let him play games; and a game well played, at the right time for playing, is as much to God's glory as is work or prayer.

The Jewish law gave not only one day in the week for rest, but also many days in the year for religious festivals : an example which the Church followed. The Jews kept the seventh day holy; but the Church from the beginning kept the first day, Sunday, as the Lord's Day, in memory of the resurrection;[1] and before long it dropped all observance of the Jewish sabbath.

The rules of the sabbath do not apply to Sunday. The Jewish idea was that all occupation on the sabbath was more or less sinful, and needed to be limited as strictly as possible; the mere cessation from employment was regarded as being in itself to the glory of God. The Christian idea is that the ceasing from ordinary occupations has value chiefly because it sets men free for the direct worship of God, but also because it provides opportunity for necessary rest and recreation. The Church's holidays—the Sundays, and the many other days which it puts on a level with Sunday—are holy-days, because the requirement is that God's worship be put first by the offering of the holy sacrifice. But the Church intends also the holy-days to be holidays.

Our Lord sharply censured the Jewish observance of the sabbath. He taught the Jews that works of necessity, of mercy, and of the service of God,[2] were lawful on the sabbath. Much more are they lawful on Sunday. Nor are games or any other innocent recreations on Sundays condemned by the Church; provided that the obligation of being present at Mass is duly observed; and provided that others are not hindered, for the commandment requires us to allow due Christian rest to others, and even to animals, as well as to ourselves.

The note of the Church's teaching about Sunday observance is not Don't, but Do. It does not lay down a

[1] Matt. xxviii. 1; John xx. 26; Acts xx. 7; I Cor. xvi. 2; Rev. i. 10.
[2] Matt. xii. 4, 5, 12.

number of prohibitions, like those imposed upon the Jews, to produce an inactive dullness; but it gives one positive command of the minimum obligation—the Lord's service on the Lord's Day. Beyond that it allows great liberty of action, in the same spirit of festival joy. The Church allows or forbids on Sunday only what it allows or forbids on such feasts as Christmass or Ascension Day. It is true that a devout Christian will often be glad to use his Sunday for other worship besides Mass, and for meditation and receiving instruction; but these are not an obligation upon all. Christian teachers act unwisely when, by the multiplying of obligations or by undue restrictions, they make Sunday burdensome and vexatious to the young and to those who are spiritually immature.

The feasts usually regarded as of obligation in the English Church are Easter, Pentecost or Whitsunday, and all Sundays; Circumcision,[1] Epiphany,[2] the Purification of St Mary,[3] the Annunciation,[4] the Ascension, SS. Peter and Paul,[5] Michaelmass,[6] All-Saints,[7] Christmass.[8] Many also observe other feast-days, such as those of the Apostles and St John Baptist,[9] Corpus Christi (the festival of the blessed sacrament),[10] St Joseph,[11] the Visitation of St Mary,[12] the Transfiguration,[13] the Holy Name of Jesus,[14] the Assumption of St Mary,[15] and her Conception[16] and Nativity.[17]

The fourth commandment is the law of holy joy in labour and in rest.

V

Honour thy father and thy mother. *Thou shalt give honour to whom honour is due.*[18] This is the law of Christian humility.

In this commandment many duties are included. The

[1] January 1 [2] January 6. [3] February 2.
[4] March 25. [5] June 29. [6] September 29.
[7] November 1. [8] December 25. [9] June 24.
[10] Usually on the first Thursday after Trinity.
[11] March 19. [12] July 2. [13] August 6.
[14] August 7. [15] August 15. [16] December 8.
[17] September 8. [18] Rom. xiii. 7.

Church Catechism explains it thus: My duty towards my neighbour is to love, honour, and succour my father and mother; to honour and obey the king and all that are put in authority under him; to submit myself to all my governors, teachers, spiritual pastors and masters; to order myself lowly and reverently to all my betters. The Christian principle is: In lowliness of mind let each esteem others better than himself.[1]

It is necessary for a Christian to recognise that he has betters. By that term the Church means all those who are in fact better than we are, and also those who hold such positions in regard to us as call for our respect. But according to Church teaching, Better does not mean Better-off. The rich are not to be regarded as our betters merely because of their wealth, unless they have some other claim upon our respect. But our Lord and his apostles recognised class distinctions, based on other considerations than those of money,[2] and taught the mutual obligations of class to class.

The Christian owes duty first to his parents.[3] That is a natural obligation, and in all natural obligations the Christian sees the will of God.

Secondly, to the Church, its universal laws, and its local bye-laws, and to the ministers of the Church.[4]

Thirdly, to the civil government, its laws and its representatives. Be subject, wrote St Peter, to every ordinance of man for the Lord's sake.[5] And St Paul taught: Let every soul be in subjection to the higher powers, for the powers that be are ordained of God.[6] And our Lord taught the same principles when he told the Jews to render unto Caesar that which is Caesar's.[7] Rebellion and revolution can sometimes be justified, when civil authority has been wrongly usurped or is unjustly used: but the normal rule is that those who are in fact accepting a government, and

[1] Phil. ii. 3.
[2] Matt. xxiii. 2; John xix. 11; Acts xxiii. 5; Rom. xiii. 7, etc.
[3] Mark vii. 8-13; Eph. vi. 1-3; Col. iii. 20.
[4] 1 Cor. ix. 1-14; 1 Thess. v. 12, 13; 1 Tim. v. 17 ff.; Heb. xiii. 7, 17.   [5] 1 Pet. ii. 13-17.   [6] Rom. xiii. 1-7.   [7] Mark xii. 17.

deriving benefits from it, may not cast off the obligation of obedience to it.

Christians are bound to take their due part, according to their positions and capacities, in bearing the burden of the State of which they are members, and to the town in which they live. They will pay rates and taxes, not only under compulsion, but willingly for conscience' sake. They are responsible for making right and conscientious use of their power to vote. No one may stand aloof from his community. As they share in the advantages which it provides, so they must share in the burdens and responsibilities it imposes.

Patriotism and the sense of nationality are natural and right. St Paul appealed to the Jewish pride of race, arguing that *Noblesse oblige*.[1] It is good that a man should feel that he is part of a body greater than his lonely self, and be ready to subordinate his private interests to the welfare of the whole. But Christianity cannot tolerate the abuse of this instinct, which prompts a man to say: My country, right or wrong. There are higher laws than that of patriotism. And in the parable of the Good Samaritan, our Lord taught that nationalism should not be debased into a narrow-minded hostility or indifference to other nations.[2] The Christian sees all the nations of the world being brought out of their separation and their conflicting interests into the brotherhood of the Church. His sense of patriotism finds its chief scope in his service and devotion to the Catholic Church.

Fourthly, the Christian owes duty to his school-teachers in childhood, and to his employers in later life.[3] The fulfilment of duty to employers is not, for the Christian, merely a matter of exchanging so much labour for so much wage; it is a service rendered to God. For example, take the extremest case, slavery. We know that to hold men as slaves is not consistent with Christianity; but the apostles, who found slavery an existing fact, were concerned to urge upon Christian slaves obedience even to hard masters, as a particular instance of Christlikeness.[4]

[1] Rom. ii. 17.23. [2] Luke x. 25-37.
[3] Eph. vi. 5-8; Col. iii. 22-25; 1 Tim. vi. 1-2; Titus ii. 9, 10.
[4] 1 Pet. ii. 18-25.

217

Our duty to our betters implies the duty of our betters to us;[1] and the underling is justified in doing all he can, within his obedience to God, to oblige those above him to fulfil their duty. But the failure of the one party in the mutual obligation does not exempt the other party from it.

There are two exceptions only to the duty of obedience. First, we may not obey human authority in anything that is against God's law. We ought to obey God rather than men.[2] And secondly, our obedience to a lower authority must sometimes give way before our duty to a higher. Christ showed this when he said to St Mary and St Joseph : Wist ye not that I must be about my Father's business?[3] and again when he said : He that loveth father or mother more than me is not worthy of me.[4]

VI

Thou shalt do not murder. *Thou shalt be kind.* My duty towards my neighbour is to hurt nobody by word or deed, and to bear no malice nor hatred in my heart.

Our Lord extended the prohibition of deeds of murder to the prohibition of words or even thoughts of unrighteous anger. Quarrels arising from selfishness are absolutely forbidden, and also the spirit of revengefulness, and the hatred of persons even if evil (as distinct from the right hatred of evil itself). The spirit of a Christian should be one of kindness, gentleness, meekness;[5] willing rather to suffer wrong, so far as he himself is concerned, than to exact his utmost rights against others.[6]

Revenge is never right, if its motive is self-gratification; but it is often right for a State or an individual to procure the punishment of evil-doers, whether for the sinner's sake, or for the sake of others, or for the vindication of righteousness. Punishment that is merely vindictive, or for the

[1] Rom. xii. 6-8; Eph. v. 25-33; vi. 4, 9; Col. iii. 19-21; iv. 1; 1 Tim. iii. 1-13; 1 Pet. iii. 7.
[2] Acts v. 29.   [3] Luke ii. 49.   [4] Matt. x. 37.
[5] Matt. v. 21, 22; Eph. iv. 26, 31, 32; Col. iii. 12-15.
[6] Matt. v. 38-42; 1 Cor. vi. 1-8; Jas. iv. 1 *ff*.

indulgence of angry passion, is not right; but the punishment of an erring child, or of a criminal, is often a duty; and the weak kindness that would remit the penalty may be a failure in true charity.

Similarly the waging of private or public war is justifiable, if the motive be right, such as self-defence, or the defence of the nation against aggression, or for the righteous punishment of the aggressor; but not for such motives as a selfish desire of self-assertion or national aggrandisement. When Christ's kingdom on earth is accepted universally and established, all occasions for war will have ceased, and towards this end all Christians should strive. But, under present circumstances, the rude appeal to war is often necessary, a lesser evil to prevent a greater. War has to be waged to establish peace. If it be possible, as much as lieth in you, be at peace with all men, says St Paul;[1] but the possibility does not lie entirely in oneself. To take the simplest case : a man would be bound to fight even to death, if that were the only way possible to defend his wife from outrage. Again, the Christian is often bound to enter into contention for the sake of being true to his principles. Our Lord said : Think ye that I am come to give peace in the earth? I tell you, Nay; but rather division.[2]

The Church has always allowed Christians to serve in the army. It is not the duty of the soldier to decide on the rightfulness of any war in which the terms of his service or his obedience to authority compel him to fight.

Our Lord has taught us to love our enemies.[3] By love he does not mean feelings of liking or intimate friendship, but practical duties of self-forgetting charity. A Christian fulfils this precept adequately if he forgoes all selfish desire of retaliation, and prays for those who have wronged him, and is willing to forgive any offender as soon as the offender desires to be forgiven. He cannot bestow forgiveness on one who will not receive it.[4]

The law of kindness enjoins upon Christians the duty of taking their due share in social work; ameliorating evil

[1] Rom. xii. 18. [2] Luke xii. 51-53.
[3] Matt. v. 43; Rom. xii. 19-21. [4] Luke xvii. 3, 4.

conditions of living; taking interest in the downtrodden
and outcast, and endeavouring to gain for them that justice
which is so much more valuable than charitable relief; and
living a life of unselfish service of their fellows, and especially
of Christ's little ones, those who from whatever cause are
unable to help themselves.[1]

VII

Thou shalt not commit adultery. *Thou shalt be pure.*
My duty is to keep my body in temperance, soberness, and
chastity.

This commandment forbids all sexual intercourse except
in wedlock, and all indulgence of the sexual powers, whether
in the single or the married state, contrary to the laws of God
and the Church. The world attaches less censure to the
man than to the woman : but Christian law knows no such
distinction. Acts of immorality are equally sinful in a man
or in a woman.

The exciting of sexual passion by the self-abuse of a male
or a female alone is condemned by Christianity as unnatural
and sinful. As this habit when fully formed is hard to break,
and has a peculiarly weakening effect upon the character of
a Christian, it is very important that parents and guardians
should take care to keep boys and girls from contracting it,
especially by giving them a clean knowledge of the mystery
of sex.

Intercourse between two of the same sex, or between a
human being and an animal, is forbidden both by the law of
nature and by the Christian Church.[2]

Under this commandment there is forbidden all unclean
speech and indulgence in unclean thoughts; not the mere
occurring of such thoughts in the mind, but the wilful
retention and enjoyment of them.

All other sins of the flesh also are forbidden, such as
intemperance in food or drink, or excessive luxuriousness or
other indulgence of the body. Temperance, self-control,

[1] 1 John iv. 7-21.
[2] Lev. xx. 15, 16; Rom. i. 26, 27. See further; Chap. xviii.

and purity of mind and body are enjoined. In the partnership of soul and body the soul is to be the ruling partner. We are to bring our bodies into subjection.[1]

Temperance is a duty, and has application to all bodily desires. The word is often wrongly applied to abstinence from alcoholic drinks only. And frequently total abstinence from alcohol is proclaimed as if it were in itself a virtue, and therefore a duty upon all. It is true that grave evils result from excessive drinking, and there are many warnings against it in holy Scripture.[2] Total abstinence may be a safe course for all; and for some it is necessary for the avoiding of temptation. But the Church does not teach that drinking in moderation is sinful. Alcohol is a gift of God. Every creature of God is good,[3] and nothing is to be rejected, if it be received with thanksgiving. Not the use, but the abuse, of alcohol is wrong. Wine, that maketh glad the heart of man,[4] and was drunk by our Lord himself,[5] and provided by him at Cana,[6] and sanctified for sacramental use, cannot be evil. The prohibition of alcohol by law is within the competence of any State; but, if pressed too far, it is of doubtful expediency, as it may encourage other evils as great as those it prevents. A dry State is not, merely on that account, a more Christian State.[7]

VIII

Thou shalt not steal. *Thou shalt be honest.* My duty is to be true and just in all my dealings; to keep my hands from picking and stealing.[8]

Dishonesty shows itself in many forms : the appropriation

---

[1] 1 Cor. ix. 27.   [2] Prov. xx. 1; xxiii. 29-32; Isa. v. 11 *ff.*, etc.
[3] 1 Tim. iv. 4.   [4] Ps. civ. 15.
[5] Luke vii. 34.   [6] John ii. 1-11.
[7] For other New Testament teaching relating to this commandment, see Matt. v. 27-32; Luke xxi. 34; John viii. 1-11; Rom. i. 24-27; vi. 12-14; viii. 12, 13; xiii. 11-14; xiv. 13-xv. 3; 1 Cor. v. 1-5, 11; vi. 9-20; ix. 24-27; 2 Cor. vi. 14—vii. 1; Gal. v. 19, 20; Eph. v. 3-7; Col. iii. 5-7; 1 Thess. iv. 2-8; 1 Tim. iv. 1-5; Titus i. 15; ii. 1-6; Heb. xiii. 4; 1 Pet. ii. 11; iv 3, 4.
[8] Eph. iv. 28.

of the goods of another without his consent; making unjust bargains by cheating; defrauding the Government or business companies; wilful failure to stand by contracts made; refusal to pay debts; fixing unfair prices; paying insufficient wages; slack performance of paid work, etc. Further, honesty is truth in act; it is justice in practice; and it broadens out into honourable conduct and generosity. Much that is legally honest is not honourable. Stinginess and meanness may be consistent with honesty, but they are contrary to the spirit of generosity.

There are great difficulties involved in the practical application of the principle of Christian honesty to commercial life, under the present conditions of a system of commerce which is out of accord with Christian law and charity. It would take too long to deal with these in detail. The Christian needs to seek particular guidance in each case; as also concerning the difficult duty of making restitution for injuries done to others. The one guiding rule in all cases is the principle of unselfishness: My duty to my neighbour is to do to all men as I would they should do unto me.

The pursuit of wealth, as a ruling purpose in life, is contrary to Christian teaching. Ye cannot serve God and money.[1] It is better to be poor than to be rich; and the love of money is a snare and a hindrance to salvation.[2] Here there is an immense conflict between the principles of Christianity and the practice of the world. The true Christian attitude is expressed in the words: Be ye free from the love of money; be content with such things as ye have, for Christ hath said, I will in no wise fail thee, nor forsake thee.[3] Ye know the grace of our Lord Jesus Christ, that, though he was rich, yet for your sake he became poor, that ye through his poverty might become rich.[4] Our Lord's teaching: Be not anxious about the morrow,[5] does not forbid ordinary prudence and provision for the future.

[1] Matt. vi. 24.
[2] Luke vi. 24; xii. 15-21; Matt. vi. 24-34; xiii. 22; 1 Tim. vi. 6-10, 17-19; Jas. ii. 1-6; v. 1-4.
[3] Heb. xiii. 5.   [4] 2 Cor. viii. 9.   [5] Matt. vi. 33, 34.

He did not say, Take no thought for the morrow. But it does very distinctly turn the mind from the pursuit even of a competence to that of higher things. Seek ye first the kingdom of God and his righteousness, and all these things shall be added unto you. It follows that much that is extolled by the world and even by some Christians under the name of thrift would be condemned by the Church as avarice and sinful love of money. At the same time it is true that the mere possession of wealth is not wrong; for the rich man can regard his wealth as a trust for the benefit of others. It is the selfish love of money, the love of it for its own sake, or for one's own sake, that is sinful.[1]

It is often said that gambling is a sin; but it is hard to see on what principle that way of risking one's money is to be regarded as sinful which would not also condemn all forms of business. The Church does not censure gambling in principle, but it warns the Christian against obvious dangers and temptations involved in it, and especially in its excess.

<h2 style="text-align:center">IX</h2>

Thou shalt not bear false wtness against thy neighbour. *Thou shalt be truthful.* My duty is to keep my tongue from evil speaking, lying, and slandering.

As truth is the character of God, it should be the character of man made in God's image. The obligation to truth also follows from the fact of our brotherhood in Christ. Putting away lying, speak ye truth each one with his neighbour, for we are members one of another.[2]

If there is no intention of deception, there is no sin; as for example in the common use of Not at home, meaning, Not receiving visitors. On the other hand, the guilt of a lie is increased by false swearing; or by the inclusion of other sins with the lie, such as the malicious injury of another's reputation by false gossip, scandal, backbiting, or slander. In cases of wilful lying, there lies on the penitent sinner the duty of making satisfaction, and of putting truth in the place of the falsehood.

[1] Mark x. 23, 24. *Cf*. Chap. xv. 2.   [2] Eph. iv. 25.

Under this commandment we may place the prohibition of all sins of speech of whatever kind, and the duty of controlling the tongue. The tongue is a gift of God, for the use of which we are responsible to him; it has become a restless evil, full of deadly poison.[1] We must let no corrupt speech proceed out of our mouth.[2] The ruling principles in speech are, as regards oneself, sincerity; as regards others, charity. Our Lord condemns idle words, that is, words uttered without purpose.[3]

The duty of speaking truth implies, as its root, the duty of thinking truth. Truthfulness begins within the mind. The things which proceed out of the mouth come forth from the heart. . . . Out of the heart come forth evil thoughts . . . false witness . . .[4] The truth-loving man is concerned first to have a right judgment in all things, to have truth in the inward parts,[5] to free himself from narrow-minded prejudice and the bias of his temperament and the influences of faulty education or environment, and to occupy his mind habitually with all that makes for truth. Whatsoever things are true, just, pure, lovely, of good report, think on these things.[6]

x

Thou shalt not covet thy neighbour's house, nor anything that is his. *Thou shalt be content with God's will.*

Covetousness, envy, jealousy are marked as sinful; but not the lawful spirit of emulation on which all progress depends. The apostles did not proclaim equality in this world, either as an existent fact or as a state of things to be aimed at. They asserted the equality in Christ of those who in the world remained unequal. Slaves remained slaves, but they were received into the Church as brothers.

On the other hand, neither the apostles nor the Church taught that a Christian must of necessity remain in the social rank or worldly condition in which he was born. It certainly was not, in their minds, a great matter that a man should get on in the world; but this was partly because they expected

---

[1] Jas. iii. 1-11.   [2] Eph. iv. 29.   [3] Matt. xii. 36.
[4] Matt. xv. 18, 19.   [5] Ps. li. 6.   [6] Phil. iv. 8.

the end of the world so soon that it was hardly worth while to consider any change of condition.[1] But the duty of efficiency in work involves the possibility of promotion and of rising above the condition in which one was born; and the rise can readily be justified, from a Christian point of view as opening the door to greater usefulness for the Lord's sake.

The Church Catechism has often been misinterpreted on this point, as if it aims at "keeping down the lower classes". Yet the words are plain enough : My duty is not to covet or desire other men's goods, but to learn and labour truly to get my own living, and to do my duty in that state of life unto which it shall please God (not, it has pleased God) to call me. The natural aspiration of all high-spirited men to make the most of themselves, and to have scope for the development of their powers, is a God-given instinct, to follow which can be wrong only if the motive or the manner be selfish. We ought to trade with the talents God has given us, that he may have the increase.[2]

Similarly, there is a righteous discontent with conditions of life which tend to deprive many men and classes at the present time not only of this scope, but even of the necessaries of life. This discontent is readily distinguishable from the uneasy selfishness that prompts a man to grudge to others the possession of good things, merely on the ground that he himself does not possess them also; and from the discontent of a man who is really quarrelling not with the selfishness of the world, but with the will of God for him.

The tenth commandment is the law of effort in the spirit of unselfishness.

---

[1] 1 Cor. vii. 20-24, 29.   [2] Matt. xxv. 14-30.

XVIII

HOLY MARRIAGE

I

CHRISTIAN marriage is a sacrament, by which a Christian man and woman are united by God, either to each alone, until the death of one or other. The two persons become by their marriage one flesh in God's sight; that is to say, they become one flesh in reality, for that which God sees is what really is. The sacrament also conveys grace to enable them to act rightly in accordance with the fact of their union, to be faithful to one another, and to live in wedlock according to God's laws.

The sexual union of man with woman is the natural state for adult mankind; and therefore, like everything that is truly natural, it is sinless, and indeed holy, as being ordained by God.

Mankind has been created for God, and man's true end is to serve God's will. Therefore the fulfilment of this or any other human desire must be brought about in accordance with God's will made known to man; or else it becomes perverted and sinful, and ceases to be truly natural. But we know that man's nature has been perverted by the Fall, so that he is prone to act for ends and gratifications of his own, apart from or against God. In no sphere of life is this perversion of human nature more obvious than in matters of sex.

Christ our Lord in his teaching recalled mankind from perverted to true nature; from that which is natural to animals to that which is natural to those who are made in the image of God, endowed not only with bodies, but also with controlling souls; from that which has become second nature to fallen man to that which would have remained natural to him, had he never rebelled against God and gone the way of his own selfishness. Christ bade men and women subject their passions to the will of God the Creator, which he reasserted; that so sexual intercourse might again become sanctified, as God from the beginning intended it to be.[1]

Christian marriage, then, was ordained as a remedy against sin;[2] providing a high road approved by God for the sexual instincts, which if not directed and controlled run riot under every impulse of passion.

Again, every human instinct is given us for a purpose. Its gratification is not an end in itself. Our instinct to eat and drink is not given merely for the gratification of appetite, but rather the pleasure we feel in eating and drinking is given us with a view to our physical and mental well-being. Similarly, the pleasure experienced in the fulfilment of the sexual instinct is given by God for the well-being of the man and the woman, through the right exercise of their powers. Also it has an end beyond them, namely, the replenishment of the world by the procreation of children. The end of Christian marriage, however, is not simply procreation, but rather procreation under conditions which will provide for the spiritual as well as for the physical nurture of the offspring.

Further, the union of man and woman is not only a union in the flesh. The distinction of male and female is a matter of the spirit as well as of the body. Christian marriage, therefore, has the purpose of binding the one to the other for mutual society, help, and comfort.

II

In marked criticism of the Mosaic Law, which with some limitations allowed polygamy and concubinage and the divorce of the wife, our Lord taught that the purpose of God the Creator was that one man should cleave to one woman. He said: From the beginning of the creation God made them male and female. For this cause shall a man leave his father and mother, and shall cleave to his wife; and the twain shall become one flesh: so that they are no more twain, but one flesh.[3]

[1] Mark x. 6-9.   [2] Marriage Service.   [3] Mark x. 6-8.

227

If we accept our Lord's word, as Christians are bound to do, we must believe that monogamy, the union of one with one, being God's intention for mankind, is the state that is most truly suitable to human nature and beneficial to mankind. Monogamy is more truly natural than polygamy or concubinage. Our Lord does not say that monogamy was in fact the primitive custom of mankind. It may be that, in this as in other matters, sin entered in at the very beginning of the race, and thwarted the purpose of the Creator. The selfish aggressiveness of the stronger sex may, in fact, have established polygamy and concubinage from the outset, or the earliest custom may have been as much promiscuity of sexual relation among mankind as we see among the animals. But if this was so, the fact would not falsify our Lord's teaching as to what was God's original purpose to which he recalls mankind. And certain notable results have appeared in the world wherever the principle of monogamy has been accepted, which go far towards establishing the truth of our Lord's words even by the light of our own experience. First, the status of women has been raised from that of being the chattels of men, with few or no rights either in sexual relation or social life; as is their status in heathendom, and as it was even in Judaism.[1] And this improvement of status has made possible the elevation of women in every department of life. Secondly, it is monogamy that has created the family, consisting of father, mother, and children, with its wholesome discipline of mutual responsibility, and its many obligations of unselfishness.

Since the divine intention for mankind is one man, one wife, it follows that divorce and re-marriage are contrary to the divine will. What God hath joined together, let not man put asunder.[2] God's act in marriage can be annulled only by God's act in death. The Mosaic Law had limited a man's right to divorce his wife to the one case of her unchastity.[3] Amid the unbridled lust of heathendom, it could

[1] Cf. Exod. xx. 17: thy neighbour's house, wife, servant, ox, ass. See section vi.
[2] Mark x. 9.   [3] Deut. xxiv. 1-4.

do no more, because of the hardness of men's hearts. Our Lord totally abolished divorce, and reasserted the divine ideal of marriage.

This teaching, that divorce is forbidden for Christians, and that no divorce enacted by man can or does break the bond of wedlock, is stated by St Mark and St Luke and also by St Paul.[1] In St Matthew our Lord is represented as if he allowed the one concession permitted by the Mosaic Law.[2] This deprives his teaching of consistency, making him say : Because of the hardness of your hearts Moses allowed divorce in cases of unchastity, but from the beginning divorce was contrary to the mind of the Creator; and I say unto you just what Moses said. But it appears plainly, from a comparison of the parallel passages in Mark and Matthew, that the Matthæan form is not the original. It is probable that the Jewish hardness of heart continued among the Jewish Christians, and that the exception given in Matthew started as a mistaken interpretation among them of Christ's teaching. The interpretation was the more plausible because some Jewish teachers of the time had greatly extended the Mosaic concession so as to allow divorce for any cause.[3]

III

The law of the Catholic Church has always forbidden both polygamy and concubinage; and has disallowed remarriage after divorce, asserting the indissolubility of the marriage-bond. But, because the Matthæan exception is found in Holy Writ, dispensations from the law are sometimes granted by authority in the Eastern Church to the innocent party in a divorce suit. It is not acknowledged, however, that the original marriage-bond has been broken; and dispensation is not granted to the guilty party. The Western Church, with a few exceptions here and there at different times, has not been accustomed to grant dispensation to either party; but holds that any new union after divorce is adulterous, so long as the original partner is living.

---

[1] Mark x. 1-11; Luke xvi. 18; 1 Cor. vii. 10, 11.
[2] Matt. v. 32; xix. 9.   [3] Matt. xix. 3.

Even the separation of husband and wife has not been encouraged. In cases where the sinfulness of one party has rendered the maintenance of wedlock intolerable, separation has been permitted, to prevent greater evil or for the sake of the children. But the allowing of separation does not carry with it any sanction of a new marriage.

The Church everywhere has allowed widowers or widows to marry again. The relation in the flesh does not remain after death. We know, indeed, little about the resurrection-body.[1] But our Lord has taught us that they who are accounted worthy to attain to the resurrection from the dead neither marry nor are given in marriage; for neither can they die any more; for they are equal unto the angels.[2] Where there is no death, there is no need for procreation. In our spiritual bodies,[3] therefore, the relations of sex will no longer be as in this life. This does not mean that the true love of man and wife, which is the essence of Christian marriage, is for this life's duration only; or that whatever relationships of love and friendship are formed here will be merged hereafter in one uniform and undistinguished love of each for all. All that is implied is that particular love and devotion will be expressed by spiritual bodies in a manner different from that of natural bodies. According to our Lord's teaching, therefore, no difficulty is involved in the thought of second marriages. On the other hand, though they are allowed, they are not highly commended in the New Testament.[4]

St Paul did not approve of the marriage of a Christian with an unbeliever. He taught : Be not unequally yoked with unbelievers; for what fellowship have righteousness and inquity? or what communion hath light with darkness?[5] He was the first to write down what has remained the judgment of the Church. The marriage of a Christian with a heathen, or a Jew, or a Mohammedan, or with a baptised person who is excommunicate, has always been repugnant to the Christian sense. Such marriages have not always been actually forbidden by the Church, nor always regarded

---

[1] Chap. xx. 3.　　[2] Luke xx. 35, 36.　　[3] 1 Cor. xv. 44.
[4] 1 Cor. vii. 34-40; 1 Tim. v. 9.　　[5] 2 Cor. vi. 14.

as meriting censure; but they have always been disapproved;
and they are not considered to be sacramental unions, because the intention of monogamy is not necessarily present
in the mind of the non-Christian. Similarly, marriages contracted by non-Christians are not held to be still binding
after the conversion of one party to Christianity. The
newly made Christian is free either to remain or to
depart.[1]

The marriage of a Christian with a catechumen preparing
for baptism and for full membership is permissible, as the
catechumen is already a Christian believer. The marriage
of a Catholic with a member of a Protestant sect is gravely
undesirable. The English marriage service assumes that
both parties are communicants. Recent Roman Catholic
ruling makes such a marriage invalid.

The marriage of Christians with near relations in blood
is forbidden by a human instinct that is almost universal,
and by the Old Testament law,[2] and by the Christian
Church.

Also, the Church took over from the Old Testament the
belief that close relationship by marriage is a bar to lawful
wedlock equally with blood-relationship. And this would
seem to be the fair conclusion from our Lord's teaching that
the twain are no more twain, but one flesh. Thus the deceased wife's sister is the widower's sister, and the deceased
husband's brother is the widow's brother, because the husband and the wife were made one.[3]

The law that relationship by marriage is an impediment
to Christian marriage has been maintained in the Church
practically without any exception. But in modern times the
stringency of the law has been greatly relaxed in the Roman
Catholic and Eastern parts of the Church, by the growing
frequency of granting dispensations to meet hard cases.
Hard cases make bad law. Still, as this law does not rest
on any explicit word of our Lord's, it may be argued that it
is a regulation of the Church dispensable by Church authority
rather than a divine law admitting of no relaxation. The
Church of England, however, maintains the law in its full

[1] i Cor. vii. 12-16. [2] Lev. xviii. 6-18. [3] But see note, page 280.

strictness, and has not admitted the lawfulness or the efficacy
or dispensation in such cases.

A table of the degrees of relationship within which people
may not marry is added to the Prayer Book. This table lays
down no restriction that is not sanctioned by the common
voice of the universal Church. In earlier times the forbidden
degrees were more numerous; as they still are in other parts
of the Church.

IV

Christian marriage, rightly contracted, is a sacrament.
That is to say, it is an outward form through which God
acts with definite and certain result, and through which his
grace is conveyed to the contracting parties.

For the validity of the sacrament, there is required (1) that
the parties in it be Christians, for only Christians are able to
receive sacramental grace; (2) that they pledge themselves
to each other openly before witnesses, freely, without constraint on either side, and with full knowledge of what they
are doing; (3) that the pledge is to monogamous union and
until death of the one or the other; (4) that their intention
is to consummate the marriage, and that they are physically
capable of marriage; (5) that neither is bound by a previous
marriage-bond, or by a solemn vow to single life; (6) that
the Church's laws of the forbidden degrees are not
violated.

If any of these conditions is lacking, the sacrament is not
valid : that is, the Church does not believe that the marriage
is ratified by God, or that sacramental grace is given.

When a Christian man and woman, under these conditions, give themselves either to other, their state as man and
wife is thereby established. The parties themselves are the
ministers of the sacrament. The function of the priest at a
marriage is to bestow upon it the Church's blessing. It is not
fitting that Catholics entering into the married state should
do so without coming to the Church for the priestly benediction; but the act of the priest is not essential to the validity
of the sacrament. Marriages of Church-members before a
civil registrar, or by any method accepted by law or local

232

custom, are valid, if the conditions mentioned above are fulfilled.

By the common custom of the Church the celebration of marriage is forbidden at certain seasons of the year, of which the chief are Advent and Lent; but this regulation has not always been observed, and the disregard of it does not make a marriage invalid.

v

Besides being a sacrament, Christian marriage is also a civil contract, recognised and regulated by the State. It is right that the State should lay down the regulations which it considers necessary for the maintenance of public morals; and as the State has to decide on questions such as the legitimacy of children and the rights of inheritance that may come into discussion in its courts of law, it is necessary for it to say under what conditions it recognises a marriage as legal. Christians are bound in conscience to comply with the laws of the State concerning marriage, provided that they do not conflict with the laws of God and the Church.

Thus, the State in different countries has made different regulations concerning the registration of marriages, the authorisation of certain places for marriages, or certain persons as civil officers of marriage, the limitation of the celebration of marriage to certain hours of the day, etc.; and in some countries a civil contract is required by law apart from any religious marriage service. If such requirements are not complied with, the State does not regard the marriage as legal. Most of the State's regulations have been enacted to prevent secret unions, and to safeguard the civil rights of the contracting parties.

The legality of a marriage, which is the concern of the State, is to be carefully distinguished from its validity as a sacrament, which depends upon the laws of God and the Church.

It has sometimes happened that a State, if it is not guided by Christian principles, or if it has to legislate for non-

Christians, has legalised marriages which are not lawful or valid according to Church law. When this is the case, Catholics are bound not to enter into any marriage contrary to the laws of the State; but they are not justified in contracting every marriage which the State regards as legal.

This conflict between Church and State exists at the present time in most countries. In England the State has legalised marriage with the deceased wife's sister and the marriage of either party in a divorce suit, after the decree of divorce has been made absolute in the courts.[1] But the Church's laws and the principles of Christianity are not thereby altered. Acts of Parliament cannot alter the laws of the Church so as to free the conscience; still less can they alter the laws of God. The new unions of those who have been divorced may be respectable in the eyes of the law and the offspring legitimate. None the less, the unions of Christians under such circumstances are sinful and adulterous. It is of the highest importance that those who are living under English law should see this clearly, that State legislation does not make allowable what Christ has not allowed; for it is probable that the variance between Church and State will grow wider as time goes on, under the influence of the general moral laxity of the age. In the matter of divorce, Christ did not hestiate to place himself in opposition both to the Jewish law[2] and to that of the Roman State.[3] So for Christians there is no choice. When the civil law is in conflict with the Christian law, we must obey God rather than man.

VI

St Paul taught that Christian marriage is typical of the union between Christ and his spouse the Church. The love which Christ has for the Church, and the subordination of the Church to him, in their mutual self-surrender, is to be copied in his members by the self-sacrificing love of the husband and the loving obedience of the wife.[4]

[1] But see page 280.   [2] Mark x. 11.   [3] Mark x. 12.   [4] Eph. v. 22-33.
234

The duty of the wife to obey her husband, which is taught in holy Scripture,[1] is emphasised by the English Church more strongly than by any other part of the Catholic Church. In every partnership one partner must in the last resort be predominant, and Christianity assigns that office to the husband. But the wife's duty of obedience implies on the part of the husband the duty of rendering honour to the wife.[2] There is to be reality of partnership; the surrender of the one to the other by the marriage-vows is complete and absolute; the responsibility of each to the other is equal. Christianity by no means leaves the woman at the mercy of the man's caprices, nor does it sanction the man making his wife the mere victim of his selfishness. Christianity, and Christianity alone, has raised woman to equality with man, to that Christian equality which is never inconsistent with subordination. The Church, in its devotion to blessed Mary and her sacred motherhood, has recognised that God, by making her the agent of the Incarnation, has magnified all womanhood.

Consistently with this, the Church does not say that there is any activity of life from which women are debarred by the divine will, except that of the sacred ministry.[3] The Church is not antagonistic to, it must be sympathetic with, that desire for fuller life and wider scope which has moved women in recent years. It cannot but be sympathetic with that desire, and opposed to the selfish exclusiveness of men. But, at the same time, the Church is opposed to the spirit of self-assertiveness that tended to mar the movement. The only ambition which the Christian Church approves, whether in men or women, is the ambition to serve.[4] And as motherhood is the natural lot of a woman, by which she may realise the fulfilment of her nature and attain to fulness of life, it follows that for most women the true sphere of ambition and of service is the home.

The English marriage service represents the married state as one of equal partnership, with equal duties of mutual

---

[1] Col. iii. 18; Eph. v. 22-24; 1 Pet. iii. 1-6.
[2] 1 Pet. iii. 7; Col. iii. 18, 19.   [3] Chap. x. 2.   [4] Luke xxii. 27.

love, honour, and service; with equal obligations to exclusive
faithfulness; and with equal acceptance of the hazards of
the future, each taking the other for better, for worse.

Not least is the equality of the husband and wife to be
shown in their sexual intercourse. The Christian principle
is : Let the husband render unto the wife her due; and likewise also the wife unto the husband. The wife hath not
power over her own body, but the husband; and likewise
also the husband hath not power over his own body, but
the wife. Defraud ye not one the other.[1] Neither party is
to be the mere instrument or victim for the gratification of the
other's lust. There must be mutual consideration and mutual
forbearance, as in all matters between one Christian and
another. Also the Christian principle of temperance and
self-control needs to be exercised in regard to sexual passion
as much as in regard to any other natural desire; and in
married life as well as before marriage. But, with these
provisos, the general rule stands, that neither party is
justified in refusing to consent to the regular fulfilment of
the purpose of marriage. Accordingly, it is not lawful to
enter into marriage with the intention of not consummating
it; and a marriage which is not capable of consummation, or
which in fact is not consummated, is not a true marriage,
and is not binding.

The limitation of family is lawful, if it be through abstinence from sexual intercourse, with free and equal consent
on either side. If the consent be not free and equal, grave
temptation is thrown upon the partner who abstains un-
willingly. St Paul would not approve of such abstinence
for any prudential or worldly reason. He says : Defraud
ye not one the other, except it be by consent for a season,
that ye may give yourselves unto prayer, and may be
together again, that Satan tempt you not for your incon-
tinency.[2]

The limitation of family is unlawful and gravely sinful if
it be achieved through the prevention of conception by any
means contrary to nature, or by destroying the developing
seed in the womb. Even in cases where child-bearing

[1] 1 Cor. vii. 3-5.   [2] *Ibid.*

would be fatal to the wife, the use of contraceptives is unlawful. The only right course in such cases is continence.
If it is argued that this is a hard teaching, overtaxing poor
human nature, the Christian answer is that Christianity
often obliges us to that which would be cruelly hard for
unaided nature, but that God's grace is sufficient to enable
us to endure. If it be said that such complete abstinence
tends to alter and impair the whole relation of the man and
wife, the Christian answer again is that by God's grace such
a result need not happen, and that anyway the ill-effects of
abstinence are as nothing when compared with the physical
and spiritual harms of sexual intercourse contrary to nature.

Parents are responsible for the maintenance, education,
and Christian nurture of their children. The desire to
provide opportunities for them at least equal to those the
parents had is both a natural instinct and a Christian duty.
The respect of parents towards their children is a duty equal
to that of the respect of children towards their parents. The
duty of parents to provide for their children is even greater
than that of children to provide for their parents.[1]

Finally, it must be borne in mind, as has been said above,
that the union of marriage is much more than carnal. It
is a union of soul with soul, as well as of body with body.

The mutual duty, forbearance, and responsibility cover
every relation of life. The surrender of either to other before
God involves the will and the affections and all the powers
of mind as well as of body. Christian marriage is a spiritual
union, by which each is to help the other, by mutual society,
help, and comfort, not only to bear the inevitable troubles
and anxieties of this life, but also to walk together in the
way that leadeth to eternal life.

VII

Let marriage be had in honour among all.[2] The Church
does not sanction any teaching that proclaims the married
state as sinful or unworthy.[3] Greater honour, however, has
been given by the Church, from St Paul's time onwards,
to the state of virginity, when it is embraced for Christ's

[1] 2 Cor. xii. 14.   [2] Heb. xiii. 4.   [3] 1 Tim. iv. 3.

sake and in obedience to his will. Blessed Mary was a virgin when she conceived our Lord, and Church tradition asserts that she remained a virgin always. Our Lord himself lived a virgin life. The Church, therefore, could not but ascribe peculiar honour to the following of so august examples.

But though virginity or celibacy is regarded in general as being higher than the married state, it is not the higher state in regard to each individual. Whichever state of life is God's will for each person is for him or her the highest state. And God's will for the great majority of mankind is marriage, for the replenishment of the earth.[1] The call to live in life-long singleness is given by God only to the few. It is a special vocation. It is a counsel, not a precept; but those who are called to it are not free in conscience to marry. If they do so, they are forsaking the higher life, which God who called them would have enabled them to live, and adopting a state of life lower than that which God meant for them.

A mere disinclination to marry is not the same as a call by God to the single life. Those who embrace religious virginity to do so for Christ's sake, believing it is the will of God for them. It may be contrary to their natural inclinations. It cannot be without self-sacrifice.

That God does call some men and women to the single life is the plain sense of our Lord's words : There is no man that hath left house, or wife, or brethren, or parents, or children, for the kingdom of God's sake, who shall not receive manifold more in this time, and in the world to come eternal life;[2] and, There are eunuchs who made themselves eunuchs for the kingdom of heaven's sake; he that is able to receive it, let him receive it.[3] Similarly St Paul taught : It is good for a man not to touch a woman. I say to the unmarried and to widows, It is good for them if they abide even as I. He that is unmarried is careful for the things of the Lord, how he may please the Lord; but he that is married for the things of the world, how he may please his wife. She that is unmarried is careful for the things of the Lord, that she may be holy both in body and spirit; but she that is

[1] 1 Gen. i. 28.   [2] Luke xviii. 29, 30.   [3] Matt. xix. 12.

married for the things of the world, how she may please her husband.[1]

This counsel of Chastity, as it is called, is generally joined with the counsels of Poverty and Obedience. As a vow of chastity effects the detachment of those who make it from close ties of intimacy with others, so that they may be the more free to serve God only, so the vow of poverty detaches them from the entanglements of this world's goods for the same purpose. No soldier on service, says St Paul, entangleth himself in the affairs of this life; that he may please him who enrolled him as a soldier.[2] All Christians are called to free themselves from the love of money; some are called to abandon for Christ's sake personal income or possessions. Our Lord did not say to all, but did say to the rich ruler: If thou wouldest be perfect, go, sell that thou hast, and give to the poor, and thou shalt have treasure in heaven: and come, follow me.[3]

The vow of obedience is more difficult than that of poverty or of chastity. Beyond the surrender of things or of persons lies the surrender of the self, the laying down of one's own will. All are called to self-abnegation, to enthrone Christ at the centre of their life, dethroning self; as our Lord taught to all his disciples: If any man would come after me, let him deny his self, and take up his cross, and follow me.[4] Each disciple must receive the Kingdom of God as a little child, in docility and simple dependence upon God.[5] The Church has taught that some are called to attain or to seek after this self abnegation by the submission of their wills in all things lawful to that of another, forsaking the direction of their lives according to their own ideas: both as a continual personal mortification, and for the more effective performance of the work of the Church by the disciplined service of many working together.

Those who rule their lives by these three counsels are usually called Religious, a word which in this connection means those who are bound by a special religious rule.

[1] 1 Cor. vii. 1, 8, 32-34.   [2] 2 Tim. ii. 4.
[3] Matt. xix. 21.   [4] Mark viii. 34.   [5] Mark x. 15.

The Religious life has existed in the Catholic Church from the earliest times. We see the beginnings of societies of consecrated widows,[1] and of virgins,[2] in New Testament times. Soon afterwards there arose the hermits, men or women living solitary lives in poverty and incessant prayer and labour. By the fourth century we see groups of monks or of nuns living in community, and the principle of holy obedience established which was necessary for the due ordering of life in common. These organised orders have multiplied during the ages of the Church's history, and have been very various in their purposes; some being founded chiefly for the development of the life of prayer and the spiritual contemplation of God, some more especially for active work in unselfish service of God and men, and some aiming at the combination of work and prayer. Some orders lay greater stress on poverty than on obedience; some on obedience more than poverty. These counsels admit of degrees of observance; but not so that of chastity, which is the essential characteristic of all forms of the religious life.

Religious communities exist in all parts of the Catholic Church at the present time as in past ages. In England they were suppresed by the rapacity of Henry VIII., with the result that the vocation to this form of consecrated life found no room for expression for some centuries. New communities, of women first, and later of men, were founded in the nineteenth century, of which many have struck their roots firmly, and are flourishing with the fruits of prayer, work, and mortification. But they are comparatively few and recent. The idea of the celibate consecrated life still remains strange to the minds of English Church-people. Yet there are doubtless many with the aptitude for such a life, who would become conscious of a direct call to it, if they knew of it. In no way has the Church in England shown its true catholicity more clearly than by the revival of the religious life.

The principle that the clergy of the Church should be celibate, for their greater detachment for the service of God,

[1] 1 Tim. v. 9, 10.   [2] 1 Cor. vii. 36-38.

is commended by St Paul,[1] but was not the rule in New Testament times.[2] In the early days, however, it became first the custom, and then the established rule of the universal Church, that the sacred ministers might not enter the married state after ordination, although those who were previously married might continue to live with their wives. the twelfth century the discipline of the Western Church has been that the clergy must live in celibacy, and that This still remains the rule of the Eastern Church. From no man who had a wife still living should be ordained. This rule is upheld in the Roman Church, with a few local exceptions. It was observed in England from its introduction until the Reformation. Then the English Church authoritatively stated the truth that bishops, priests, and deacons are not commanded by God's law either to vow the estate of single life or to abstain from marriage.[3] It proceeded to abrogate not only the Roman law, but also the common rule of the universal Church, by adding : Therefore it is lawful for them, as for all other Christian men, to marry at their own discretion, as they shall judge the same to serve better to godliness.

In the opinion of many the English Church has exceeded its powers in giving a general dispensation from the primitive and continual rule of the whole Church that marriage after ordination is unlawful. Others, however, argue that the rule, being one of Church discipline only, and not a principle divinely revealed, is capable of being abrogated by a part of the Church.

It is obvious that there are advantages in being free from a rule of compulsory celibacy; for thereby many temptations are avoided. But it is also true that the married state involves the clergy in other temptations of various kinds. It does not even save them from all temptations of the flesh. And in spite of the common practice of English clergymen marrying, it remains tthat St Paul's teaching sets forth celibacy as the higher state for all those who are dedicated to the divine service.

[1] 1 Cor. vii. 32-34.   [2] 1 Tim. iii. 2, 12; 1 Cor. ix. 5.
[3] Article of Religion XXXII.

241

XIX

DEATH AND AFTER DEATH

I

DEATH is the separation of the soul from the body. The body suffers the dissolution which befalls all material things; and the soul, the person, passes into a new stage and condition of life. The dust returns to the earth as it was, and the spirit returns unto God who gave it.[1]

St Paul has taught us to consider death as the result of sin: Through one man sin entered into the world, and death through sin; and so death passed unto all men, for that all sinned.[2] It is probable, indeed, that there was death in the animal world before the creation of mankind. But if that was so, it would not contradict St Paul's teaching. He seems to suggest what has remained the common opinion in the Church, that human beings, having not only a bodily nature akin to that of the other animals, but also immortal souls capable of union with God the Father of spirits,[3] were intended by him to be delivered from the common law of nature by being endued with the supernatural gift of immortality in body as in soul. We may suppose that, had it not been for sin entering in, the passing from one state of existence to another, which we call Death, would have been without the painful separation of soul and body and all its attendant misery; the body and the soul together passing joyously, by virtue of their unbroken union with God, from the glory of life here to the higher glory of heaven. But sin did enter; and death became death such as we know it in this fallen world, the result and penalty of sin.

Christ our Saviour endured for us the pain of death,

---

[1] Eccles. xii. 7.   [2] Rom. v. 12.   [3] Num. xvi. 22; Heb. xii. 9.

suffering the utmost that Satan, who has the power of death,[1] could do against him. And we believe that, by the obedience of the Son of God in our human nature, dying as a sacrifice for sin, mankind is redeemed from the guilt and the power of sin. If by the trespass of the one the many died, much more did the grace of God, and the gift by the grace of the one man, Jesus Christ, abound unto the many. If by the trespass of the one, death reigned through the one, much more shall they that receive the abundance of grace and the gift of righteousness reign through the one, even Jesus Christ. Where sin abounded, grace did abound more exceedingly; that as sin reigned in death, even so might grace reign through righteousness unto eternal life through Jesus Christ our Lord. For the wages of sin is death; but the free gift of God is eternal life in Christ Jesus our Lord.[2]

Each one, therefore, who seeks it in faith and repentance, may be restored to that union with God which was broken by sin, and may receive through that union the gift of the eternal and supernatural life, the life wherewith God lives eternally. That life is received by us even while we are in this world, and it is nourished in us by sacramental grace. It is the beginning, and the pledge, of the glory that shall be ours hereafter through and in Christ. And, as man in his completeness is both body and soul, it is the pledge also of the glory of our human bodies in the resurrection.[3]

But mankind, redeemed from the guilt and power of sin by the sacrifice of Christ, is not also delivered from all the consequences of sin. The eternal consequences and punishment of sin, which we call Eternal Death, is done away for those who are in Christ: but other penalties remain for mankind to endure, and among them the suffering of the pains of physical death. Death is the last onslaught of the power of Satan. It is the symbol of that eternal death merited by mortal sin. It is man's last penance; to be accepted and endured as such in penitential and joyful acceptance of God's chastisement. Death is the last opportunity of glorifying God offered in this world to man, the sinner saved.

[1] Heb. ii. 14.   [2] Rom. v. 15, 17, 21; vi. 23.   [3] Chap. xx. 3.

243

II

It is commonly believed that, as there would not have been the pains of death if sin had not entered into the world, so also there would have been no sickness. Sickness, physical and mental, seems to be one of the results of the Fall. Cases are recorded in the New Testament where the person's own sin is represented as being closely connected with his sickness or death. Thus, Christ said to the infirm man whom he healed at Bethesda : Sin no more, lest a worse thing befall thee;[1] and St Paul said to the bad communicants at Corinth : For this cause many among you are weak and sickly, and not a few sleep (in death).[2] But there are many more cases of sickness recorded in which no hint is given that the sickness was caused by the person's own sinfulness. And our Lord taught, in one case anyway, that there was no such connection, when he spoke of a man born blind : Neither did this man sin, nor his parents; but that the works of God should be made manifest in him.[3]

Sickness, then, may be the result and the sign of spiritual evil which was done by the sufferer himself or was inherited by him, the disorder of the soul being displayed in the disorder of the body or mind. On the other hand, sickness may have many another origin. It may, like any other human trouble, be the result of purely natural causes. It may be the effect of the unprovoked assaults of evil spirits. It may be a divinely given opportunity for growth in resignation, patience, and all holiness.[4] And these various possible causes of sickness and suffering are not mutually exclusive.

In every case, it is right and necessary that the patient should see that his soul is right with God, or is put right; so that the sickness, from whatever cause it has come, may bring to him the spiritual blessing which God intends, under whose providence the sickness has been allowed to come. Therefore the Church urges the duty of penitence and confession of sin on all who are suffering from sickness, and especially on those who are in danger of death. Ministra-

[1] John v. 14.
[2] 1 Cor. xi. 30.
[3] John ix. 3; cf. Luke xiii. 4, 5.
[4] Heb. xii. 5-11.

tion to the sick has always been a chief part of the work of the priests of the Church.

There is implanted in all men the desire for perfect health, which is not only the common instinct to escape from the burden and pain of sickness, but also arises from resentment against sickness as being a state not truly natural to man. There is no doubt but that this desire for health is good, and comes from God, who wills both the spiritual well-being of his creatures, and also all physical and mental health that is consistent with their spiritual well-being. We are therefore not only justified, but we are even bound, to use all means of healing provided by medical science, so far as our circumstances admit. To make use of science is to make use of a gift of God. My son, said the wise man, in thy sickness be not negligent; but pray unto the Lord, and he will make thee whole. Leave off from sin, and cleanse thy heart from all wickedness. Then give place to the physician, for the Lord hath created him; let him not go from thee, for thou hast need of him. There is a time when in their hands there is good success. For they shall also pray unto the Lord, that he would prosper that which they give for ease and remedy to prolong life.[1] Similarly, those who are well are bound to use every means to keep well that are possible for them within their duty to God.

Some devout Christians, however, too readily regard their sickness as calling them only to resignation; and, through a mistaken submission to what they think to be God's will, they fail to exert a resolute determination towards health. Thus they retard or hinder their recovery, which may be what God is intending for them.

Apart from the power of intercession by which Christians can aid the healing work of the physicians, the Church has spiritual powers of healing peculiar to itself. The Church is able, by spiritual ministration to the sick person and the power of prayer, to apply to the soul, and through the soul to the body and mind, the healing power of Christ.

[1] Ecclus. xxxviii. 1-14.

245

Christ himself performed miracles of healing on many who sought his help, and from many who were possessed he cast forth evil spirits. The power of the Lord was with him to heal.[1] His human nature was the vehicle of divine powers of healing for the body as well as for the soul. The power that was in him went forth to meet men's need.[2] And he was able to exercise this divine power, not in virtue of his own Godhead, but by the human energy of prayer.[3] This ministry of healing, though frequent in its occurrence, was not the principal purpose or occupation of Christ's ministry. He came to preach, to bear witness, to save men from their sins. But also he healed their sicknesses, because he was moved with compassion for them, even though in some ways his miracles of healing made his principal work more difficult to fulfil.[4]

This lesser ministry of healing, as well as the more import-ant ministrations, was committed by Christ to the Church, to continue as his representative. His instruction to the apostles, when he sent them out two and two, was : Preach, saying, The kingdom of heaven is at hand. Heal the sick, raise the dead, cleanse the lepers, cast out devils.[5] And his charge to the Church after his resurrection is summed up in the words : Preach the gospel to the whole creation . . . And these signs shall follow them that believe . . . they shall lay hands on the sick and they shall recover.[6] It is not promised that every laying on of hands would effect a cure : but that divine healing through the laying on of hands would be sufficiently frequent to be a sign that men might look for. We cannot know in any case whether God wills to cure, in answer to the faithful prayer : but we do know that the prayer will not go unanswered, and that the answer may be the effecting of a cure through the agency of the Church. If it appears that such cures are less frequent in these days than in New Testament times, the reason probably is that the Church in this respect has lost faith.

In the primitive Church we see two forms of the ministry of healing. One was by the exercise of personal powers

[1] Luke v. 24.   [2] Mark. v. 30.   [3] Mark ix. 29. Chap. iv. 4.
[4] Mark i. 41, 45.   [5] Matt. x. 8.   [6] Mark xvi. 15-18.

given to various individuals. Thus St Paul speaks of certain people at Corinth possessing gifts of healing, akin to the gifts of tongues, or prophecy, or other special powers wrought through them by the Holy Spirit.[1] The other form of healing was a sacramental function of the priesthood. Thus, St James writes: Is any among you sick? let him call for the elders of the Church, and let them pray over him, anointing him with oil[2] in the name of the Lord; and the prayer of faith shall save him that is sick, and the Lord shall raise him up; and if he have committed sins, it shall be forgiven him. Confess therefore your sins one to another, and pray one for another, that ye may be healed. The supplication of a righteous man availeth much in its working.[3] This ministry of the elders has continued in the Church to the present day, in the sacrament of unction. There seems no reason, however, for thinking that the personal gifts of healing are no longer to be found in individual Christians.

The sacrament of unction is administered by a priest, with oil that has been consecrated to this purpose by the bishop. The usual custom is to anoint the several organs of the senses, the eyes, ears, lips, etc., and the hands and feet, the priest meanwhile praying God's forgiveness for all sins of which these have been the instruments. The anointing is strictly a way of spiritual healing, a healing of the sinful spirit of the patient by the conveyance to him of divine pardon and grace. Hence sacramental unction is not given to children who are too young to have sinned wilfully. Nor is it given to those who are unbaptised, as Christ has provided for them the sacrament of baptism for the remission of sins. With these exceptions, all who are judged to have repentance and faith should be anointed.

With the prayers for forgiveness are added prayers for protection from evil spirits, and for the spiritual consolation and support of the sick person, and for restoration to health if God shall will, or else for a happy death.

The sacrament of unction may be used in any case of serious illness. It is not the custom of the Church to

---

[1] 1 Cor. xii. 9, 28, 30.   [2] Mark vi. 13.   [3] Jas. v. 14-16.

administer it in cases of lesser ailments which are not usually a cause of death. In such cases the laying on of hands is used with prayer; and oil blessed by a priest for the purpose of healing may be used also. On the other hand, it is not necessary to delay the sacramental anointing till death seems imminent. The prayer for the recovery of the patient, which is always said, implies that the sacrament is not meant to be used only when recovery seems humanly impossible. But, great though the power of the sacrament be for recovery, still more valuable is it for the greater and more important work of preparing the soul for its passage through death to the life beyond the grave, fortifying it against temptations and the attacks of Satan, that it may not for any pains of death fall from God. If it be a blessed thing to be restored for a time to the life of this troublesome world, far more blessed is it to be brought, by the grace of God, safely and peacefully through the peril of death to assured salvation for all eternity.

Every Christian stricken with serious illness should endeavour to prepare himself for death which may be near, without delaying until perhaps his failing strength may make him incapable of preparation. He should seek for the prayers of those around him and the Church, that he may have true faith and repentance. And he should call for the priest of the Church, that he may make humble confession of his sins, and receive the last sacraments, that is, absolution, holy communion (called Viaticum, the food for the last journey), and holy unction.

Also the sick person should set his worldly affairs in order, making due provision for those who are dependent upon him, paying his debts, and making a will if necessary : so that no trouble may arise, nor any injustice be suffered by others, after his death. He should also make offerings for the purposes of religion and charity, according as his circumstances may permit.

Then, with humble confidence, and trust in God's mercy, he can place himself within the divine compassion, accepting patiently and tranquilly whatever issue of his sickness God may send.

III

The soul passes into the next stage of existence without loss of personality. The person is the same person on either side of death. And every person is responsible before God for the life lived in this world, and for the use or misuse he has made of the natural and supernatural talents God has given him. That is the solemn warning of both Testaments: God shall bring every work into judgment with every hidden thing, whether it be good or whether it be evil.[1] We shall all stand before the judgment-seat of God.[2]

God is the judge of all the earth.[3] The divine right of judgment is committed to the Incarnate Son: As the Father hath life in himself, even so gave he the Son also to have life in himself; and he gave him authority to execute judgment, because he is Son of man.[4] It is fitting and necessary that the divine Son, whose human nature has been made the channel of eternal life to men, should also be the agent of judgment. He who is the Saviour is also the Judge; for the judgment is the bestowal or the witholding of the life which brings salvation.

The judgment of God in Christ upon each soul is not to be thought of as taking place only at the last day; although it is of that final act of judgment that holy Scripture most often speaks.[5] The crises of human history are manifestations of divine judgment;[6] and as it is with nations, so also is it with individuals. God is continually judging, and at times we can see the divine judgment made manifest. There is no creature that is not manifest in his sight; but all things are naked and laid open before the eyes of him with whom we have to do.[7] Already in this life we are come to Jesus, the mediator of the new covenant; therefore already are we come to God the judge of all.[8] The continual offering of salvation involves a continually present judgment. So our Lord

---

[1] Eccles. xii. 14.   [2] Rom. xiv. 10, 12; 2 Cor. v. 10.
[3] Gen. xviii. 25.   [4] John v. 26, 27.   [5] Chap. xx. 4.
[6] Mark xiii., where the destruction of Jerusalem is regarded as a coming of Christ in judgment.
[7] Heb. iv. 13.   [8] Heb. xii. 23, 24.

taught : He that heareth my word, and believeth on him that
sent me, hath eternal life, and cometh not into judgment,
but hath passed out of death into life. The hour cometh,
and now is, when the (spiritually) dead shall hear the voice
of the Son of God; and they that hear shall live.[1]

We are each of us working out, by our obedience or self-
will, by our use or misuse of grace, Christ's present judgment on us. We are now determining what will be Christ's
pronouncement concerning us at the last day. For Christ's
judgment, both now and in its final declaration, is no arbitrary
decree of reward or of punishment : at each moment it is the
declaration of the truth about the state of each of us in
relation to God, and of the immediate and necessary consequence of that state. In this sense, each of us is continually
judging himself.

But we are right in thinking of the great crisis of death
especially as the occasion of judgment. Then is ended the
life here, for which we must give account. It is appointed
unto men once to die, and after this cometh judgment.[2]
Then the period of life's probation, during which we can win
or cast away our salvation, is past and gone. The soul, when
it passes through death, is either saved or lost eternally. No
further chance of salvation for a lost soul after this life has
been revealed to us. The soul then stands at the parting of
the ways—towards heaven or towards hell. Its eternal
destiny is fixed, according as it is then seen by God to be
united with him, or of its own will separated from him.
If a tree fall toward the south, or toward the north, in the
place where the tree falleth, there shall it be.[3]

Of the final salvation of one who dies in the grace of God,
with signs of repentance and faith, we can have a sure and
certain hope,[4] a hope which is certain because of the sure
promises of God to those who are in the state of salvation.
But we cannot have absolute certainty; for God alone knows
the real state of any soul.[5]

The Church does not presume to assert of any departing
soul that it is eternally lost. The Church must, indeed,

[1] John v. 24, 25.   [2] Heb. ix. 27.   [3] Eccles. ix. 3.
[4] Burial Service.   [5] See also Chap. vii. 2.

refuse Christian burial and the offering of Mass for those in whose case the neglect of the sacraments, or the evidences of the absence of faith and repentance, seems to afford no ground for any hope. The Church is the guardian of the holy rites of religion, and may not suffer them to be profaned. Therefore it refuses them to those who die unbaptised, or excommunicate, or by wilful suicide, or in the act of any other grievous and open sin. It does not thereby damn the sinful soul nor assert its damnation. It only determines that there is no evidence to show that the soul departed is in a state of grace.

The teaching of our Lord seems to suggest that the heathen will be judged by standards that they were able to see by the natural conscience, and not by the standards of Christianity which they did not know.[1] God's condemnation rests upon wilful sin, not upon ignorance. The servant that knew not his Lord's will, and did things worthy of stripes, shall be beaten with few stripes.[2] In the same way, our belief in God's justice and mercy leads us to think that he can make allowances for the many Christians on whom the world has been hard, and who have never had a real chance. They are his children, though they have not known him. It seems natural to believe that Christ, who offered the gospel to the souls of those who had sinned long before his coming on earth,[3] will offer the same gospel to those who have been more sinned against than sinning; and that no soul will be finally lost until knowingly and wilfully it refuses salvation. But such thoughts can only be our inferences from what we know of the character of God : the Church cannot teach with authority on this subject more than has been given to it to teach.

Death, with its dread determination of eternal destiny, awaits each one of us. The Christian should live always in such a way as to be always prepared for death and for judgment. Death is certain; the time is uncertain. We can count with security only upon the present. Now is the acceptable time : behold, now is the day of salvation.[4] Each

[1] Matt. xxv. 31-45. [2] Luke xii. 48.
[3] 1 Pet. iii. 18-20. [4] 2 Cor. vi. 2.

is given time enough, but not more than enough. If our
soul is indeed right with God now, we need not fear the
impending judgment. If there is the least doubt as to our
soul's state now, we have much reason to fear death. Even
at the eleventh hour a sinner can turn to God in repentance,
and be saved: but how can we know that death's hasty
coming will allow us one hour or one moment? How can
we be sure that our soul, if it has become fixed in sin, will
then be able to repent? It is a fearful thing to fall into
the hands of the living God.[1]

IV

The Church believes and teaches that few of those who are
saved and who die in the state of grace are immediately fit
and ready to enter heaven and to see God. This belief arises
not so much from the consideration of the badness of all
Christians. Many of those who die in the Lord have not
been bad, when judged by the standards of the world or of
the Church. It arises from the consideration of the supreme
holiness of God and the wondrous glory of heavenly bliss.
The reward that is set before us is so great that ordinary
good people, as they are at their death, would not be capable
of appreciating it. There is need of preparation, and of,
further spiritual development, after death. It is true, indeed,
that God has power to cause each of those who are saved
to attain in a moment to perfect sanctification. But all we
know of the working of God's grace in man leads us to expect
that the growth in holiness will be gradual beyond death,
as it is in the life here, and that the departed will pass in
orderly progression from glory to glory.

Few, again, during this life have done adequate penance
for their sins. They are forgiven for Christ's sake; but
their share in the consequences of sin yet remains to be
endured.

The Church teaches that, between this world and heaven,
there is a state of existence to be passed through by all those
who are destined for perfected union with God; by all, that is,

[1] Heb. x. 31.

except those in whom all the effects of sin have been done away while still in this world.

This state is beyond our powers of direct comprehension. We can think and speak of it only in picture language, using terms of time and of place such as we know in this world. We can learn about it only in a parable. Strictly speaking, ideas of earthly place are not applicable to disembodied souls, nor ideas of earthly time to a state of existence that is outside time.

This state of existence of the saved after death, this ante-chamber of heaven, is commonly called Purgatory. Other names given to it by English writers are the Intermediate State, and Paradise.[1] We speak of those whom we think of as being in this state as the Faithful Departed, or the Holy Souls.

Little has been clearly revealed to us about Purgatory. But the common consent of the Catholic Church leads us to think of it as being, on the one hand, a state of safety, rest, and refreshment; and on the other hand, of penance, purgation, and painful progress.

It is a state of safety. The soul is at rest after the turmoils of this troublesome world. The perils of its probation are over. Temptation has ceased. Sin can no longer exercise dominion. The soul is sure of salvation and of sanctification. It cannot now go astray and be lost. And the grace of God still remains with it for its refreshment and re-creation after the ravages which sin has wrought. Blessed are the dead which die in the Lord from henceforth : yea, saith the Spirit, that they may rest from their labours; for their works follow with them.[2] I am persuaded that death shall not be able to separate us from the love of God.[3] The souls of the righteous are in the hand of God, and there shall no torment touch them. They are in peace. Their hope is full of immortality. And having been a little chastised, they shall be greatly rewarded. God hath care for his elect.[4]

---

[1] Luke xxiii. 43; but more usually in the language of the Church Paradise denotes heaven.
[2] Rev. xiv. 13.   [3] Rom. viii. 38, 39.   [4] Wisd. iii. 1-9

THE   KING'S   HIGHWAY

But there is pain in purgatory, such pain as can exist together with peace and joy.

There is the pain of penance, in the acceptance of whatever of punishment shall be given to the soul, on account of all sins for which sufficient satisfaction has not been made during this life. We shall not come out thence until we have paid the last farthing.[1] Thus our Lord shows us the rich man suffering punishment in the life beyond the grave because he had wasted the good things of this life, and had not laid up treasure in heaven by charitableness and generosity. We are shown him punished indeed, yet not lost, nor outside the grace of God. He had grace to humble himself before Abraham and Lazarus, whom formerly he had despised and neglected; and we see newly awakened his charitable concern for his brethren.[2]

The two words, Son, remember, make for us a picture of the pain and the blessedness of purgatory—the pain of remembering former sins and wasted opportunities; the blessedness of our abiding sonship. The painful penance to be endured by us is not simply punishment. It is not arbitrarily imposed by God. Rather, we believe that all God's penances are remedial, when they are accepted in the spirit of sonship. They are the expression of the love of God towards his sinful children. God dealeth with us as with sons; for what son is there whom his father chastiseth not?[3]

Purgatory, as the name implies, is a state of purgation; where, by the grace of God and in the fire of the divine love, the sin-stained character is cleansed and purified, and the effects remaining upon it from past sinfulness and old habits of sin are done away. To each shall be given that penance, that remedy, which is fitting to his state and previous life. Each man's work shall be made manifest; for the day shall declare it, because it is revealed in fire; and the fire itself shall prove each man's work of what sort it is. If any man's work shall be burned, he shall suffer loss; but he himself shall be saved : yet so as by fire.[4]

Again, we believe that part of the pain of purgatory is that

[1] Matt. v. 26.   [2] Luke xvi. 19-31.
[3] Heb. xii. 7.   [4] 1 Cor. iii. 13-15.

which is caused by, and is the means of spiritual progress. The soul learns to advance in the painful road of self-knowledge and repentance. Its spiritual perception is no longer hindered by the distractions of this life, but can truly compare itself with the vision of the perfection of human nature in Christ. And it strains upwards in the painful, yea blissful, anticipation of heaven, now clearly apprehended, but not yet attained.[1]

v

The value and importance of praying for the faithful departed has been part of the belief of the whole Church from the earliest times. The Church has always been greatly concerned with its duty of helping them. And naturally so, since the departed members are so many more in number than those who are in this life.

There seems to be no argument that can be brought forward against praying for the dead that would not equally be against all intercessory prayer; except such as may arise from the mistaken idea that, because the departed are said to sleep in Christ,[2] they are in a state of unconsciousness and incapable of any change. And indeed the Church, in encouraging prayers for the dead, has only given its sanction to what is a powerful instinct of the heart of man. The loving heart cannot but desire good for the loved ones within the veil; and every earnest desire of a Christian heart in union with Christ is prayer, even if it be not expressed in a form of prayer.

As the state and condition of each soul is hidden from us, prayers for the departed cannot be closely particularised. The prayers in common use are general in their form; such as : May the souls of the faithful departed, through the mercy of God, rest in peace. Rest eternal grant unto them, O Lord, and let light perpetual shine upon them. Grant them a place of refreshment, light, and peace, both now and in the day of resurrection.

The Church has often quoted with approval the example

---

[1] Chap. xx. 6.   [2] 1 Thess. iv. 14.

of Judas Maccabæus, of whom we read that he caused a sin-offering to be offered for the dead, doing therein very well and honestly, in that he was mindful of the resurrection : for if he had not hoped that they should have risen again, it had been superfluous and vain to pray for the dead. And also in that he perceived that there was great favour laid up for those that died godly, it was a good and holy thought. Whereupon he made a reconciliation for the dead, that they might be delivered from sin.[1] And the Church, having the true sacrifice to offer, has been accustomed both to remember before God the departed with the living at every Mass, and also frequently to offer the holy sacrifice with the special intention of the welfare and advancement of the holy souls. It is a good and Catholic custom for the relations of one who has departed to procure that Masses be said for him, and to make offerings for that purpose.

By holy communion we are renewed in our spiritual union with the departed, who, like ourselves, are in Christ and live by his life, being still members of his mystical body. On either side of death the faithful are united with Christ, and it follows that they cannot be separated from one another. By holy communion the gulf of death is spanned; we stretch our hands across the narrow sea : we are joined in the bond of mutual prayer with our dear ones who rest in Christ.

This is the only communion with the dead which is permitted to Christians. The Church has always forbidden as sinful and harmful, all attempts to enter into direct communication with the dead. The spurious comfort which spiritism offers to mourners by calling back the dead into contact with this world has always been disallowed, either as being a false pretence, or as being in reality a trafficking with evil spirits posing as departed souls of men and women. Ignorance of the Catholic faith has often encouraged the cult of spiritism, as at the present time in England. The Christian, however, is taught to submit to the cessation of communion through the senses, and to be content with the assurance of faith that the souls of the righteous are in the

[1] 2 Macc. xii. 41-45.

hand of the good God. The prophet asked the bereaved
mother: It is well with the child? And she answered, It
is well.[1]

VI

The word Saints, or holy ones, is a common title in the
New Testament of faithful members of the Church living in
this world.[2] All who have been called to sonship in holy
baptism have been called to be saints.[3] They have been set
upon the high road of sanctification; and, if they abide in the
grace of God given to them, God will make them holy.

In the language of the Church, however, the term Saints is
usually reserved for those in whom God has not only begun
the good work, but has also perfected it,[4] and who are
believed to have attained already to the glory of the heavenly
state and the blessed vision of God, their destined end.

The saints in heaven are a great multitude which no man
can number, out of every nation;[5] many more in number
than those whose names are known to us. Very many,
doubtless, have already passed from the discipline of purgatory to their eternal reward. Some, also, we believe,
needed no purgation after death; either because their
baptismal innocence was never sullied by sin, or because,
by the depth of their penitence and by their heroic endurance
of suffering for Christ's sake, their penance and preparation
for glory was completed in this life. All these are com-
memorated yearly on the festival of All Saints.[6] Those
also are particularly honoured as saints about whose sanctity
something particular is known; as for example St John
Baptist, St Joseph, St Peter and St Paul and the other
apostles, and many of the martyrs who died for Christ, and
other men and women who were pre-eminent in their confession of him and their sufferings for his sake and the
gospel's.[7] Thus it has come to pass that the roll of the
Church's heroes has become very large. There is hardly a
day in the Church's calendar without some special com-
memoration of a saint at Mass.

[1] 2 Kings iv. 26. [2] Acts ix. 32; Eph. v. 3, etc. [3] 1 Cor. i. 2.
[4] Phil. i. 6. [5] Rev. vii. 9. [6] November 1. [7] Mark x. 29.

It is right that the saints should thus be remembered with
honour. The Church in its warfare is encouraged by the
thought of those who have gone before, and have entered
into their reward. We are reminded of the great cloud of
witnesses that surrounds us,[1] and our minds are raised above
the turmoils and imperfections of this small part of the
Church which is here on earth to that larger part that lives
in joy and security within the veil. We rejoice to think that
we are now fellow-citizens with the saints, and of the household of God, being built upon the foundation of the apostles
and prophets.[2] And we embrace in our minds the catholicity
of the Church, rejoicing not only in those saints who in their
lifetimes were English, but equally in those who were Syrians,
or Greeks, or Africans, or Italians, or French. As a regiment
honours not only its own heroes, but those of the whole army,
so we honour not only the English saints, but the saints of
the whole Church, for they are ours.

And, day by day, the example of the saints is set before us.
We remember that their holiness is not beyond our aim;
for to us, as to them, God offers sufficient grace. What
they did, we can do; what they were, we may be; what they
are, we may become : for what they had, we have; difficulties, hindrances, and temptations not greater than theirs, and
sacramental grace not less. It is true, indeed, that Christ
our Lord is himself our great and supreme example : for
in him all virtues are equally and perfectly displayed. But
it is also true that by the study of the saints we can see more
clearly the holiness of Christ, for in each of them was
reproduced supremely one or more of the virtues of Christ.
Also, the saints give us what the sinless Christ could not give,
the example of sinners being made holy.

Chiefly it is right to venerate the saints because by doing
so we give glory to God. God has made all men for himself
and in his image. God's grace is given to all Christians that
they may become like him. The saints are those who have
been enabled to fulfil the purpose of their creation. They
are those who have, by God's grace, been faithful to their
high calling in Christ Jesus.[3] They are the great proofs and

1 Heb. xii. 1.   2 Eph. ii. 20.   3 Phil. iii. 14.

258

examples of the power of grace, the choicest fruits of God's new creation. By the veneration of the saints we do not take away from the honour due to God only; for in honouring them we are honouring the husbandry of God.[1]

We have considered the Catholic custom of asking for the help of the prayers of the saints.[2] But, in the Catholic Church, which is the communion of the saints, it is not only by their intercessions that we are benefited. The whole Church is a living brotherhood, a body whose members are so closely joined together that the good in each is available for the benefit of all. If one member of a body suffer, all the members suffer with it; and if one member is honoured and glorified, all the members rejoice with it.[3] For every good deed done, every virtue manifested, every pain faithfully endured for Christ's sake, every working-out of the passion of Christ in any member of his, go to make up a rich treasury of merit, in union with the merit of his sacrifice, which is available for the salvation and sanctification not only of that one member, but also of all. This is true even to ourselves. Not only for our own sakes do we endure, but for the good of all. Much more is it true of the saints. I rejoice, said St Paul, in my sufferings for your sake, and fill up on my part that which is lacking of the afflictions of Christ in my flesh for his body's sake, which is the Church.[4] In so far as anyone's union with Christ is real and living, his acts and sufferings are the acts and sufferings of Christ wrought in him, and are part of that one sacrifice which taketh away the sins of the world.

The saints in their glory in God's presence have not yet attained to their fulness of blessedness. They yet await the glory of their resurrection bodies.[5] Their spiritual union with Christ is perfected and glorified; but the glory of their souls is not yet manifested in the glorified flesh.

St Mary alone is believed to have attained to that fulness of glory. The Church teaches that she alone awaits no new perfection at the day of resurrection; but has already, from

[1] 1 Cor. iii. 9.   [2] Chap. xiv. 5.   [3] 1 Cor. xii. 26.
[4] Col. i. 24.   [5] Chap. xx. 3.

259

the time of her falling asleep in this world, received her bodily glory. Her reward is in this respect different from that of all other saints, as her vocation was different from theirs; they were true servants of Incarnate God, but she alone was the human agent of his Incarnation.

This belief has, for many centuries, been celebrated yearly on the festival which is called the Falling Asleep, or, the Assumption into heaven of blessed Mary.[1] There also arose a tradition, accepted by many that after her burial her body was not to be found by those who visited her tomb. And no relic of her body has been known to exist anywhere in the world. But the belief in blessed Mary's full glory in heaven in body and soul is not necessarily bound up with belief in this tradition.

The honour assigned by God to blessed Mary was pre-eminent, to be the Mother of Christ who is Almighty God.[2] And in accordance with her great vocation, she was endowed with divine grace from her birth and before her birth, as the whole Church has commonly believed and taught. Many Christians have also believed that at the moment of her conception in the womb of her mother Anne she was saved miraculously from that taint of sin and faulty inclination towards self-will, apart from God's will, which is common heritage of all other children of men; and that the redemptive grace of Christ, which saves us from the guilt and power of sin, saved her from any contact with it. This doctrine of St Mary's immaculate conception without original sin is an inference from the fact of her motherhood of Christ, and from the fact that she passed her whole life without committing any sin. It has been taught in the Roman Catholic Church in modern times as a necessary part of the Christian faith; but not so in the Eastern Church. The English Church has given no definite pronouncement on the subject. It does not assert that belief in the doctrine is necessary for faithful Church membership; but it follows mediæval custom in commemorating St Mary's conception,[3] and does not commemorate the conception of any other saint.

The pre-eminent honour of St Mary still remains to her in

---

[1] August 15.   [2] Chap. iv. 1.   [3] December 8.

heaven. Christ has not ceased to be truly man, nor has Mary ceased to be Christ's Mother. The Church, therefore, venerates her above all saints, and has loved to ascribe to her every title of honour. She is called the Queen of heaven, for she is exalted above the angels, and above the saints who reign in Christ.[1] She is the Queen-Mother of him who is King of kings and Lord of lords[2] acknowledged and crowned by her divine Son in heaven. She is called our Advocate, because we think of her as being of all the saints the most closely united with Jesus Christ, and because we have learnt to know the power of petitions commended to her intercession.

But no title that can be given to St Mary can exceed the greatness of that earliest title given to her by the authority of the whole Church—the Mother of God. And yet let us note that it was chiefly for the glory of Jesus Christ, and to establish the truth of his true divinity and humanity, that that name was solemnly given to her. The fact of her motherhood is our justification in giving her every honour than can be given to a human being. Devotion to the blessed Mother is the safeguard of the true belief in the Incarnation. And remembrance of her motherhood will prevent us from forgetting in our devotion the infinite gulf that separates her, as a created being, from him who is her Creator and the Creator of all. For we can never rest in the thought of the Mother. The word itself suggests the thought of the Son who is infinitely greater than his human Mother. The image of blessed Mary which is dearest to the Christian heart is not that of the Virgin crowned in the glory of heaven;[3] but that of the Virgin in the greater glory of her motherhood, holding in her arms her Son, the babe of her body, who deigned to take from her all he could take, his human nature, but who in his own person from all eternity is the Lord God.

[1] Rev. xxii. 5.   [2] Rev. xix. 16.   [3] Rev. xi. 1, 2.

XX

THE END

I

THE end of all things is at hand.[1] Each man's experience of
this world is only for a brief while. For each one this
world ends at his death.

And again, the end of all things is at hand. The whole
human race will come to the end of its earthly history. There
will be the ending of this stage, which has lasted since the
creation of the material world, or from man's first appearance
in it; there will be a summing-up[2] of all human experience
here, and the beginning of a new age for mankind.

This tremendous crisis which is to come in the history of
mankind is what we mean when we speak of the End of the
World, and the Last Day.

Holy Scripture pictures the total destruction of the material
universe. Thou, Lord, in the beginning hast laid the
foundation of the earth, and heavens are the works of thy
hands; they shall perish, but thou continuest; and they all
shall wax old as doth a garment, and as a mantle shalt thou
roll them up, and they shall be changed; but thou art the
same, and thy years shall not fail.[3] The day of the Lord will
come, in the which the heavens shall pass away with a great
noise, and the elements shall be dissolved with fervent heat,
and the earth and the works that are therein shall be burned
up.[4] We do not know whether such passages are to be taken
as predictions of actual events, or as parables of the completeness of the change that is to be, and of the utter
removing of all that is evil.

[1] 1 Pet. iv. 7.
[3] Heb. i. 10-12.
[2] Matt. xxviii. 20.
[4] 2 Pet. iii. 10.

THE END

Whatever be the fate awaiting this material world, we believe that the final state will show the triumphant vindication of God and righteousness : the world passeth away, and the lust thereof, but he that doeth the will of God abideth for ever.[1] Whatever shall be the new heavens and new earth that we look for, therein will dwell righteousness.[2] At the end of the world we shall see the fulfilment of the prophesied triumph of the kingdom of God, of which Christ is the victorious king.

And we believe that the kingdom of God is already established on earth, within this age, in his Catholic Church. Christ has delivered us out of the power of darkness, and translated us into the kingdom of the Son of his love.[3] By our membership in his Church, which is our heavenly citizenship,[4] we are already delivered out of this present evil world,[5] and belong to the kingdom which is eternal. And whatever is meant by the shaking of material creation, which Jewish prophecy connected with the manifestation of the Messiah, we know that the Catholic Church will remain, a kingdom which cannot be shaken.[6]

We believe in one Lord Jesus Christ, whose kingdom shall have no end.[7]

II

The final events in the history of this world will be the second coming of Christ, the resurrection of the dead, and the general judgment.

Christ has entered in our human nature into heaven, now to appear before the face of God on our behalf.[8] As the Jewish high-priest entered with the blood of the sacrifice into the holy of holies, leaving the people outside the veil expectant of his return; so we think of Christ as having entered within the veil as our forerunner, opening the highway by which mankind may draw near to God.[9]

There he is preparing a place for us, that we may be with

---

[1] 1 John ii. 17; *cf.* 1 Cor. vii. 31.   [2] 2 Pet. iii. 13.
[3] Col. i. 13.   [4] Phil. iii. 20.   [5] Gal. i. 4.
[6] Heb. xii. 22-29.   [7] Nicene Creed.
[8] Heb. ix. 24.   [9] Heb. vi. 20; x. 20.

him where he is.[1] His eternal sacrifice is present on the throne of God, preparing heaven to be the place where mankind redeemed from sin may acceptably worship God.[2] He prepares heaven to be our place, by making us through his sacrifice prepared for it.

He is our great high-priest, separated from sinners, and made higher than the heavens.[3] And, having been once offered to bear the sins of many, he shall appear a second time, apart from sin, to them that wait for him, unto salvation.[4]

We believe that he shall come again with glory.[5] It was said to the apostles at his ascension : This same Jesus, who was received up from you into heaven, shall so come in like manner as ye beheld him going into heaven.[6] The New Testament is full of the thought of the coming of our Lord Jesus Christ with all his saints,[7] which the Church understood would be the fulfilment of the age-long Jewish expectation of the manifestation of the Messiah and of the great and terrible day of the Lord.[8] The Lord himself shall descend from heaven, with a shout, with the voice of the archangel, and with the trump of God.[9] Behold, he cometh with the clouds, and every eye shall see him.[10] The Son of man shall come in his glory, and all the angels with him.[11] Then shall all the tribes of the earth see the Son of man coming on the clouds of heaven, with power and great glory : and he shall send forth his angels, with a great sound of a trumpet, and they shall gather together his elect.[12]

Thus the Church speaks to us in the imagery of Jewish expectation.

And yet he who will thus come again is the same Jesus who said, Lo, I am with you always, even unto the consummation of the age;[13] and, Where two or three are gathered together in my name, there am I in the midst of them;[14] and, He that

[1] John xiv. 3.   [2] Heb. ix. 23.
[3] Heb. iv. 14; vii. 26; viii. 1.   [4] Heb. ix. 28.
[5] Nicene Creed.   [6] Acts i. 11.   [7] 1 Thess. iii. 13.
[8] Mal. iv. 5.   [9] 1 Thess. iv. 16.   [10] Rev. i. 7.
[11] Matt. xxv. 31.   [12] Matt xxiv. 30; xxvi. 64.
[13] Matt. xxviii. 20.   [14] Matt. xviii. 20.

THE END

eateth my flesh and drinketh my blood abideth in me and I in him.[1] It is not only in the future that our Lord's promise is fulfilled: Where I am, there shall also my servant be;[2] and, if I go and prepare a place for you, I come again and receive you unto myself, that where I am, there ye may be also.[3] Such passages speak to us of Jesus present with us now. Our high-priest is out of sight, but not apart from us. Christ-for-us is not complete without the mystery of Christ-in-us.

And so the second coming does not mean the return of Christ from absence from us. It means a new manifestation to us of Christ who is ever present.[4]

The eternal Son, who, being God, is in all things and all things in him, through whom all things were made, and in whom all things consist,[5] took to himself our flesh and blood,[6] for us men and for the salvation.[7] The word of God was made flesh, and dwelt among us,[8] in the body of his humiliation.[9] In that body now glorified he is present still, in another mode, in the blessed sacrament, in which we show forth the Lord's death till he come.[10] And again in another mode, that same Jesus, whom not having seen we love, on whom though now we see him not yet we believe,[11] shall be seen at the last day, made manifest to all men in the revelation of his eternal glory and majesty.

We do not know when that great day of final revelation will come. The knowledge has been withheld from human minds, even from the human mind of the Son himself: of that day and hour knoweth no one, not even the angels in heaven, neither the Son, but the Father only.[12]

We have been told that the world must first be evangelised. Our Lord said: This gospel of the kingdom shall be preached in the whole world for a testimony unto all the nations; and then shall the end come.[13] Each nation must

---

1 John vi. 56.   2 John xii. 26.   3 John xiv. 3.
4 1 Cor. 1, 7; 2 Thess. ii. 1, 8; 1 John iii. 2, etc., with R.V. marginal readings.
5 Col. i. 16, 17.   6 Heb. ii. 14.   7 Nicene Creed.
8 John i. 14.   9 Phil. iii. 21.   10 1 Cor. xi. 26.
11 1 Pet. i. 8.   12 Matt. xxiv. 36.   13 Matt. xxiv. 14.

first hear the good things, and make its answer to the challenge of the gospel. By the world-wide extension of the Church, the nations will have the offer of Jesus as their Saviour and Master, before they meet him as their final Judge. All men will have their chance of faith and repentance.[1] Witness will be borne in every nation to the righteousness and love of God revealed in Christ; and Christ crucified will make his appeal.

The result will not be that all the nations, or the majority of each nation, will accept the gospel or respond faithfully to the challenge. Indeed, holy Scripture rather leads us to expect that in each new nation Christ will suffer a repetition of his experience among the Jews, being rejected by the many, and accepted only by the few. The mystery of human sin and the powers of evil will fight against Christ and his Church even to the end. The Church, like Christ himself, will ever fight what seems to be a losing battle. Christ, when he comes in glory, will not come to a converted world. He will be manifested in a world whose forces are arrayed against him,[2] and where, in the face of turmoils and persecutions, many even of those who have accepted him will have fallen away from him. Only a faithful remnant will welcome the final manifestation of Christ. So Christ himself has said : God will avenge his elect : howbeit, when the Son of man cometh, shall he find faith on the earth?[3] Because iniquity shall be multiplied, the love of the many shall wax cold; but he that endureth to the end shall be saved.[4]

Hence the coming of Christ is depicted as that of an avenging conqueror : I saw the heaven opened, and behold, a white horse, and he that sat thereon, called Faithful and True; and in righteousness he doth judge and make war, and out of his mouth proceedeth a sharp sword, that with it he should smite the nations; and he shall rule them with a rod of iron; and he treadeth the wine-press of the fierceness of the wrath of Almighty God.[5] Behold, he cometh with the clouds;

[1] 2 Pet. iii. 9.
[2] Rev. xix., etc.
[3] Luke xviii. 8.
[4] Matt. xxiv. 12, 13.
[5] Rev. xix. 11, 15; cf. Rev. vi. 14-17.

and every eye shall see him, and they which pierced him; and all the tribes of the earth shall mourn because of him.[1]

We know, from our Lord's words, that the day of divine vengeance will come suddenly upon an unexpectant world, absorbed in its life of eating and drinking, marrying and giving in marriage, without thought of him. In an hour that men think not, said Christ, the Son of man cometh.[2] And so St Paul taught: The day of the Lord so cometh as a thief in the night.[3] Therefore the Christian must live detached in spirit from the things of this world; like the wise virgins watchful and ready for his coming.[4] The end of all things is at hand: be ye therefore of sound mind, and be sober unto prayer.[5] Watch; for ye know not on what day your Lord cometh.[6]

We know not whether we shall, together with this generation, be overtaken[7] by the day of the Lord, or whether each of us shall separately enter into it by death.[8] In either case, we know not whether the dread moment is near or distant. The knowledge is withheld from us, in order that we may live in daily expectation; fearing because we know not how short our time is,[9] and also gladdened because amid the trials of this life we see our redemption drawing nigh.[10] We have not here an abiding city, but we seek after the city which is to come.[11] And, seeing that the things of this world are all to be dissolved, what manner of persons ought we to be in all holy living and godliness, looking for and earnestly desiring the presence of the day of God?[12]

III

At Christ's coming all men shall rise again with their own bodies.[13] I look for the resurrection of the dead, and the life of the world to come.[14]

---

[1] Rev. i. 7.   [2] Matt. xxiv. 32-51.
[3] 1 Thess. v. 1-11; cf. Matt. xxiv. 43; 2 Pet. iii. 10.
[4] Matt. xxv. 1-13.   [5] 1 Pet. iv. 7.
[6] Matt. xxiv. 42; Mark xiii. 28-37.   [7] 1 Thess. v. 4.
[8] Chap. xix. 3.   [9] Ps. lxxxix. 47.   [10] Luke xxi. 28.
[11] Heb. xiii. 14.   [12] 2 Pet. iii. 11. 12.
[13] Athanasian Creed.   [14] Nicene Creed.

The thought that death is not the end of man, but that there is existence and the continuance of personality beyond death, is not found only among Christians. The untutored instincts of many primitive races have clung to some vague hopes of an after-life. Pagan philosophy voiced the repugnance of mankind at the thought of this life being all, and has often endeavoured to lift the veil. Human reason has made its conjecture that the wealth of various powers possessed by men implies an ampler scope for their expression than this life's brief span can afford—that man is too richly equipped for this world only.

When men realise that they are not material only, but also spiritual, it is natural for them, even without any revelation from God, to feel that the death of the body will not be the end of personal life. And when they realise that they are not only spiritual, but also material, and that the soul and flesh together are one man,[1] and that the material part is not a mere temporary clothing of the soul, they are already near to belief in a resurrection; they cannot form any clear conception of themselves after death, except as being in some way still united with bodies.

The Jews, like other races, found or recovered their belief in a future life only gradually, partially, vaguely. Because they knew that God entered into personal relationship with men, they were bound to come to the belief that that relationship with him, the living and eternal God, could not be merely temporary. They were in fact confessing belief in a future life, when they sang such words as : O God, thou art my God.[2] And so our Lord taught that the doctrine was asserted in Exodus, where God is represented as saying, long after the death of the patriarchs : I am the God of Abraham, Isaac, and Jacob. God is not a God of the dead, but of the living.[3] Since he declared he is still their God, they are alive and in living relation with him; for all men live unto him.

But the Jews were far from realising this clearly. The common Jewish outlook was such as is expressed in the

[1] Athanasian Creed.   [2] Ps. lxiii. 1.
[3] Matt. xxii. 31, 32; Luke xx. 38.

words : I shall go unto the gates of the grave; I am deprived
of the residue of my years. I said, I shall not see the Lord,
even the Lord, in the land of the living. The grave cannot
praise thee, death cannot celebrate thee; they that go down
into the pit cannot hope for thy truth. The living, the
living, he shall praise thee, as I do this day.[1] Or, My life
draweth nigh unto the grave; I am counted with them that
go down into the pit : cast off among the dead, like the slain
that lie in the grave, whom thou rememberest no more, and
they are cut off from thy hand. Wilt thou shew wonders
to the dead? Shall they that are deceased arise and praise
thee? Shall thy loving-kindness be declared in the grave,
or thy faithfulness in destruction? Shall thy wonders be
known in the dark, and thy righteousness in the land of
forgetfulness?[2]

It is only in the latest written books of the Old Testament
that the conviction of a full life beyond the grave and a
resurrection from the dead appears in clear light; as, for
example, in Daniel and Esdras : Many of them that sleep in
the dust of the earth shall awake, some to everlasting life
and some to shame and everlasting contempt. And they
that be wise shall shine as the brightness of the firmament,
and they that turn many to righteousness as the stars for
ever and ever.[3] Those that be dead will I raise up again
from their places, and bring them out of their graves; for I
have known my name in Israel. The earth shall restore
those that are asleep in her, and so shall the dust those that
dwell in silence, and the secret places shall deliver those
souls that were committed unto them.[4] I know, said Martha
of her dead brother, that he shall rise again in the resurrection at the last day.[5] But the Sadducees held to the old
doubtfulness and lack of hope.[6]

The Christian belief in resurrection and future life has
a clearness and a certainty other than any Jew had. It is
because we know that Christ rose from the dead that we
believe in the resurrection of the dead.[7] And because

[1] Isa. xxxviii. 10-18.   [2] Ps. lxxxviii. 3-12.
[3] Dan. xii. 2, 3.   [4] Esdr. ii. 16; vii. 32.   [5] John xi. 24.
[6] Luke xx. 17.   [7] Chap. v. 3.

through sacraments received by faith we are united with the risen Lord and share his life, we believe that we shall ourselves attain to the resurrection unto life. Indeed the possession by us even now of the eternal life in Christ is the actual beginning of our resurrection life, and the pledge that it will be perfected in us if we continue to abide in Christ.

The eternal life of our souls united with Christ will be manifested at our resurrection in the glory of our resurrection bodies. As Christ rose by a bodily resurrection, so shall we: for we have his promise: He that eateth my flesh and drinketh my blood hath eternal life, and I will raise him up at the last day.[1] But not yet, while we remain in this world, is that perfect glory attained in body or soul. Rather, the aim of the Christian is to know him and the power of his resurrection, and the fellowship of his suffering, becoming conformed unto his death; if by any means we may attain unto the resurrection from the dead. Not that we have already attained, or are already made perfect: but we press on, if be that we may apprehend that for which also we were apprehended by Christ Jesus.[2]

There will be a resurrection of the lost also, as well as of those who are saved in Christ. The hour cometh, in which all that are in the tombs shall hear the voice of the Son of man, and shall come forth; they that have done good, unto the resurrection of life; and they that have done ill, unto the resurrection of judgment.[3] It is necessary that those who are lost shall have bodies in the resurrection, for the body as well as the soul belongs to human nature; but Christian revelation gives us no information about the bodies of the lost. We need to think here only of the resurrection unto life, as it alone is the subject of Christian hope.

St Paul teaches us that the spiritual bodies[4] of the saved will be in some way like to our Lord's resurrection body: The Lord Jesus shall fashion anew the body of our humiliation, that it may be conformed to the body of his glory.[5] It does not follow, and indeed it can hardly be supposed,

---

[1] John vi. 54.　　[2] Phil. iii. 10-12; cf. Rom vi. 4-11.
[3] John v. 28, 29.　[4] 1 Cor. xv. 44.　　　[5] Phil. iii. 21.

that in all points our bodies will be like to the body of him who is the Son of God.

As to the relation of our resurrection bodies to our present bodies, it is not those actual particles which happen to compose our ever-changing bodies at the moment of death that will receive the resurrection-change and be made into our spiritual bodies. That, indeed, is one of the pictures of the resurrection given in holy Scripture:[1] and at some times it found acceptance with Church teachers. But it is not the only nor the most prominent picture. When we are dealing with what can be shown to us only in parables, we are concerned, not with the details of the parables regarded as literal statements of fact, but with the general meaning to be gathered from them. And that general meaning seems to be this. In the resurrection we shall have bodies which will in a true sense be our bodies, the true outward and visible signs of our souls with which they are united. Our resurrection bodies, however, will not be as our bodies are in this world: flesh and blood cannot inherit the kingdom of God, neither doth corruption inherit incorruption.[2] They will be spiritualised and glorified, expressing in their glory the glory of our souls. But there will be as real a connection between our bodies then and our bodies now as there is between our bodies now and those which we had, say, when we were children; the identity in either case being established, not by the permanence of the material particles, but by the unchanging soul through all the stages of its material and spiritual manifestation.

Thus, St Paul uses the analogy of the grain of wheat which is sown that it may die, and that the undying germ of life may find new expression in the perfected ear of corn.[3] Similarly, the body born into this world is at once the same and not the same as the resurrection body. That which thou sowest is not quickened, except it die; and thou sowest not the body that shall be, but a bare grain; but God giveth it a body, and to each seed a body of its own. Again, in a different picture, he teaches: The dead shall be raised

1 John v. 28; Rev. xx. 13, etc.
2 1 Cor. xv. 50. 3 1 Cor. xv. 35-49.

incorruptible, and we, who are alive in this world at the coming of Christ, shall be changed; for this corruptible must put on incorruption, and this mortal must put on immortality.[1] He uses this picture of the new clothing again in another form, when he says : We know that if the earthly house of our tabernacle be dissolved, we have a building from God, a house not made with hands, eternal, in the heavens.   For verily in this we groan, longing to be clothed upon with our habitation which is from heaven; not that we would be unclothed, but clothed upon, that what is mortal may be swallowed up of life.[2]

It is a notable fact that, where there has been any thought of a future life, that expectation, even among the heathen, has usually been shown in the reverent treatment of the bodies of the dead, and in rites of burial.   The Christian Church alone knows with certainty of the bodily resurrection, and accordingly it has always attached the greatest importance to giving Christian burial to those who have died in grace. The duty of burying the dead is one of the charitable works laid upon the faithful; and burial, rather than cremation, is the Christian custom.   The bodies are buried in consecrated ground, with solemn chant and prayer that speak not only of human grief and sin's penalty, but also of triumph and thanksgiving and hope.   They are placed with the feet towards the east, symbolising the expectation that they shall rise and face Christ, the Sun of righteousness, at the dawning of the last day.   All this is natural, as a parable of the sure and certain hope of resurrection to eternal life through our Lord Jesus Christ.[3]

IV

God commandeth men that they should all everywhere repent : inasmuch as he hath appointed a day, in the which he will judge the world in righteousness by the Man whom he hath ordained; whereof he hath given assurance unto all men, in that he hath raised him from the dead.[4] When the Son of man shall come in his glory and all the angels with

[1] 1 Cor. xv. 52, 53.
[3] Burial Service.
[2] 2 Cor. v. 1-4.
[4] Acts xvii. 30, 31.

him, then shall he sit on the throne of his glory: and before him shall be gathered all the nations; and he shall separate them one from another, as the shepherd separateth the sheep from the goats.[1] The Son of man shall send forth his angels, and they shall gather out of his kingdom all things that offend, and them that do iniquity, and shall cast them into the furnace of fire: there shall be the weeping and gnashing of teeth. Then shall the righteous shine forth as the sun in the kingdom of their Father.[2] And I saw a great white throne, and him that sat upon it, from whose face the earth and the heaven fled away; and there was no place for them. And I saw the dead, the great and the small, standing before the throne; and the books were opened: and another book was opened, which is the book of life: and the dead were judged out of the things which were written in the books, according to their works.[3]

In such phrases holy Scripture depicts the general judgment of the last day. We have learnt to think of Christ's judgment as continually present, and particularly at the great crisis of death.[4] And again we are taught to expect a final manifestation of righteous judgment, when the Lord shall come. We believe that he shall come again with glory, to judge both the living and the dead.[5]

Holy Scriptures does not narrowly distinguish one manifestation of divine judgment from another. What describes one describes all; there is only one justice and only one judge, the Incarnate Son of God. What seems especially to characterise the picture of the judgment of the last day is its openness, in the face of all men and angels.

Truly, we need the asurance which such a final picture gives us. We need to be assured by divine revelation that evil, which seems so often to be triumphant in this world, will not triumph for ever. In the end God's righteousness will be vindicated, and right will be shown to be right. Christ must reign until he hath put all his enemies under his feet.[6]

[1] Matt. xxv. 31-33.
[2] Matt. xiii. 41-43.
[3] Rev. xx. 11, 12; Dan. vii. 10 ff.
[4] Chap. xix. 3.
[5] Nicene Creed.
[6] 1 Cor. xv. 25.

Also we need the assurance that every good dead we have been enabled to do by God's grace, every struggle faithfully endured, will not be forgotten before God, but will in the end receive the reward it has merited. For it is not only our ill deeds and our misuse of divine grace that will be reckoned in the judgment, but also whatever good we have been or done.[1] This was St Paul's confidence: I have fought the good fight, I have finished the course, I have kept the faith; henceforth there is laid up for me the crown of righteousness, which the Lord, the righteous judge, shall give me at that day: and not only to me, but also to all them that have loved his appearing.[2] If the Lord will take into account whatever has been evil in Christians, much more will he take into account whatever has been good; for that is his own, the fruit of his Spirit within us, the working out of his grace given to us.

The righteousness of Christians is meritorious in the sight of God, not in itself, but in union with the righteousness of Christ and his availing sacrifice, through which alone we and our good deeds are made well-pleasing before God. By God's good grace and mercy we may each of us be filled with the fruits of righteousness, which are through Jesus Christ, unto the glory and praise of God.[3] And every fruit of righteousness shall earn for us its due reward —that is, the reward which is due, not to us, but to Christ in us.[4]

And the heathen, who have not known Christ, nor ever been united with him by sacraments, shall not go without reward, if they have been true to the law written in their hearts.[5] It is to the nations, that is, not only to Christians, that the Lord promises to say in the judgment: Come, ye blessed of my Father, inherit the kingdom prepared for you.[6]

This hope of reward, then, is set before us. And it is set before us for our encouragement during this time of stress and trial. It is the encouragement which God knows we need in our weakness. It is not given to us to be our motive. We may not make a bargain with God, that we will endure

---

[1] Eccles. xii. 14.   [2] 2 Tim. iv. 8.   [3] Phil. i. 11.
[4] Chap. xvi. 2.   [5] Rom. ii. 15.   [6] Matt. xxv. 34.

so much of pain and suffering in this world for the sake of so
much greater reward and happiness in the next. We are
called to endure for Christ's sake[1] not for the sake of our
own advantage. But we have the encouragement of knowing that, if we endure to the end, we shall attain our reward, for his sake; and at the last hear his blessed word:
Well done, good and faithful servant, thou hast been faithful;
enter thou into the joy of thy Lord.[2]

v

Beyond this final judgment—irrevocable, inevitable, in-
fallible—there are revealed to us two final and eternal states,
heaven and hell.

Hell is prepared for the devil and his angels.[3] God is
holy. All that is evil is alien to God's nature. That which
is evil cannot abide in God. That which is permanently
evil must be permanently separated from the beneficial action
of the love of God. This is what is meant by the wrath of
God. The wrath of God is the love of God refused by
angels or men. We say the sun rises and sets: while in fact
the sun remains unchanged, but the earth revolves. So
God's love abides steadfast, but his self-willed creatures can
turn away from it. God does not change: he cannot be
changed by the actions of those whom he has made. It is
not that God is moved to personal anger by the rebellion of
sinful beings, and in his indignation chooses to inflict
tremendous punishment on the rebels: but those who choose
evil choose what is opposite to God, and therefore choose to
exclude themselves from the love of God.[4]

It cannot be denied that the doctrine of hell is a difficult
one. The central difficulty is that we cannot see how human
beings, made by God for the attainment of perfected union
with him can finally refuse him, and of their own will
become fixed in evil, rejecting his offered love. And,
although we see that the belief in hell necessarily follows
from our belief in the holiness and righteousness of God, it

---

[1] Mark viii. 35.   [2] Matt. xxv. 21.   [3] Matt. xxv. 41.
[4] Rom. ix. 22; Eph. v. 6; John iii. 36; Rev. vi. 16; xi. 18; xvi. 19.

may seem to us that it cannot easily be reconciled with our conviction of his love and almighty power. It seems to leave at the last his loving will for the salvation of all men imperfectly fulfilled. The lost, indeed, glorify God, whose righteousness is vindicated by his just judgment upon them; but it may seem to us that that is a less satisfactory manifestation of his glory than if, somehow or other, in the end all conscious beings were brought to willing submission to God and acceptance of him.

This difficulty in our minds arises from the fact that we understand so little about evil, its origin and its power.[1] God has revealed to us that there is hell, and that hell is everlasting. That is his solemn warning to us. He has not revealed to us the explanation of hell, for that is not necessary.

At various times there have been teachers who, arguing from their own notions of the loving-kindness of God, have asserted the ultimate salvation of all. But they have done so without the support of Church authority or of holy Scripture. From the beginning to the end of the New Testament[2] it stands written that hell is the final and eternal doom of the ungodly. The revelation of hell is as clear and certain as the revelation of heaven. What we believe about hell we have learnt from the teaching of Christ himself.

Hell is revealed to us in Scripture as everlasting fire,[3] in imagery drawn from the perpetual burning of the refuse of Jerusalem in the valley of Hinnom. It seems plain that this is a parable, and that the fires of hell cannot mean what we mean by fire. But this by no means removes from us the terror of hell. A fearful picture has a fearful meaning : a terrible parable implies a terrible reality.

Another picture of hell is that of darkness, and exclusion from the light and joy of God; Cast ye the unprofitable servant into the outer darkness; there shall be the weeping and gnashing of teeth.[4] This brings into prominence what to the modern mind appears to be the essential characteristic

---

[1] Chap. ii. 1.   [2] Matt. iii. 12; Rev. xx. 10, 15.
[3] Matt. xiii. 30; xxv. 41; Mark ix. 48; John xv. 6, etc.
[4] Matt. xxii. 13; xxv. 30.

of the state of the lost souls : deprivation of union with God, the eternal losing of him, the failure to gain the true end of man. No picture of hell can be more dreadful than that contained in our Lord's words : I never knew you; depart from me, ye that work inquity.[1] Depart from me under a curse.[2] This loss of God, who is life, is eternal death.[3]

The two pictures are combined at the end of the New Testament. For the fearful, and unbelieving, and abominable, and murderers, and fornicators, and sorcerors, and idolaters, and all liars, their part shall be in the lake that burneth with fire and brimstone; which is the second death. And : There shall in no wise enter into the city anything unclean, but only they that are written in the Lamb's book of life. Blessed are they that wash their robes, that they may have the right to come to the tree of life, and may enter in by the gates of the city. Without are the dogs, and the sorcerers, and the fornicators, and the murderers, and the idolators, and every one that loveth and maketh a lie.[4]

Such, then, is the dread warning that remains ringing in our souls, as we close the last pages of holy Writ. If we sin wilfully, after we have received the knowledge of the truth, there remaineth a certain fearful expectation of judgment. It is a fearful thing to fall into the hands of the living God.[5] The fear of hell is, indeed, no worthy motive for obedience to God. The only pure motive is the love of God revealed to us in Jesus Christ our Saviour. But good is it for us to turn away from sin, even if it be at first only through fear.

The state of hell is not to be thought of as belonging to the future only. God's judgment is continually present; the separation from God, which is the essential pain and misery of hell, is the necessary consequence even now of unrepenting persistence in wilful sin.

The separation becomes complete, and the doom irrevocable, only when the impenitence has become fixed and

---

[1] Matt. vii. 23.
[2] Matt. xxv. 41 (R.V. marg.).   [3] Rev. xx. 14; xxi. 8.
[4] Rev. xxi. 8, 27; xxii. 14, 15.   [5] Heb. x. 26, 27, 31.

unchangeable.   The only sins which cannot be forgiven are
the sins which cannot be repented of.   And we believe that,
while this life's probation lasts, no souls so utterly fall away
from God as to be beyond the possibility of recovery, if they
will, by the grace of God.

Take heed therefore, brethren, lest haply there shall be in
any one of you an evil heart of unbelief, in falling away from
the living God : but exhort one another day by day, so long
as it is called Today; lest any of you be hardened by the
deceitfulness of sin : for we are become partakers of Christ,
if we hold fast the beginning of our confidence firm unto the
end; while it is said, Today if ye shall hear his voice, harden
not your hearts.[1]

VI

By heaven we mean the presence of God, and the enjoyment of him, for whom mankind was created, to attain to
whom is man's purpose in life.   We shall be in heaven,
when all sin and all the effects of sin have been done away,
and our union with God is made perfect.   Then, in his
unveiled glory and holiness, we shall see him as he is,[2] and
share, body and soul, in the joy of the Lord in which the
angels and the saints now rejoice exceedingly.

Holy Scripture paints for us in glowing colours many
pictures of the happiness of heaven, which is, of course,
altogether above our powers of direct apprehension.   Let
two quotations suffice : These which are arrayed in the
white robes, who are they, and whence came they?   These
are they which came out of the great tribulation, and they
washed their robes and made them white in the blood of the
Lamb.   Therefore are they before the throne of God; and
they serve him day and night in his temple; and he that
sitteth on the throne shall spread his tabernacle over them.
They shall hunger no more, neither thirst any more; neither
shall the sun strike upon them, nor any heat; for the Lamb
which is in the midst of the throne shall be their shepherd,
and shall guide them unto fountains of waters of life : and
God shall wipe away every tear from their eyes.[3]   And there

[1] Heb. iii. 12-15.   [2] 1 John iii. 2.   [3] Rev. vii. 13-17.

shall be no curse any more: and the throne of God shall be
in the city; and his servants shall do him service; and they
shall see his face; and his name shall be in their foreheads.
And there shall be night no more; and they need no light
of lamp, neither light of sun; for the Lord God shall give
them light: and they shall reign for ever and ever.[1]

Heaven is God's presence. The enjoyment of heaven is
the enjoyment of the presence of God without any hindrance
of sin. Therefore the enjoyment of heaven, which is eternal
life perfected, is in some degree entered upon even in this
world, in so far as our union with God through Christ is real,
and the effects of our sins done away. In this sense, true
and living membership of the Catholic Church is the
beginning of heavenly joy, the beginning of eternal life.
The words cited above are in some measure applicable to
faithful Christians in this world. The joy we look for is the
perfection of that which in part is already ours to enjoy.
Even in this world God has prepared for them that love him
such good things as pass man's understanding.[2]

Already in the Catholic Church we are of the company of
those who in heaven see the King's face.[3] There is one
Church, on earth, in purgatory, and in heaven. And hereafter, the Church, which now in part is militant and suffering,
will altogether be triumphant, purified, glorified; and the
whole company of the blessed will attain to perfected glory
and eternal bliss without alloy, in the presence of God and
Jesus our King. That is the end of the King's highway.

In the olden time God's prophet spoke of the safe highway which God would make for his people back from their
exile into the promised land: A highway shall be there, and
a way, and it shall be called the way of holiness: the wayfaring men shall not err therein. The redeemed shall
walk there: and the ransomed of the Lord shall return, and
come with singing unto Zion; and everlasting joy shall be
upon their heads; they shall obtain gladness and joy, and
sorrow and sighing shall flee away.[4]

[1] Rev. xxii. 3-5.   [2] 1 Cor. ii. 9.
[3] Chap. xix. 6.   [4] Isa. xxxv. 8-10.

Back from our exile, caused by human sin, God has indeed made a way for us, by the Incarnation and Death of his Son, that through him we may enter into the holy place, and gain the destined end of mankind.

Jesus said, I am the way, and the truth, and the life : no one cometh unto the Father, but through me.[1] Because God Incarnate is the truth and light, the grace and life, of God given to man, he is the way in whom and through whom alone we can come to union and atonement with God. And he is the sacrifice offered for us through which our right to enter in is assured to us.

Therefore we have boldness to enter into the holy place by the blood of Jesus, by the way which he dedicated for us, a new and living way, through the veil : that is to say, a way of his flesh, his Incarnation, and the extension of his Incarnation, which is the Catholic Church and the sacraments. And we have Jesus, our great high-priest over the house of God, which is the Church, the kingdom which cannot be shaken.

Let us therefore draw near with a true heart, in fulness of faith, and hope, and love.[2]

God has given us himself to be our way home to him.

And we will go along the King's highway; we shall not turn aside to the right hand nor to the left.[3]

[1] John xiv. 6.   [2] Heb. x. 19-25.   [3] Num. xx. 17.

NOTE to Chapter xviii, HOLY MARRIAGE
Prohibited Degrees (See pages 231 and 234)

The prohibition on the marriage by a man of his deceased wife's sister, and by a woman of her deceased husband's brother, was removed in 1946 by the promulgation of a new Canon 99, embodying a revised Table of Kindred and Affinity.

INDEX

INDEX

Godparents, 80 f.
Gospel, 11, 26, 143
Grace, 36, 43, 45, 60, 64 f., 69 f., 81, 85, 87 f., 124, 132, 197 f., 208, 243, 252 f., 258
Greeks, 28 f., 120

Hail Mary, the, 181, 190
Heathen, 14, 22 f., 30, 74, 78, 89, 167, 197, 199, 206, 228, 231, 251, 274
Heaven, 4, 13, 60 f., 77, 102, 109, 250, 252, 255, 257, 275 f., 278 ff. See Eternal Life.
Hell, 13, 23, 89, 250, 275 ff. See Death Eternal
Heredity, 10, 20
Heretics, 120, 125, 131 f., 148
Holiness, 5, 7, 15, 109, 111, 138
Holy days, 214 f., 257
Honesty, 221 f.
Hope, 23, 199 f., 202, 250, 270, 274
Humility, 91, 215

Idolatry, 27, 211
Image of God, 11, 13 f., 18, 21, 23, 42, 47
Images, 211
Immanence, 4
Immortality, 1, 13, 111, 242
Imprecatory Psalms, 171
Incarnation, 36 ff., 45, 54, 59, 65, 69, 71, 101 ff., 104 ff., 142, 145, 211, 235, 260 f., 279 f. See Divinity of Christ.
Incense, 103
Infallibility of Christ, 43, 142
    of the Church, 135, 144, 156 f.
    of the Pope, 157
Intercession, 108, 114, 191, 255
Intermediate state. See Purgatory
Interpretation, Mystical, 158 ff., 170 ff.
    Private, 131, 149 ff., 161
Invocation of saints and angels, 181, 261
Israel. See Jews

Jerusalem, Council of, 117, 163
Jesus, Name of, 37 f.
Jews, 29 ff., 44, 51 f., 68, 99, 103 f., 157 ff., 167, 188, 229, 268 f.

John, St., 62 f., 84, 103
John the Baptist, St., 34 ff., 39, 44
Joseph, St., 37 ff.
Joy, 97, 206 f., 215, 279
Judgment, 10, 13, 34 f., 41, 112, 153, 249 f., 266 f., 270, 272, 276 f.
Justification, 109, 198 f.

Kindness, 218 ff.
Kingdom of God, 32, 40 ff., 45, 52, 58, 73, 77, 80, 85, 162 f., 219, 263. See Messiah
King's highway, 15, 69, 78, 168, 227, 263, 279 f.
Knowledge of God, 1 ff., 7, 11, 21, 23, 27, 29 f., 142 ff., 151

Laity, Duties of, 123
    Priesthood of, 74, 85, 107
Last day, 262 f.
Limitation of family, 236 f.
Liturgy, 98
Lord's Prayer, 98, 100, 174 ff.
Lord's service, 98, 100, 215
Lord's Supper, 98
Love. See Charity
Love of God, 5 ff., 8, 11, 23, 26, 53, 55 f., 90, 93, 97, 257, 275

Man a sacrament, 9, 64 f., 103
Marks of the Church, 137 ff.
Marriage a sacrament, 69, 226 ff. 232
    Civil contract of, 232 ff.
    Consummation of, 232, 236
    Laws of, 158, 227 ff.
    Legality of, 233
    Mixed marriages, 230 f.
    of clergy, 120, 240 f.
    Partnership of, 234 ff.
    Prohibited degrees, 231 f., 280
    Prohibited seasons, 233
    Purposes of, 226 ff.
    Second marriages, 230
    See Affinity, Divorce, Monogamy
Mary, Blessed, 36 ff., 59, 61, 69, 73, 93, 108 f., 235, 238, 259 ff.
    Assumption of, 260
    Conception of, 260

283

Mary, Mother of God, 34 *f.*, 260 *f.*
  Sinlessness of, 36, 260
  Virginity of, 37 *f.*, 238
Mass, 98 *ff.*, 107, 114, 168 *f.*, 180, 214 *f.* See Altar, Communion, Eucharist
  Attendance at, 100, 114
Matter, 4, 64, 68 *f.*, 102, 105, 211
Meditation, 192 *ff.*
Membership of Christ and the Church, 3, 60 *f.*, 65 *ff.*, 68, 74, 76, 79, 81, 85, 91, 94, 108, 114, 126, 130, 143, 164 *f.*, 176
Merit, 110, 259, 274
Messiah, 31 *ff.*, 40, 44, 48, 52, 159, 263 *f.*
Ministry of the Church, 116 *ff.*, 136 f. See Order, Priesthood
  Charismatic, 118
  Maintenance of, 123
  Protestant, 130
Miracles of Christ, 43 *ff.*, 47, 246
Missionary duty, 149, 154, 205 *f.*, 265 *f.* See Evangelisation
Mixed chalice, 100
Modernism, 131, 149 *ff.*
Money, 188, 222 *f.*
Monogamy, 158, 165, 227 *ff.*, 231
Mosaic Law, 31, 41, 158 *f.*, 209, 213, 227, 229
Mysteries, the Holy, 98

Nature, 4, 8 *f.*, 18, 70, 226, 230
Nazareth, Christ's life at, 38 *f.*

Obedience to the Church, 164 *f.*, 187, 190
  Religious, 239 *ff.*
Order, Sacrament of, 40, 69, 116 *ff.*, 121, 136 *f.* See Ministry, Priesthood
Orders, Minor, 122
Ordination of Christ, 40

Pain, 5, 9, 14, 205, 207. See Evil, Sickness
Papacy, 134 *ff.*, 140 *f.*, 157
Paradise, 253
Parents, duties of, 237
Patriotism, 217
Paul, St., 49, 58, 62, 82

Penance, 95, 122, 243, 252, 254, 257
  Sacrament of, 90 *ff.*, 180
Pentecost, 61, 73, 79, 83, 177
Perfection, Counsels of, 239 *ff.*
Personality, 1, 6, 28, 37 *f.*, 249, 268
Peter, St., 46, 62, 79, 84, 135 *f.*, 140 *f.*, 163
Pharisees, 35, 51
Philosophy, 28, 268
Poverty, Religious, 239
Prayer, 11, 45, 49, 53, 158, 167 *ff.*, 183 *ff.*, 246
  Acts of, 176, 211
  Corporate, 167 *ff.*
  Efficacy of, 177 *ff.*
  Mental, 192 *ff.*
  Private, 189 *ff.*
Preaching, 155
Predestination, 10, 18, 53
Preparation for Christ, 27 *ff.*
Priesthood, Christian, 69 *f.*, 91, 94, 101, 116 *ff.*, 130, 154 *f.* See Order, Ministry
  of Christ, 33, 40, 60, 73, 101, 106 *f.*, 118 *f.*, 168, 263 *f.*, 280
  of Laity. See Laity
  Representative, 94, 119, 121
Probation, 18, 250 *ff.*, 253, 278
Prodigal Son, the, 24 *ff.*, 96 *ff.*
Prophetic office of Christ, 32 *f.*, 40, 73
Prophets, the, 3, 32, 34, 40, 105, 143
Propitiation, 28, 60, 105, 107. See Sacrifice
Protestantism, 130 *ff.*, 136, 170, 231
Psalter, 31, 169 *ff.*
Purgatory, 252 *f.*, 257, 279
Purity, 220
Purpose of life, 2, 12, 14, 18, 22, 25, 43, 81 *f.*, 258, 276, 278

Real Presence, 110 *ff.*, 107
Reason, 2 *f.*, 15, 28 *f.*, 48, 144, 150, 268
Recreation, 213 *f.*
Redemption, 3, 26, 33, 55, 57, 101, 243, 260

INDEX